THE CULTURAL CONSTRUCTION OF
SEXUALITY

Nancy Cook
Brock 2006

The Cultural Construction of
SEXUALITY

Edited by
Pat Caplan

TAVISTOCK PUBLICATIONS
London & New York

First published in 1987 by
Tavistock Publications Ltd
11 New Fetter Lane
London EC4P 4EE
Reprinted 1987

Published in the USA by
Tavistock Publications
in association with Methuen, Inc.
29 West 35th Street
New York, NY 10001

© 1987 Pat Caplan

Typeset in Great Britain by
Scarborough Typesetting Services
and printed by
Richard Clay
(The Chaucer Press) Ltd
Bungay, Suffolk

British Library Cataloguing in
Publication Data
The cultural construction of
sexuality.
1.   Sex customs
I.   Caplan, Patricia
155.3   HQ12

ISBN 0-422-60870-X
ISBN 0-422-60880-7 Pbk

Library of Congress Cataloging
in Publication Data
The Cultural construction of
sexuality.
(Social science paperbacks; 353)
Includes bibliographies and
indexes.
1. Sex – cross-cultural studies.
I. Caplan, Patricia.   II. Series.
[DNLM: l. Cross-Cultural
Comparison.
2. Identification (Psychology)
3. Sex.   4. Sex Behavior.
HQ 1075   C968]   GN484.3.C85
1987   306.7   86-22982

ISBN 0-422-60870-X
ISBN 0-422-60880-7 (pbk.)

Contents

List of contributors   vii
Preface   x

Introduction   1
Pat Caplan

1 Questions of identity   31
   Jeffrey Weeks

2 'Facts of life' or the eroticization of
   women's oppression? Sexology and the
   social construction of heterosexuality   52
   Margaret Jackson

3 Reason, desire, and male sexuality   82
   Victor J. Seidler

4 A note on gender iconography: the vagina   113
   Shirley Ardener

5 Social and cognitive aspects of
   female sexuality in Jamaica   143
   Carol P. MacCormack and Alizon Draper

6 Honour and shame: the control of
   women's sexuality and group identity in Naples   166
   Victoria Goddard

7 Beyond the Samoan controversy in anthropology:
   a history of sexuality in the eastern interior of Fiji   193
   Allen Abramson

8 'Selling her kiosk': Kikuyu notions of sexuality
   and sex for sale in Mathare Valley, Kenya   217
   Nici Nelson

9   Rank, gender, and homosexuality: Mombasa as a
     key to understanding sexual options   240
     Gill Shepherd

10 Celibacy as a solution?
     Mahatma Gandhi and *Brahmacharya*   271
     Pat Caplan

Name index   296
Subject index   301

List of contributors

Allen Abramson is currently lecturing in social anthropology at University College, London, where he is also completing a PhD. He has previously taught at the University of Edinburgh. His field-work was in Fiji, and he has published articles in *Critique of Anthropology* and other journals.

Shirley Ardener is Director of the Queen Elizabeth House Centre for Cross-Cultural Research on Women, Oxford. A social anthropologist, she has carried out field-work in West Africa. She has published widely and is editor of *Perceiving Women* (Dent 1975), *Defining Females* (Croom Helm 1978), *Women and Space* (Croom Helm 1981), *The Incorporated Wife* (with Hilary Callan, Croom Helm 1984), and *Images of Women in Peace and War* (with Sharon MacDonald and Pat Holden, Macmillan 1987).

Pat Caplan teaches anthropology at Goldsmiths' College, London. She has carried out research in Tanzania, Nepal, and southern India, and has published *Priests and Cobblers: Social Change in West Nepal* (Chandler 1972), *Choice and Constraint in a Swahili Community* (Oxford University Press 1975), *Women United, Women Divided* (edited with J. Bujra, Tavistock 1978), and *Class and Gender in India* (Tavistock 1985). She is currently writing up her research on gender in Tanzania, with specific reference to food, health, and fertility.

Alizon Draper is a postgraduate student at the London School of Hygiene and Tropical Medicine. She has done field-work in Tanzania (1981) and Jamaica (1983–85).

Victoria Goddard is an Argentine anthropologist who lectures at Goldsmiths' College, London. She did field-work in Naples, southern Italy in the 1970s, and her main area of interest is women in the informal sector. She has published articles in *Critique of Anthropology, Anthropology Today,* and the *Institute of Development Studies Bulletin.*

Margaret Jackson works at Goldsmiths' College, London, teaching on courses in Teacher Education and in Women's Studies. She is a lesbian and revolutionary feminist and has been involved in the Women's Liberation Movement for about ten years, particularly in the areas of sexuality and violence against women. She has published several articles on sexuality in journals and edited collections and was joint author of *The Sexuality Papers* (Hutchinson 1984). She is currently completing a PhD on the social construction of heterosexuality.

Carol P. MacCormack is Senior Lecturer in Social Sciences at the London School of Hygiene and Tropical Medicine. She has carried out field-work in West Africa over a number of years, and also in Tanzania, Kenya, Sudan, Pakistan, Burma, and Jamaica. She has edited two books – *The Ethnography of Fertility and Birth* (Academic Press 1982) and *Nature, Culture and Gender* (with Marilyn Strathern, Cambridge University Press 1980), and published a number of articles in journals and edited collections.

Nici Nelson lectures in anthropology at Goldsmiths' College, London. She has done research in Nairobi, Kenya, on which she has published a number of articles, and also in Lesotho. She is the author of *Why Have the Women of Village India Been Neglected?* (Pergamon 1979), and the editor of *African Women in the Development Process* (Cass 1981).

Victor Jeleniewski Seidler is Senior Lecturer in the Sociology Department at Goldsmiths' College, London. He was one of the editors of *One-Dimensional Marxism* (Allison and Busby 1980), and is the author of *Kant, Respect and Injustice* (Routledge and Kegan Paul 1986). He is currently working on a book on Simone Weil with Lawrence Blum. He is a member of the Masculinity Research Group at Goldsmiths' College.

Gill Shepherd is Research Officer at the Overseas Development Institute. She carried out field-work among Comorians in Mombasa, Kenya, in the 1970s, and has published a number of articles on the topic in *Africa, Paideuma,* and various edited collections. She subsequently did work for Oxfam in East and North-East Africa on rural development and population. She has also published on development research in Sudan, Kenya, and Botswana, and has taught at the University of Sussex, and at Goldsmiths' College, London.

Jeffrey Weeks is the author of four books on the social organization of sexuality: *Coming Out* (Quartet 1977), *Sex, Politics and Society* (Longman 1981), *Sexuality and its Discontents* (Routledge and Kegan Paul 1985), and *Sexuality* (Ellis Horwood/Tavistock 1986). He has edited *The Family Directory* (British Library 1986), and is also an editor of *History Workshop Journal.* He is a Visiting Research Fellow at the University of Southampton and currently works in educational administration in London.

Preface

This book arose out of a seminar series organized in 1984 by the Anthropology Department of Goldsmiths' College as one of the regular inter-collegiate anthropology seminars of London University. The topic of sexuality was chosen because there seemed to be little attempt to grapple with this concept within anthropology, even though in recent years there has been a flood of academic writing on the subject of sex and sexuality by sociologists, historians, and psychologists. The final seminar series consisted of ten papers, most by anthropologists, but some by sociologists and social historians. Two of the original contributors withdrew before publication, and two more were added.

Because sexuality is such a broad topic, it would be impossible to cover all aspects of it in a single volume. This collection does not, then, purport to be comprehensive. The articles included in it are diverse both in their subject matter and in their theoretical concerns, but from them emerge a number of common themes. The first three articles are by social historians who consider sexuality in western society (Weeks, Seidler, and Jackson). The remainder are by anthropologists who direct their gaze mainly at non-western societies, although both Ardener and Caplan also consider western material, and Goddard's area of study, Naples, lies within Europe.

In a circular to the participants, I expressed the hope that the seminar series would explore sexuality from both an empirical and a theoretical viewpoint, and relate it to gender, power, class, state, kinship, and marriage, as well as to symbolic systems, in specific historical contexts. I also hoped that the series would avoid the obvious pitfall of becoming a compendium of bizarre exotica, but would aim at an understanding of how and why sexuality is constructed the way it is.

Pat Caplan, 1986

Introduction

Pat Caplan

Sex, sexuality, and gender

The word 'sex' has different meanings. In common parlance, it
applies to the categories of male and female (as in 'the female
sex'). In this regard, it is often thought in western society to be a
'natural' quality, and hence one that cannot be changed.
However, in recent years, a distinction between sex, in the
physiological sense, and gender, which is a cultural construct, a
set of learned behaviour patterns, has been proposed and is now
widely used. Much work over the last two decades, particularly
by feminist scholars, has examined the relationship between sex
in this sense, and gender.

Another way in which the word 'sex' is widely used is of
comparatively recent origin; people talk of 'having sex', usually
meaning coitus. In the 1965 version of the Oxford English
Dictionary, this use of the word does not appear, but it is
included in the 1975 version, defined as 'pertaining to sexual
instincts, desires or their manifestations'. Here again, we note the
implication that there is some kind of innate force in people,
often referred to as a 'drive' or an 'instinct' which compels them
to seek sexual outlets, the so-called 'hydraulic' model of
sexuality.

The fact that two versions of the OED only ten years apart can
show differences in their definition of the word 'sex' suggests
that there are shifts in meaning over time. This has been borne
out in recent years by the work of historians of western societies,
who have shown that sexual behaviour and practice, morality,
and ideology are constantly in a state of flux.

What is the relationship between sex in the modern sense, or to
use the more abstract term, sexuality, and gender? These two

different meanings tend to coalesce in many people's minds, with the implication that gender is expressed through sexuality, and that each sex has a specific sexuality. However, probably the most important first step in studying sexuality is to differentiate it from gender, and to explore the articulation between them (Vance 1984b). We may therefore ask under what circumstances and to what extent can sexuality and gender be independent variables? Various writers have suggested that we are only likely to find sexuality thought of as a 'thing in itself' when there is a severance of sex from reproduction; others suggest that the division comes from the 'commoditization' of sex under capitalism. The first use of the term 'sexuality', according to the OED, appeared in 1800, which suggests that the concept came into existence with modern society.

But when we talk about sexuality, are we considering behaviour or a set of ideas and, if both, what is the relationship between them? It is clear that in modern western society, one's sexual orientation is a very important part of one's identity. Perhaps this is because, as Brake (1982) perceptively suggests, gender here is not so much ascribed on the basis of physiological sex as of *achieved* sex, and a vital part of that achievement is sexual behaviour and identity. People are encouraged to see themselves in terms of their sexuality, which is interpreted as the core of the self. But what is sexual in one context may not be so in another: an experience becomes sexual by application of socially learned meanings. Our heads, it has been said, are our most erogenous zone.

In our society, heterosexual relations are seen as the norm, and homosexual relations are stigmatized. Nonconformity to the norms of heterosexuality threatens the dominant ideology's view of sex as 'innate' and 'natural'. Male homosexuality threatens male solidarity and superordination because some men take on what are thought of as female characteristics. Lesbianism is likewise seen as threatening to male superiority because the women who engage in it appear not to need men. Sex-change operations, on the other hand, while they arouse enormous public interest, do not appear to be condemned; it is as though surgery removes not only organs but also anomalies, making a correct fit between sex, gender, and sexuality.

By contrast, one of the contributors to this volume, Shepherd, shows that in Mombasa, homosexual relations are scarcely stigmatized, and she suggests that this is not unrelated to the fact that gender and sexuality are conceptually separate in people's minds. Being in a homosexual relationship does not change one's gender, which is essentially assigned by biological sex.

The history of sexuality in the west

Because the dominant ideology in western society suggests that sexual activity is 'natural', innate, and instinctual, there is a reluctance to concede that sexuality has a history – as Snitow has put it, 'We treasure sex as a retreat from time' (Snitow, Stansell, and Thompson 1984: 2). Yet recent work carried out by historians, particularly of the nineteenth century, demonstrates that there have been considerable shifts in sexual behaviour and the meanings attached to it.

The work of a number of historians shows how the dominant Anglo-American definition of women as especially sexual creatures was reversed and transformed between the seventeenth and nineteenth centuries into the view that women were less lustful than men. Cott's (1978) work on the ideology of what she terms female 'passionlessness' links it to the rise of evangelical Christianity between the 1790s and the 1830s. Ministers portrayed women as more sensitive to the call of religion than men, but the tacit condition for their elevation was the suppression of female sexuality, or, as another historian of the same period puts it, 'The mutation of the Eve myth into the Mary myth' (Basch 1974: 9).

By the latter half of the nineteenth century, medical opinion had also become an authoritative sector of public opinion. Women were usually characterized by medical men as having sexual anaesthesia: 'In women . . . the sexual desire is dormant, if not non-existent', wrote W. R. Greg in 1853, while William Acton, fellow of the Royal Medical and Chirurgical Society and author of *The Functions and Disorders of the Reproductive Organs* (1857), stated that woman 'was so pure-hearted as to be utterly ignorant of and averse to any sensual indulgence' (both quoted in Basch 1974: 8–9).

Cott (1978) points out that there have been two recent challenges to the idea of female sexual anaesthesia in the nineteenth century. One maintains that this was an ideology which did not necessarily reflect actual behaviour. Gordon and Dubois (1983), for example, quote a nineteenth-century survey of middle-class married women which found that 40 per cent admitted to experiencing orgasm occasionally, and 20 per cent frequently.

Cott's second point is that a number of works have contested the standard twentieth-century view of nineteenth-century women as victims of sexual repression, by pointing out the advantages for women of such an ideology. The early nineteenth-century writer Hannah More, for instance, attacked the notion that women were made for man's pleasure, because, like Mary Wollstonecraft, she wished to emphasize women's moral and intellectual powers. As Cott says, 'Their two critiques arose from shared indignation that women were degraded by their sexual characterization' (Cott 1978: 227). Furthermore, women might well have hailed 'passionlessness' as a way of asserting control in the sexual arena, even if that control consisted of denial. It gave women an opportunity to restrict sexual intercourse within marriage, and thus limit family size. It has been suggested that this form of 'domestic feminism' may help to account for the beginnings of a drop in the birth rate in the late nineteenth century.

Victorian ideas about male sexuality were different. Men were thought to be full of sexual desires. Yet these were perceived as dangerous, not only to women, but to men themselves. The widespread belief, reinforced by medical theory of the period, that loss of sperm led to weakness, served as a negative sanction against sexual indulgence (Caplan, this volume). Thus women who denied their husbands sexual relations except when procreation was desired could be seen as actually helping them to control their 'baser natures'.

Masturbation, the 'solitary vice', was even more strongly condemned than heterosexual excess: it was said to lead to a whole range of diseases, including insanity, not only in the practitioner, but even in his descendants (Ellis 1942: 249). Masturbation by women was also considered highly reprehensible and abnormal, and some doctors even practised clitoridectomy on women patients to 'cure' them of this 'perversion' (Ehrenreich and English 1979: 111; Foucault 1980: 217).

A major part of the politics of sexuality in the Victorian period revolved around the struggle of women for 'social purity'. By this was meant a single sexual standard for men and women. Women attacked equally drunkenness and lust. Campaigns such as that of Josephine Butler and her allies to repeal the Contagious Diseases Act focused on prostitution and on the injustice of punishing women for being prostitutes while imposing no sanctions on their male clients. Walkowitz's (1980) study of Victorian prostitution points out that working-class women who, earlier in the century, had moved in and out of prostitution, while remaining largely within their own communities, were increasingly stigmatized, and subject to the sanctions of the state. It thus became more difficult for them to leave prostitution, which was increasingly taken over by pimps.

In this collection Nelson discusses women who 'sell sex' in Nairobi. At the time of her original field-work in the 1970s, these women were relatively unstigmatized, at least within their own squatter community, and prostitution was not their sole means of earning a living, since they also brewed and sold beer. However, during the 1980s, beer-brewing has become increasingly criminalized, and, at the same time, there is growing condemnation by the wider society of the women in this squatter settlement as 'immoral'. It is possible that prostitution may become more institutionalized and organized here too, precisely because of the intervention of the state, as in Victorian England.

If changes in the definition of prostitution can be discovered, so can they for homosexuality. Mary McIntosh (1968) has pointed out that the concept of 'homosexual' is a relatively recent historical construct, which came into use around the turn of the century, an insight further elaborated by Weeks in much of his work (e.g. 1977 and this volume). The very word 'homosexual' was only coined in 1869, and did not come into common usage until the 1880s and 1890s (Weeks 1979: 164). This is not to say that there was no homosexual behaviour prior to that: there certainly was, but it did not constitute an identity. Similarly, two women living together in the nineteenth and early twentieth centuries would have been assumed to be friends (Smith-Rosenberg 1975); by the middle of the twentieth century, they would more likely be called lesbians. Their behaviour might, in fact, not be very different; what changed was how it was labelled (Faderman 1982).

Furthermore, identification with the role of homosexual has different meanings for women and men. Men have involved themselves in (homo)sexual politics because they wished to resist victimization. For many women, however, identification as a lesbian may have less to do with sexual orientation than it does with identification with female oppression; 'coming out' as a lesbian may spring less from eros than from anger. Indeed, in a recent influential article, Adrienne Rich seeks to show that lesbianism has a history which is less concerned with a genitally defined sexuality than it is with a continuum of women identifying with and nurturing other women (Rich 1980).

There is a widely held view of nineteenth- and twentieth-century sexuality as moving from repression to sexual permissiveness. This position states that the Victorian period was characterized by a repression of sexuality which had begun in the seventeenth century, and thus coincided with the rise of capitalism. The official repression of sexuality has thus been interpreted as a necessary part of the work ethic, although the enormous growth in prostitution in the nineteenth century is often cited as an example of the moral hypocrisy of the period and the breadth of the gap between ideology and actual behaviour.

Permissiveness in sexual matters is often said to have followed in the wake of Freud, whose libido theory has become part of the western folk model of sexuality. Freud, while following a much earlier philosophical tradition which held that sexual freedom and civilization were antithetical, claimed to find in his work that on the individual level, sexual repression frequently led to neurosis. Twentieth-century critics of sexual repression such as Reich (1936) and Marcuse (1966) have argued that through sexual liberation could come personal liberation, even social revolution, because the free expression of sexuality is antithetical to the exercise of power. Although as the historian Eric Hobsbawm has pointed out, there are probably no well-organized revolutionary movements or regimes which have not developed puritanical tendencies (1970: 38–9), the ideas of Reich and Marcuse were enthusiastically taken up in the 1960s, particularly by student protest movements, with the slogan 'Make love not war'.

However, the French historian of ideas, Michel Foucault, rejects a view of the history of sexuality as moving from repression to permissiveness, arguing that while ostensibly there was a growth of prudishness and silence about sexual matters in the eighteenth and nineteenth centuries, on other levels there was a veritable explosion of discourse. 'What is peculiar to modern societies, in fact, is not that they consigned sex to a shadow existence, but that they dedicated themselves to speaking of it ad infinitum, while exploiting it as *the* secret' (1981: 35).

Foucault's periodization of the history of sexuality thus differs from the one accepted until recently. The latter, which centres on mechanisms of repression, supposes two great ruptures: the first in the seventeenth century, with the advent of the prohibitions on sex, and the second in the twentieth century with the loosening of repression and prohibitions. But Foucault suggests that the crucial periods were the eighteenth century, with the rise of pedagogy, medicine, and demography, and the nineteenth century, with the medicalization of sex and, at the end of the century, the rise of psychiatry.

Foucault's chief interest is in mechanisms of power, and he maintains that sexuality must not be seen as a drive, which is alien and disobedient to power, but 'As an especially dense transfer point for relations of power . . . it is not the most intractable element in power relations, but rather one of those endowed with the greatest instrumentality' (1981: 103). He suggests that sexuality has been used in the exercise of power in four ways: firstly through a 'hysterization' of women's bodies – the female body was viewed as thoroughly saturated with sex, which was the reason for woman's hysteria and her 'nervous disorders'. Secondly, there was in the eighteenth century the beginnings of a 'pedagogization' of sex – a preoccupation with the sexuality of children, particularly the practice of masturbation, leading to increasing measures to restrain it through the organization and lay-out of schools, and ideas about how children in the home were to be socialized. Thirdly, there was increasing 'socialization' of procreative behaviour – in other words, reproduction became a social issue, through concern about population levels and eugenics, and debates about birth-control. Finally, there was a 'psychiatrization' of perverse pleasure around the turn of the century. The rise of psychoanalysis gave a name and a being to certain forms of sexual behaviour, notably homosexuality. Foucault also proposes that psychoanalysis 'allowed individuals to express their incestuous desires in discourse' (1981: 129) and that westerners have continued to be 'confessing animals', the confessional moving from the church to the analyst's couch. In these ways, he maintains, sex has become the explanation for everything.

In this volume, Seidler considers the work of Foucault and the extent to which it is useful in examining both male and female sexuality. While conceding that Foucault's analysis contains enormous insight, Seidler concludes that his failure to take gender sufficiently into account, and to allow that the history of sexuality is different for women and men, ultimately weakens his analysis. Seidler examines male heterosexuality in western society, showing that since the Enlightenment, masculinity has been identified with reason, whereas femininity is thought to embody irrationality and unreason. For these reasons, Seidler concludes, men fear intimacy in relations, preferring to remain in control, and thus to appear 'rational'.

His work points not only to a historically specific construction of heterosexuality, but also to the need to consider the power element in sexual relations. Both of these points are also made forcefully in this volume by Jackson's study of the writings of sexologists, who replaced the nineteenth-century idea of sex as nasty with the principle of erotic pleasure for both partners. However, as her account makes clear, they did nothing to change the relative position of women to men; women were to remain subordinate, and their sexuality was not allowed any autonomy.

The politics of sex

Until recently, it would have been unthinkable to connect sex with politics. Marxism dismissed sex as superstructural, and unrelated to class struggle. By the early 1960s, the 'problem' of sexuality appeared to be on its way to being solved with the increasing growth of permissiveness in the west. But by the late 1960s, women were realizing that neither political movements nor sexual permissiveness had solved their problems, and that there did exist a 'sexual politics' initially voiced most powerfully in Kate Millett's work of that title (1969). One of the first slogans of the emerging women's movement was 'The personal is political': gender relations and sexuality were perceived to be about power, and therefore about politics, just as much as, for example, the black civil rights and anti-Vietnam war movements in the United States.

Much of the debate about sexuality in the west in recent years, then, has arisen out of feminist struggles for autonomy in the area of sexuality and reproduction, with campaigns being waged in such areas as contraception, abortion, and child care, and, most recently, genetic engineering and the new reproductive technologies. Another major site of struggle has been the area of violence against women. Feminist campaigning has led to a gradual, albeit often grudging, recognition on the part of the wider society of the frequent incidence of battering and rape, both inside and outside marriage, and, more recently, of the frequency of the sexual (including incestuous) abuse of children, especially females. Women in all western countries in the 1970s campaigned around these issues by setting up refuges for battered women and rape crisis centres, and by demonstrating and campaigning for changes in the law as well as in the way in which it is implemented. Books such as *Against Our Will*, Susan Brownmiller's study of rape (1976), were especially influential.

By the end of the decade, another issue had asserted itself: pornography, with Andrea Dworkin's *Pornography: Men Possessing Women* (1981) and Susan Griffin's *Pornography and Silence* (1981) as seminal texts. Much feminist energy began to be expended on campaigns against pornography. The famous phrase attributed to T. Grace Atkinson – 'If porn is the theory, rape is the practice' – encapsulated a view held by many women that the increasing amount of both soft- and hard-core pornographic material flooding the west has contributed in no small measure to the physical dangers which women face in their daily lives.

In the last year or two, this view has been challenged, not only by people outside the women's movement arguing for greater sexual permissiveness, but from within the feminist movement itself. A number of debates, mainly emanating from the United States, have aroused great passions. On the one hand, there are the radical feminists, who hold that sexuality in a male-dominated society inevitably involves danger for women. They identify with a lesbian-feminist community, and condemn pornography, as well as practices such as sado-masochism and 'cruising' (promiscuous sex with strangers). 'Libertarian' feminists, on the other hand, both lesbian and heterosexual, support any consensual activity bringing pleasure, including the use of pornography, and condemn what they term 'vanilla sex' (Ferguson *et al* 1984: 107). The libertarian feminists, then, assert the primacy of pleasure, whereas radical feminists assert the value of emotional intimacy. Libertarians also argue that campaigning against pornographic material is to focus on symbols rather than reality, as there is no clear connection between visual representation and actuality, nor any proof that looking at pornography incites men to commit acts of rape and battering.

Some British feminists have also joined the debate (e.g. Brown 1981; Coward 1982; Kuhn 1984), although it has been less prominent here than across the Atlantic, possibly because in the United States, civil liberties and feminism are under strong attack from the powerful forces of the New Right.

In her introduction to the collected papers from the Barnard conference on sexuality held in 1982, Carol Vance suggests that the reason why the feminist movement has been powerfully affected by pornography is that our culture is visually illiterate. Furthermore, like other participants in that conference (which specifically excluded anti-pornography campaigning groups), she doubts the capacity of feminism to analyse sexuality as successfully as it has analysed gender (Vance 1984a). Rubin in the same volume also maintains that feminism cannot analyse sexuality, since it was developed to analyse gender relations, and 'simply lacks angles of vision which can encompass the social organisation of sexuality' (1984: 309).

But sexuality, like gender, is socially constructed. For this reason, as Barrett has pointed out, sexual relations *are* political, and therefore they can be variously constituted (1980: 43). In the next section, I turn to the discipline of anthropology, to consider whether cross-cultural comparison can shed any further light on the meaning of sexuality.

The contribution of anthropology

Social anthropology has a reputation for interesting itself in the (preferably bizarre) sexual practices of exotic peoples. This reputation is perhaps not greatly deserved – Vance, for instance, remarks that anthropology as a discipline has not been especially concerned with the study of sexuality (1984c: 393, fn 7). Even so, undergraduate studies may be enlivened by learning that in the heat of sexual passion, Trobrianders bite off their partners' eye-lashes (Malinowski 1929), or that in parts of Papua New Guinea, ritual sodomy is practised by adult males on boys being initiated into manhood (Herdt 1982). But then, so what? Cross-cultural comparison may serve to reassure us that everything is normal – somewhere in the world – or that sexuality is, must be, culturally constructed. But what do such statements *mean*?

In the nineteenth century, anthropologists interested them-selves in questions relating to sex and gender, and contributed to current debates on 'the woman question'. As Elizabeth Fee has pointed out, marriage, the family, and sexual roles were assumed until about 1860 to belong to the natural condition of humanity. However, between 1860 and 1890, anthropologists demonstrated that the ideal family of the Victorian middle class was not a result of the operation of the laws of nature, but of a 'long and painful evolutionary struggle away from nature'. Fee shows that 'By thus presenting "civilized" marriage as the end-point of social evolution, these men provided a solid, historical, evolutionary justification for the role of women in their own culture' (Fee 1973: 24). They also showed just how far Victorian England had risen above the 'savage state'. Sexuality was identified with animality, and 'savages' were equated with nature. It is not there-fore surprising to find that the Victorians regarded the sexual habits of primitive peoples as more 'animal' than their own. Many anthropologists saw the struggle against sexual instincts as the earliest triumph of man against nature.

Towards the end of the century, and particularly in the writing of Herbert Spencer, some of these ideas were tied in with social Darwinism to arrive at the view that 'The development of rigidly defined sex roles (with males dominant) and the tight controls clamped on sexuality (particularly female sexuality) were not historical accidents but adaptations to social survival' (Fee 1973: 34). Like others before and after him, Spencer argued that civilization depended on the control of sexuality.

By the early twentieth century, anthropology had to reckon with psychoanalysis, and especially with the work of Sigmund Freud. Some anthropologists engaged with the ideas of the new science and contributed to debates about the nature of sexuality.

In his influential book *Sex and Repression in Savage Society* (1927), Malinowski challenged some of the ideas of Freud, particularly on the universality of the Oedipus complex, by seeking to demonstrate that there was no such phenomenon in matrilineal societies like the Trobriands.

While he appears in some contexts to be a sexual radical, in other respects Malinowski showed himself to be not only imbued with conventional ideas about male and female roles, but also unable to understand the political implications of his ideas. In 1931, he debated the nature of marriage with Briffault, in a discussion conducted over the radio and only published twenty-five years later (Montagu 1956). Briffault argued that anthropology was characterized by a series of 'Adam-and-Eve' assumptions about the nature of women and sexual relations, and that this was being used as ammunition against the feminist movement (Montagu 1956: 37). Malinowski, while indignantly refusing to be labelled an 'Adam-and-Eve' anthropologist or an anti-feminist, maintained that 'Marriage is regarded in all human societies as a sacrament, that is, as a sacred transaction establishing a relationship of the highest value to man and woman' (Montagu 1956: 64) and that 'True scientific anthropology teaches us another lesson. Individual marriage sanctioned by religion as well as by law exists throughout humanity, primitive and civilised alike' (Montagu 1956: 67). Here, as in *Sex and Repression*, he maintained that mating was a very similar process cross-culturally: 'Man still has to court his prospective mate and she still has to choose to yield to him. The woman still has to bear and the man to remain with her as her guardian' (Malinowski 1927: 227). It is extraordinary that Malinowski was able to question the universal applicability of concepts like the Oedipus complex, while assuming that marriage was similar everywhere, primarily because he thought male-female relations were as well.

The same assumption was, however, not made by the American anthropologist Margaret Mead, who, in 1925, was beginning her first field-work (Mead 1928). Her research in Samoa, and later work carried out elsewhere in the Pacific (Mead 1930, 1935), had considerable influence upon theories of gender and sexuality, affecting not only her own profession, but also the views of the wider society, particularly in North America. It is popularly supposed that Mead 'proved' (in *Sex and Temperament in Primitive Society*) that gender is socially constructed, rather than biologically based. Furthermore, she appeared to have demonstrated, in her work on Samoa, that it was possible for a society to exist in which adolescence was not marked by the *Sturm und Drang* typical of western societies, but could be a painless transition into adulthood, provided that sexuality was not repressed. Mead's work was for a long time perhaps the most frequently quoted argument for the primacy of nurture rather than nature, of culture rather than instinct.

In this volume, Abramson considers the work of Mead in Samoa, and Freeman's 1983 critique of it, in the light of his own field-work on Fiji.[1] He shows that in this area, while there is an ideal of female virginity prior to marriage, which is zealously upheld by the elders, there is also a reality of fairly promiscuous pre-marital behaviour on the part of boys and girls which makes attainment of the ideal unlikely. Abramson suggests that both Mead and Freeman were right; Mead, by living as she did outside the village boundaries, was able to hear of the activities of the youth, which Freeman, drinking *kava* with the chiefs in the village, would never have heard. Polynesian sexuality is thus both repressed and promiscuous, suggests Abramson, and the dynamics of the situation, and hence its potential for bringing about social change, lie precisely in this contradiction.[2]

Questions of the kind Mead had asked continued to interest some American anthropologists, particularly those of the 'culture and personality school' but in Britain the entrenchment of structural-functionalism in the second quarter of this century meant that they were ignored for a long time. Issues of sex and sexuality were felt to be more properly dealt with by psychologists and psychoanalysts, not anthropologists. There were, of course, some exceptions. In addition to Malinowski's *The Sexual Life of Savages* (1929), works such as *Facing Mount Kenya* (1938), Jomo Kenyatta's study of his own people the Kikuyu, *The Muria and their Ghotul* (1947), by Verrier Elwin on the *ghotul* (or young people's house) of the Indian Muria, or *Married Life in an African Tribe* (1940), Isaac Schapera's account of married life among the Tswana of South Africa, were remarkable for their sexual frankness. Books such as these may have helped anthropology to acquire its afore-mentioned popular reputation, but they did little to theorize sexuality, much less gender.

None the less, some of the work of British anthropologists during this period did involve questions of gender and sexuality. Research and debates on kinship, marriage, incest, and the family touched upon these areas, even when, as usually was the case, they were not directly addressed. One reason for this was that the anthropology of this period shied away from the political implications of its work. For example, the question of whether patriarchy replaced matriarchy was disregarded, and descent systems were considered merely as patrilineal or matrilineal; the power element was thus overlooked, at least as far as gender relations were concerned (Coward 1983).

While questions of kinship and marriage did not directly address gender or sexuality, the study of ritual and symbolism often obliged anthropologists to grapple with them because plainly they were of concern to their informants. Work on initiation rituals, for instance, contains a good deal of material on sexuality, notable examples being Gregory Bateson's *Naven* (1936), Kathleen Gough's study of female initiation rites on the Malabar coast (1955), and Audrey Richards's *Chisungu*, a study of the Bemba girls' rite (1956); later came the work of Victor Turner on rituals of initiation for both males and females among the Ndembu of what is now Malawi (Turner 1967, 1968).

Another area of symbolism which touches upon sexuality is the study of the human body and how it is viewed. Even before the work of Mary Douglas first appeared in the 1960s, there had been studies of right- and left-handedness (Hertz 1909), and later of hair (Leach 1958), which showed an association between body symbolism and views of society, including gender relations. Douglas argued that the body, common to all humans, has to be viewed as a metaphor for society; there is a clear correlation between how people see their bodies and how they see their own society. Societies, like other bounded groups, are vulnerable at their intersection with other groups, i.e. their margins. Thus much attention is paid in many societies to the orifices of the human body, for here matter passes from outside to inside, and vice versa. Societies which deem it important to maintain their separateness will also guard their margins carefully, and this may be symbolized through taboos on food, commensality, and sex (Douglas 1966, 1970).

Numerous examples show that it is particularly the bodies of women which are made to serve as social symbols. Yalman's seminal essay 'On the Purity of Women in the Castes of Malabar and Ceylon' (1963) was an early example, although more recent studies have also emphasized that in caste societies, women, and particularly their sexuality, serve as important boundary markers (e.g. Fruzzetti 1982; Bennett 1983). Similarly, two studies of gypsies in England and California have shown how gypsy identity is maintained through strict rules of purity and pollution, the main burden of which falls upon women (Okely 1983; Sutherland 1975). Perhaps the most extreme examples of the lengths to which it is posible to go in this regard are various forms of operation on the female genitalia, ranging from clitoridectomy in many parts of sub-Saharan Africa, to the 'pharaonic' forms of infibulation practised in much of north-eastern Africa (Kennedy 1970; Hosken 1976; El Saadawi 1980).

Work on 'honour and shame' in Mediterranean and Middle Eastern societies also demonstrates the importance to the group of control of women's sexuality, a theme which is taken up by Goddard in this volume. She shows how this is used as a metaphor by working-class Neapolitans resisting the incursions of the Italian state. The women represent the privacy of the group; they also symbolize the importance of a kinship-based society in contradistinction to one organized through a centralized state. For this reason, women are not allowed to work in factories (mainly owned and operated by northern 'foreigners') and their sexuality is controlled by an ideal of chastity.

Edwin Ardener suggested in 1972 that ritual and symbolism were the areas *par excellence* where anthropologists might search for the world views of 'muted' groups such as women. A number of interesting works do indeed reveal that women, perhaps because of a relatively powerless position, may express themselves through ritual. For instance, Safa-Isafahani (1980) shows how secluded Iranian women, apparently conforming to strict Islamic norms of behaviour, none the less play dramatic games (*baziha*) at weddings and other events, in which they reveal quite different views of their sexuality and gender roles.

In this volume, Shirley Ardener examines vaginal iconography in three areas – among the Bakweri of Cameroon, in Greek myth, and among American feminist artists – showing how women in these different times and places have used the exposure of their genitals as a form of symbolic political protest. Feminist artists, for instance, have attempted to change the significance of vaginal iconography from one in which it is either hidden in shame or else displayed for men in pornography, to one in which their depictions of vaginas serve as condensed symbols of female power, just as do those of Bakweri women when they are insulted by men.

Edwin Ardener's above-quoted remarks were taken by some as a sign that anthropology was beginning once again to become aware of issues of sex and gender, although he was also criticized for characterizing women as 'muted' when the major problem seemed to be that anthropologists had rarely bothered to ask them any questions (Mathieu 1978). Feminist scholars accused the profession, not without reason, of being totally androcentric; women had been rendered apparently passive – like the Nuers' cows, they were just there, pawns in marriage alliances, mothers, wives, daughters to be given away by men.

In the last fifteen years, however, there has been a steady spate of anthropological works which have looked specifically at women. Latterly, there has also been some interest in gender relations. Advances in both empirical and theoretical knowledge have been enormous.[3] But in much of the recent writing on these topics by anthropologists, both feminist and non-feminist, there is often the kind of conflation of sexuality with gender to which I have alluded above. Rubin, for instance, in her influential 1975 article, stated that gender and sexuality were linked: 'A sex-gender system is a set of arrangements by which a society transforms biological sexuality into products of human activity and in which these transformed needs are satisfied' (1975: 159). This definition has been widely quoted and used, but it is one which Rubin herself has recently repudiated: 'In contrast to my perspective in "The Traffic in Women", I am now arguing that it is essential to separate gender and sexuality analytically to more accurately reflect their separate social existence' (Rubin 1984: 308). However, Rubin is cautious about whether it is possible to separate gender and sexuality in non-western societies. She argues that in kinship-based societies, kinship sculpts sexuality which is embedded in numerous other social relations. Ortner and Whitehead seem to agree, pointing out that the sexuality of such societies demonstrates a greater concern with the pig herd, military honours, and the estate than with sexuality *per se*, showing 'the power of social considerations to override libidinal ones' (1981: 24). Is there then a fundamental difference in this respect between such societies and modern western society?

One of the most important contributions made by the new feminist scholarship is the breaking down of the dichotomy between the public and private spheres. As the historian Smith-Rosenberg has argued, new questions relating to 'The events, the causal patterns, the psychodynamics of private places (the household, the family, the bed, the nursery, and kinship systems) . . . have in turn altered our categories of significant public institutions, and our analytic approach to the public world' (1976: 185). Writing 'people's history', then, which includes the history of both women and men, involves a rethinking of categories, causes, and effects, even of periodization and theories (Kelly-Gadol 1976: 809–10).

Anthropologists have perhaps been more aware than other scholars of the links between the public and domestic spheres, focusing as they have for so long on kinship-based societies where such a dichotomy is of less significance. Even they, however, until recently have not always made full use of their own insights, largely because of their gender blindness. Accordingly, the understandings gained from studies of precapitalist societies have only recently been applied to complex societies, largely as a result of feminist scholarship in such areas as the relationship between the family and the state, or class and gender. However, the use of such concepts as production and reproduction, and the examination of the articulation between them, have forced a rethinking of pre-existing categories, not only in considering complex societies, but also kinship-based ones (e.g. Weiner 1976). The opening of such avenues has made it impossible to ignore gender relations, since they are seen to be fundamental in any kind of society.

If, then, we look to anthropology for answers to questions about sexuality, it can indeed show us that sexuality, at least in kinship-based societies, is not a 'thing in itself'; but while it can give us a picture of a culturally specific form of sexuality, the lack of historical specificity makes cross-cultural comparison difficult. Can we then envisage a discussion of sexuality which combines the insights of feminism, anthropology, and history?

Anthropology, history, and politics

A recent article by Ross and Rapp (1984) discusses the potential fruitfulness of collaboration between anthropology and history. They suggest that three layers in the analysis of sexuality can be discerned: that of kinship and the family, of communities, and of world systems. In the first regard, we need to consider kinship terminologies, incest prohibitions, and inheritance practices. Ross and Rapp point out: 'Inheritance patterns actually integrate family members and their sexuality into national and even international movements in law and in class formation' (1984: 108). The work of Goody on production and reproduction as well as bridewealth and dowry springs to mind here (particularly Goody 1973, 1976), but so too does that of a number of social historians (e.g. MacFarlane 1978, Flandrin 1979, Stone 1979). Unfortunately, however, such studies are for the most part 'gender-blind' (see Whitehead 1977).

Secondly, we can consider sexuality with reference to communities, which are the termini of world-wide economic, social, political, and cultural systems; these are to some extent autonomous, but are also affected by the larger world. Ross and Rapp show that this ambiguity is exhibited by, for example, peer groups, who often regulate sex and marriage, both of which are, of course, crucial to the politics and economics of family and community life. In Europe, the loss of the traditional peer-group regulation of courting seems to have been one of a cluster of forces leading to increased illegitimacy rates, along with urbanization and proletarianism, and the growth of class formation. Ross and Rapp also point out that sexuality is often a source of tension between peer groups of youth and adults, a topic which is discussed in two articles in this volume.

Abramson examines two aspects of sexuality in Fiji – a cult of virginity and chastity for women, voiced by the elders, and a reality of free sexual relations prior to marriage, instigated by the 'wild' young men of the village. One of the puzzles in this situation is why these same young men eventually become elders themselves and uphold a version of morality which they know to be unattainable.

MacCormack and Draper examine the phenomenon of high rates of fertility among the working class in Jamaica, where knowledge of contraception is widespread. Although a woman's own mother will seek to prevent her engaging in sexual activity, the birth of her first child, albeit out of wedlock, does confer adult status upon her. Such children are welcomed by kin, including grandmothers, and frequent childbearing helps create large kinship networks which are an important source of economic support. (In this respect, the findings of MacCormack and Draper resemble those of Stack (1975a) and Tanner (1974) on black Americans in the ghettoes of the northern cities of the USA.) The link between mothers and daughters is symbolized in the careful burying of each umbilical cord under a tree, a custom brought across the Atlantic by slaves from West Africa.

A third level of analysis discussed by Ross and Rapp is that of 'world systems', including universal religions, and of legal systems backed by the power of the state. Like Foucault, they suggest that a feature of the recent past has been the increasing intervention of the state into the arena of sexuality. They conclude that it is not accidental that contemporary (western) culture tends to reify sex as a thing-in-itself, for

> 'The separation with industrial capitalism of family life from work, of consumption from production, of leisure from labour, of personal life from political life, has completely re-organized the context in which we experience sexuality. . . . Modern consciousness permits, as earlier systems of thought did not, the positing of "sex" for perhaps the first time as having an "independent" existence.'   (Ross and Rapp 1984: 121).

Yet this separation is in fact ideological, as another historian, Padgug, points out. Although under capitalism, sexuality and the economy *appear* to have become separate from each other, yet the links between them are innumerable, and both spheres remain significant in the production and reproduction of social reality (1979: 16). He suggests that sexuality may be defined both as a set of categories which order experience and make it meaningful, and as a set of relationships which are historically and culturally specific.

Part of the problem is that we are still bound by the terms of our own discourse, and even the act of putting together a book on sexuality further contributes to the contradiction: it supposes that there is something called sexuality which can be analysed, and it

also contributes to the 'explosion of discourse' which is undoubtedly the product of particular historical circumstances.[4]
For example, we are constantly tempted to dichotomize, and to
hierarchize those dichotomies. Sexuality is thought of in terms
of binary opposites: male–female, heterosexual–homosexual,
marital–extra-marital, and in each case, one of these pairs is
privileged, is seen as the 'normal'.

We are bound by our own discourse in another way – who we
are often determines the questions we ask and of whom we ask
them, as some of the commentators on the Mead–Freeman
debate alluded to earlier have pointed out. In this volume, there
is an example of how an author's own sex can determine the lines
of inquiry. Both Goddard and Abramson, for instance, look at
societies in which female virginity is valued, and women's
sexuality is supposed to be controlled; the actuality in both
instances is that there is frequent premarital sexual intercourse,
However, Abramson and Goddard offer quite different explanations for this contradiction between ideal and reality. The former
suggests that Fijian women are relatively passive pawns of male
desires and machinations, while Goddard shows how women
strategize within a set of constraints defining and controlling
their sexuality in order to achieve their own ends.

Identity: sex, gender, and sexuality again

What then of the question posed earlier, the relationship between
sexuality and gender? A theme which arises out of a number of
papers in this volume is that of identity or selfhood. Several
authors suggest that sexuality is an integral part of identity on
both a personal and a social level; it is part of being male or
female, as well as adult. This emerges strongly in MacCormack
and Draper's article, which demonstrates that in Jamaica, it is not
only sexual activity, but that attested to by the birth of a child,
which confers adulthood on both young women and men.[5]

Weeks, too, shows how homosexuality has become 'an
identity' in the west. But male gays and lesbians do not change
their gender, although, as suggested earlier, the lack of 'fit'
between their sex, gender, and sexuality is one reason why they
are regarded with suspicion by society at large; in anthropological terms, they constitute an anomaly. Shepherd's article,

however, shows that in Mombasa there is a different relationship between gender identity and sexuality, since the former is assigned on the basis of biological sex, not sexual behaviour. Lesbians, whether dominant or not, remain women, and dress as women. Similarly, homosexual males retain their male gender, even when they behave as passive partners. Their roles as patrons or clients are, in this stratified society, far more important constituents of their identity than their sexual proclivities.

However, Unni Wikan, in an article published a few years ago on Oman (an area which has strong historical links with Mombasa), takes quite the opposite viewpoint. She maintains that male homosexual prostitutes (xanith), of whom there are quite a number in Oman, are actually transsexuals: 'A socially acknowledged role pattern whereby a person acts and is classified as if he/she were a person of the opposite sex for a number of crucial purposes' (1977: 104). Wikan thus suggests that xanith may change their gender, and that they effectively 'become women'. They may become men again by marrying a woman and successfully consummating the marriage. Thus she argues that 'It is the sexual act, not the sexual organs, which is fundamentally constitutive of gender . . . behaviour and not anatomy, is the basis for the Omani conceptualisation of gender identity' (Wikan 1977: 309).

Wikan's article provoked a long-running debate. Shepherd herself questioned Wikan's formulation of a gender triad in Oman (Shepherd 1978), suggesting that the xanith's identity is less that of transsexual than homosexual, a role with a well-established tradition in Islamic societies.

Wikan countered her arguments by noting that although psychologists and others working on western culture have found it useful to distinguish true transsexuals from effeminate homosexuals and transvestites, yet for the Omanis among whom she worked, the role of xanith is the only one open to them. Some of her xanith informants told her that they desired to escape from a male role and 'become women'. Wikan argues strongly, contra Shepherd, that they do not become homosexual prostitutes for reasons of poverty, nor because of the segregation of the sexes, but because they experience particular desires.

There are parallels between Wikan's Omani material, and a brief account by Evans-Pritchard of homosexual relations among the Azande. In the precolonial period, a warrior might take a boy as a 'wife', and have him perform numerous services of a wifely nature, including sexual intercourse *inter crura*. This was a temporary expedient, before marriage to a woman. When the boy grew up, he married in the normal way, but during his period as a 'wife' he was known as a woman. Such homosexual marriages were in no way stigmatized, but lesbian relationships between women, which were not unknown in the harems of princes, were regarded with horror by men, largely because it enabled women to have control of their own sexuality (Evans-Pritchard 1970).

What these case studies reveal is a number of possible combinations of sex, gender, and sexuality, leading to different 'identities'. In many instances, these are not fixed and immutable – *xanith*, Mombasa's male homosexuals, and Azande boy wives move into the role of heterosexual husband apparently unproblematically, provided they can meet the necessary criteria, i.e. successfully consummate a marriage or pay the necessary bride-wealth. Such examples suggest that our own classifications, which privilege sexuality above all other criteria, impose a peculiar rigidity on our conceptions of gender.

It is probably when we consider homosexuality that we are most likely to examine the relationship between gender and sexuality. No doubt this is because of our own ethnocentrism. Yet in speaking of homosexuality, we are of course also implicitly discussing heterosexuality, which is equally socially constructed, as Jackson and Seidler show in this volume. Do we then need a sexuality, just as we need a gender, in order to be human? Is it true, as Foucault suggests, that it is only through our sexuality that we appear to gain access to our bodies and our identities? Here perhaps lies the difference between our present society, and those in past time, or other parts of the world.

But this is to suppose that somewhere, even if it is embedded among layers of kinship, economics, and politics, there is a something which we can label sexuality. The view that desire itself, as opposed to its varying forms, might be socially constructed, appears rarely in the literature, although Heider's work on the Dugun Dani makes a strong plea for such a view (Heider 1976).

In my own article on Gandhi, I seek to show that *brahmacharya* is a concept which extols abstinence from sexual activity. Hindu tradition values celibacy, although it is recognized that for most people, a stage of life as a 'householder' is appropriate; this should, however, be followed by an old age devoid of sexual activity, devoted to contemplation. Gandhi suggested that it was possible to combine being a householder with celibacy, a state which he saw as higher and purer than one of sexual activity. In this respect, his thought echoes much Christian teaching on the primacy of the spirit over the flesh, as well as late Victorian, western campaigns for 'social purity'. Gandhi did not minimize the difficulty of achieving *brahmacharya* and implicit in his writings on the subject is the notion that humans, particularly males, are subject to strong sexual urges, which can only be controlled, not eradicated, although successfully maintaining such control confers great power on the *brahmachari*.

In her article in this volume, Nelson suggests that such a flesh–spirit dichotomy is absent in African thought, and it is therefore not surprising to find that it should be African societies (e.g. Nelson's Nairobi) and those of the African diaspora (MacCormack and Draper on Jamaica) which view sex as an integral part of healthy living. Eurasia, on the other hand, finds sexuality much more problematic as is evidenced by the remainder of the articles.

Part of the problem of sex for many societies is that (at least in its heterosexual form) it can lead to pregnancy. In her article, Shepherd suggests that high and low fertility rates are an important key to the understanding of sexuality in different cultural contexts. Elsewhere, she develops this notion further (personal communication). She suggests that in inland Africa and societies of the African diaspora where, broadly speaking, the desire for children is very high, fertility and sexuality are hardly conceptually distinguished, and the biological sex of individuals is important. Sex is considered to be a good thing because of children, and impediments to procreation, such as homosexuality, or oral and anal sex, are regarded as wicked. In such societies, there is no highly elaborated virginity cult. The biological sex of individuals is important.

In the west, on the other hand, where the desire for children is much less, and where contraception can help to control fertility, sex is free and open, and homosexuality occurs along with the acceptance of other sexual practices which do not lead to pregnancy. There is no virginity cult because sex has become widely divorced from fertility. For these reasons, biological sex is decreasingly important, and there is more questioning of the institutionalized differences in male and female gender identities. In such circumstances, gender becomes an aspect of selfhood, not of parenthood.

The Mediterranean, Asia, and the Middle East, is an area interstitial to the other two in its attitudes to sexuality. Here, fertility is valued, but only with a partner of the right status, and it is strongly frowned upon with the wrong partner for producing the wrong sort of children. Sexuality is limited by virginity cults, strong negative sanctions against women's adultery, purdah, and other institutions. In these areas, rank is more important than either biological sex (unlike Africa) or gender identity (unlike the west). Shepherd would place her own Mombasa material into this category.

Thus control of female fertility is inextricably linked to control over people's sexual behaviour. This may range from the ideal of chastity for women posited in the Mediterranean (Goddard) or Fiji (Abramson), to exhortations to chastity even for married couples by Gandhi (Caplan). Where the birth of children is unequivocally welcomed, as it is in Nairobi and Jamaica, women's sexuality is less likely to be controlled, although in the former case there may be, as Nelson suggests, some condemnation of a woman who produces children out of wedlock, i.e. for herself. A situation in which sexual activity is considered good for health, rather than harmful, also seems to correlate with a greater degree of autonomy for women.

Conclusion

We may then ask whether these examples enable us to answer the question posed earlier: is there a qualitative difference in sexuality in 'modern' societies? Is it the case that in kinship-based societies sexuality is embedded in other institutions, and cannot be isolated, whereas in modern societies, sex has not only become a form of consumerism, but also a 'thing in itself'? Yet while we in the west may have a concept of sexuality as something separate from reproduction, from marriage and so forth, it is really not possible to analyse sexuality without reference to the economic, political, and cultural matrix within which it is embedded. It would be more accurate to say, perhaps, that in modern society we have an *idea* of sexuality as a specific concept, but we cannot in actual fact understand it without contextualizing it; if we fail to do this, we are, as Ross and Rapp suggest, reifying sex (1984). Foucault expresses this another way by showing how the idea of sex conflates disparate areas, and then this unity becomes a causal principle – in this way, sex itself comes to constitute a form of explanation.

If we accept such arguments, it follows that they somewhat invalidate those quoted earlier which preach a sexual free-for-all. Such views risk jettisoning the insights already gained, namely that sexual practices cannot exist in a vacuum. What people want, and what they do, in any society, is to a large extent what they are made to want, and allowed to do. Sexuality, as many of the articles in this volume make plain, cannot escape its cultural connection.

Notes

1 The Mead–Freeman debate has intensified since the publication of Freeman's book. For a summary of the arguments and a helpful list of references, see Glick (1983).
2 Other commentators on Samoa have made a similar point: see Ortner (1981), and two Samoan writers quoted by Glick (1983).
3 For reviews of some of this work, see Stack (1975b), Quinn (1977), Rogers (1978), Tiffany (1980), Atkinson (1982).
4 A few of the most important recent works include Weeks (1981, 1985), Coward (1983), Phillips (1984), Snitow, Stansell, and Thompson (1984), Vance (1984a), and Metcalfe and Humphreys (1985). In addition, a number of journals have had special numbers on sexuality: these include *Radical History Review* (1979), *Cambridge Anthropology* (1979), *Signs* (1980), *m/f* (1981), *Feminist Review* (1982).
5 Morakvasic (1981) similarly shows how Yugoslav women use pregnancy, which is as frequently followed by abortion as birth, as a means of affirming their femininity, and allowing their husbands to feel truly masculine.

References

Acton, W. (1857) *The Functions and Disorders of the Reproductive Organs in Youth, in Adult Age, and in Advanced Life.* London.

Ardener, E. (1972) Belief and the Problem of Women. In J. Lafontaine (ed.) *The Interpretation of Ritual.* London: Tavistock.

Atkinson, J. M. (1982) Review Essay: Anthropology. *Signs* 8 (2) Winter.

Barrett, M. (1980) *Women's Oppression Today*. London: Verso.

Basch, F. (1974) *Relative Creatures: Victorian Women in Society and the Novel, 1837–67*. London: Allen Lane.

Bateson, G. (1958) *Naven*. Stanford, Calif.: Stanford University Press. (First published 1936.)

Bennett, L. (1983) *Dangerous Wives and Sacred Sisters: Social and Symbolic Roles of High Caste Women in Nepal*. New York: Columbia University Press.

Brake, M. (1982) *Human Sexual Relations: a Reader*. Harmondsworth: Penguin.

Brown, B. (1981) A Feminist Interest in Pornography – Some Modest Proposals. *m/f* 5 and 6.

Brownmiller, S. (1976) *Against Our Will: Men, Women and Rape*. Harmondsworth: Penguin.

Cott, N. F. (1978) Passionlessness: an Interpretation of Victorian Sexual Ideology, 1790–1850. *Signs* 4 (2).

Coward, R. (1982) Sexual Violence and Sexuality. *Feminist Review* 11.

—— (1983) *Patriarchal Precedents: Sexuality and Social Relations*. London: Routledge & Kegan Paul.

—— (1985) *Female Desire: Women's Sexuality Today*. London: Paladin.

Douglas, M. (1966) *Purity and Danger: an Analysis of Concepts of Pollution and Taboo*. London: Routledge & Kegan Paul.

—— (1970) *Natural Symbols: Explorations in Cosmology*. London: Barrie and Jenkins.

Dworkin, A. (1981) *Pornography: Men Possessing Women*. London: The Women's Press.

Ehrenreich, B. and English, D. (1979) *For Her Own Good: 150 Years of the Experts' Advice to Women*. London: Pluto Press.

Ellis, H. (1942) *Studies in the Psychology of Sex*. New York: Random House. (Originally published in seven volumes between 1896 and 1928).

El Saadawi, N. (1980) *The Hidden Face of Eve: Women in the Arab World*. London: Zed Press.

Elwin, V. (1947) *The Muria and their Ghotul*. London: Oxford University Press.

Evans-Pritchard, E. (1970) Sexual Inversion among the Azande. *American Anthropologist* 72.

Faderman, L. (1982) *Surpassing the Love of Men*. London: Junction Books.

Fee, E. (1973) The Sexual Politics of Victorian Social Anthropology. *Feminist Studies* 1.

Ferguson, A., Philipson, I., Diamond, I., Quinby, L., Vance, C., and Snitow, A. (1984), Forum: The Feminist Sexuality Debates. *Signs* 10 (1).

Flandrin, J.-L. (1979) *Families in Former Times: Kinship, Household and Sexuality*. Cambridge: Cambridge University Press.

Foucault, M. (1980) *Power and Knowledge*. Hassocks: Harvester Press.

—— (1981) *The History of Sexuality*. Harmondsworth: Penguin.

Freeman, D. (1983) *Margaret Mead and Samoa: the Making and Unmaking of an Anthropological Myth*. Harmondsworth: Penguin.

Fruzzetti, L. M. (1982) *The Gift of a Virgin: Women, Marriage and Ritual in Bengali Society*. New Brunswick, NJ.: Rutgers University Press.

Glick, P. B. (1983) The Attack on and Defence of Margaret Mead. *RAIN* 58, October.

Goody, J. (1973) Bridewealth and Dowry in Africa and Eurasia. In J. Goody and S. J. Tambiah (eds) *Bridewealth and Dowry*. London and New York: Cambridge University Press.

—— (1976) *Production and Reproduction: a Comparative Study of the Domestic Domain*. London: Cambridge University Press.

Gordon, L. and Dubois, E. (1983) Seeking Ecstasy on the Battlefield: Danger and Pleasure in Nineteenth Century Feminist Sexual Thought *Feminist Review* 13.

Gough, K. (1955) Female Initiation Rites on the Malabar Coast. *Journal of the Royal Anthropological Institute* 85.

Greg, W. R. (1853) *The Sin of Great Cities*. London.

Griffin, S. (1981) *Pornography and Silence: Culture's Revenge against Nature*. London: The Women's Press.

Heider, K. G. (1976) Dani Sexuality: a Low Energy System. *Man* 11 (2).

Herdt, G. H. (ed.) (1982) *Rituals of Manhood*. Berkeley and Los Angeles, Calif.: University of California Press.

Hertz, R. (1909) The Preeminence of the Right Hand: A Study in Religious Polarity. In R. Needham (ed.) (1960 edn.) *Death and the Right Hand*. London: Cohen & West.

Hobsbawm, E. J. (1970) Revolution is Puritan. In P. Nobile (ed.) *The New Eroticism*. New York: Random House.

Hosken, F. P. (1976) Genital Mutilation of Women in Africa. *Munger Africana Library Notes* 36.

Kelly-Gadol, J. (1976) The Social Relation of the Sexes: Methodological Implications of Women's History. *Signs* 1.

Kennedy, J. G. (1970) Clitoridectomy in Nubia. *Man* 5 (2).

Kenyatta, J. (1961) *Facing Mount Kenya: The Tribal Life of the Kikuyu*. London: Mercury Books. (First published 1938.)

Kuhn, A. (1984) Covering Up Sex. *New Statesman*, 24 February.

Leach, E. (1958) Magical Hair. *Journal of the Royal Anthropological Institute* 88: 147–64.

MacFarlane, A. (1978) *The Origins of English Individualism: the Family, Property and Social Transition*. Oxford: Blackwell.

McIntosh, M. (1968) The Homosexual Role. *Social Problems* 16.

Malinowski, B. (1927) *Sex and Repression in Savage Society*. London: Routledge & Kegan Paul.

—— (1929) *The Sexual Life of Savages*. London: Routledge & Kegan Paul.

Marcuse, H. (1966) *Eros and Civilization*. Boston: Beacon Press.

Mathieu, N.-C. (1978) Man-Culture, Woman-Nature? *Women's Studies International Quarterly* 1 (1).

Mead (1928) *Coming of Age in Samoa*. Harmondsworth: Penguin. (1943 edn.)

28 The Cultural Construction of Sexuality

—— (1930) *Growing up in New Guinea*. Harmondsworth: Penguin. (1942 edn.)
—— (1935) *Sex and Temperament in Three Primitive Societies*. New York: Dell Publishing Company.
Metcalfe, A. and Humphreys, M. (eds) (1985) *The Sexuality of Men*. London: Pluto Press.
Millett, K. (1969) *Sexual Politics*. New York: Doubleday.
Montagu, M. F. A. (ed.) (1956) *Marriage, Past and Present: a Debate Between R. Briffault and B. Malinowski*. Boston: Porter Sargent.
Morakvasic, M. (1981) Sexuality and the Control of Procreation. In K. Young, C. Wolkowitz, and R. McCullagh (eds) *Of Marriage and the Market: Women's Subordination in International Perspective*. London: C.S.E. Books.
More, H. (1799) *Strictures on the Modern System of Female Education*. London: T. Cadell and W. Davies.
Okely, J. (1983) *Traveller Gypsies*. London and New York: Cambridge University Press.
Ortner, S. B. (1981) Gender and Sexuality in Hierarchical Societies: The Case of Polynesia and Some Comparative Implications. In S. Ortner and H. Whitehead (eds) *Sexual Meanings: the Cultural Construction of Gender and Sexuality*. London: Cambridge University Press.
Ortner, S. and Whitehead, H. (eds) (1981) *Sexual Meanings: the Cultural Construction of Gender and Sexuality*. London: Cambridge University Press.
Padgug, R. A. (1979) On Conceptualising Sexuality in History. *Radical History Review* 20, spring/summer (special issue on sexuality).
Phillips, E. (ed.) (1984) *The Left and the Erotic*. London: Lawrence & Wishart.
Quinn, N. (1977) Anthropological Studies on Women's Status. *Annual Review of Anthropology* 6.
Reich, W. (1972) *The Sexual Revolution*. London: Vision Press. (First published 1936.)
Rich, A. (1980) Compulsory Heterosexuality and Lesbian Existence. *Signs* 5 (4).
Richards, A. (1982) *Chisungu: A Girl's Initiation Ceremony among the Bemba of Zambia*. London: Tavistock. (First published 1956.)
Rogers, S. C. (1978) Women's Place: a Critical Review of Anthropological Theory. *Comparative Studies in Society and History* 20 (1).
Ross, E. and Rapp, R. (1984) Sex and Society: A Research Note from Social History and Anthropology. In A. Snitow, C. Stansell, and S. Thompson (eds) *Desire: The Politics of Sexuality*. London: Virago.
Rubin, G. (1975) The Traffic in Women: Notes on the Political Economy of Sex. In R. Reiter (ed.) *Toward an Anthropology of Women*. New York: Monthly Review Press.
—— (1984) Thinking Sex: Notes for a Radical Theory of the Politics of Sexuality. In C. Vance (ed.) *Pleasure and Danger: Exploring Female Sexuality*. London: Routledge & Kegan Paul.

Safa-Isafahani, K. (1980) Female Centred World Views in Iranian Culture: Symbolic Representation of Sexuality in Dramatic Games. *Signs* 6 (1).

Schapera, I. (1971) *Married Life in an African Tribe*. Harmondsworth: Penguin. (First published 1940.)

Shepherd, G. (1978) Transsexualism in Oman? *Man* 13 (1).

Smith-Rosenberg, C. (1975) The Female World of Love and Ritual. *Signs* 1 (1).

—— (1976) The New Woman and the New History. *Feminist Studies* 3.

Snitow, A., Stansell, C., and Thompson, S. (eds) (1984) *Desire: The Politics of Sexuality*. London: Virago.

Stack, C. (1975a) *All Our Kin: Strategies for Survival in a Black Community*. New York: Harper & Row.

—— (1975b) Review Essay on Anthropology. *Signs* 1 (1).

Stone, L. (1979) *The Family, Sex and Marriage in England, 1500–1800*. Harmondsworth: Penguin.

Sutherland, A. (1975) *Gypsies: the Hidden Americans*. London: Tavistock.

Tanner, N. (1974) Matrifocality in Indonesia and Africa and among Black Americans. In M. Rosaldo and L. Lamphere (eds) *Woman, Culture and Society*. Stanford, Calif.: Stanford University Press.

Tiffany, S. (1980) Anthropology and the Study of Women. *Annual Review of Anthropology* 6.

Turner, V. (1967) *The Forest of Symbols: Aspects of Ndembu Ritual*. Ithaca: Cornell University Press.

—— (1968) *The Drums of Affliction; a Study of Religious Processes among the Ndembu of Zambia*. Oxford and London: Clarendon Press and International African Institute.

Vance, C. S. (ed.) (1984a) *Pleasure and Danger: Exploring Female Sexuality*. London: Routledge & Kegan Paul.

—— (1984b) Pleasure and Danger: Toward a Politics of Sexuality. In C. S. Vance (ed.) *Pleasure and Danger: Exploring Female Sexuality*. London: Routledge & Kegan Paul.

—— (1984c) Gender Systems, Ideology and Sex Research: an Anthropological Analysis. In A. Snitow, C. Stansell, and S. Thompson (eds) *Desire: The Politics of Sexuality*. London: Virago.

Walkowitz, J. (1980) *Prostitution and Victorian Society*. London: Cambridge University Press.

Weeks, J. (1977) *Coming Out: Homosexual Politics in Britain from the 19th Century to the Present*. London: Quartet Books.

—— (1979) Movements of Affirmation: Sexual Meanings and Homosexual Identities. *Radical History Review* 20.

—— (1981) *Sex, Politics and Society: the Regulation of Sexuality since 1800*. New York: Longman.

—— (1985) *Sexuality and its Discontents*. London: Routledge & Kegan Paul.

Weiner, A. (1976) *Women of Value, Men of Renown*. Austin: University of Texas Press.

Whitehead, A. (1977) Review of Jack Goody's Production and Reproduction. *Critique of Anthropology* 3 (9/10).

Whitehead, H. (1981) The Bow and the Burden-strap: a New Look at Institutionalized Homosexuality in Native North America. In S. Ortner
and H. Whitehead (eds) *Sexual Meanings: the Cultural Construction of
Gender and Sexuality*. London: Cambridge University Press.

Wikan, U. (1977) Man Becomes Woman: Transsexualism in Oman as a
Key to Gender Roles. *Man* 12 (2).

—— (1978) The Omani Xanith: a Third Gender Role? *Man* 13 (3).

Yalman, N. (1963) On the Purity of Women in the Castes of Ceylon and
Malabar. *Journal of the Royal Anthropological Institute* 93.

1 Questions of identity

Jeffrey Weeks

'Sexual identity and sexual desire are not fixed and unchanging. We create boundaries and identities for ourselves to contain what might otherwise threaten to engulf or dissolve into formlessness.'
(Wilson 1983: 194)

Sexual identity: snare or delusion?

The very idea of a *sexual* identity is an ambiguous one. For many in the modern world – especially the sexually marginal – it is an absolutely fundamental concept, offering a sense of personal unity, social location, and even at times a political commitment. Not many, perhaps, say 'I am a heterosexual' because it is the taken-for-granted norm, the great unsaid of our sexual culture. But to say 'I am gay', 'I am a lesbian', or even 'I am a paedophile . . . or sado-masochist' is to make a statement about belonging and about a specific stance in relationship to the dominant sexual codes. It is also to privilege *sexual* identity over other identities, to say in effect that how we see ourselves sexually is more important than class, or racial, or professional loyalties. As the song puts it: 'I am what I am, my own special creation' and in saying that we are ostensibly speaking of our true essence of being, our real selves.

Yet, at the same time, we now know from a proliferating litera-ture that such identities are historically and culturally specific, that they are selected from a host of possible social identities, that they are not necessary attributes of particular sexual drives or desires, and that they are not, in fact, *essential* – that is naturally pre-given – aspects of our personality (Weeks 1985). So there is a real paradox at the heart of the question of sexual identity. We are increasingly aware, theoretically, historically, even politically, that 'sexuality' is about flux and change, that what we so readily deem as 'sexual' is as much a product of language and culture as of 'nature'. Yet we constantly strive to fix it, stabilize it, say who we are by telling of our sex. It seems, as Jane Gallop (1982: xii) has put it, that 'Identity must be continually assumed and immediately called into question'; or alternatively constantly questioned yet all the time assumed. For it is provisional, precarious, dependent on, and incessantly challenged by social contingencies and psychic demands – but apparently necessary, the foundation stone of our sexual beliefs and behaviours. Over the past century, in particular, the search for identity has been a major characteristic of those whom our culture has designated as outside the norms, precisely *ab*normal: male homosexuals, lesbians, and a whole catalogue out of the pages of Krafft-Ebing (paedophiles, transvestites, bisexuals . . .). The defining categorizations of the sexologists have provided the basis for a multiplicity of self-definitions, self-identifications; sexual identities.

So what do we mean when we use the term 'sexual identity'? Does it offer us the 'truth of our beings', or is it an illusion? Is it a political trap that imprisons us into the rigid and exlusive categorizations of those arbiters of desire, the sexologists? or is it a necessary myth, the precondition of personal stability? Is it a snare . . . or a delusion, a cage . . . or an opportunity? The debate over sexual identity may seem arcane and specialized to some, especially when a great deal of the evidence of it comes from discussions about the execrated sexualities. It is, however, actually central to any discussion about sexuality in the modern world, illuminating its meaning and political connotations, which is probably why sexologists have been obsessed with the question, even when they did not use the term; and why modern sexual radicals find the concept so problematic, even as they deploy the term all the time.

Identity as destiny

Let us start by looking at the history of the concept itself. Its theoretical roots lie in the valiant efforts of the early sexologists, in the last decades of the nineteenth century and the early years of the present century, to capture the essence of that mysterious but all-powerful force of sex by categorizing its diverse manifestations and thus attempting to make sense of its incessant flux. Tissot's awful warnings in the eighteenth century about the disastrous effects of masturbation had already marked a crucial transition: what you did was now more than an infringement of divine law; it determined what sort of person you were. Desire was a dangerous force which pre-existed the individual, wracking his (usually his) feeble body with fantasies and distractions which threatened his individuality and sanity.

This search for the primeval urge in the subject itself was the decisive step in the individualizing of sex. By the 1840s Henricus Kaan (see Ellenberger 1970) was writing about the modifications of the 'nisus sexualis' (the sexual instinct) in individuals, and other formative works followed: on the presence and dangers of childhood sexuality, the sexual aetiology of hysteria, and the sexual aberrations. Karl Heinrich Ulrichs (see Ellenberger 1970), himself homosexually inclined, published twelve volumes on homosexuality (given its name by Benkert in 1869) between 1864 and 1879, an achievement that was greatly to influence Carl Westphal's 'discovery' of the 'contrary sexual impulse' by 1870, and Krafft-Ebing's wider speculations on sexual aberrations thereafter (Ellenberger 1970; Weeks 1985: Chapter 4).

But two moments are particularly important in this emergent discourse, imparting elements which were to inflect its course profoundly. The first was the impact of Darwinism. Charles Darwin's *Origin of Species* had already hinted at the applicability of the theory of natural selection to humans. With Darwin's *The Descent of Man, and Selection in Relation to Sex* another element was added: the claim that sexual selection (the struggle for partners) acted independently of natural selection (the struggle for existence) so that survival depended upon sexual selection, and the ultimate test of biological success lay in reproduction (Darwin 1871). This led to a revival of interest in the sexual 'origins' of individual behaviour and a sustained effort to delineate the dynamics of sexual selection, the sexual impulse, and the differences between the sexes. Biology became the privileged road into the mysteries of nature, and its findings were backed up by the evidence of natural history in all its wondrous peculiarity and order.

The second decisive moment was the appearance of Richard von Krafft-Ebing's *Psychopathia Sexualis* which went through various ever-expanding editions from 1886 to 1903. A compendium, in its last edition, of 238 case histories, it represented the eruption into print of the speaking pervert, the individual marked for ever by his or her sexual impulses (Krafft-Ebing 1931). His success amongst certain circles, of esteem as well as (especially in England) scandal, encouraged many others:

between 1898 and 1908 there were over 1,000 publications on homosexuality alone. In his *Three Essays on the Theory of Sexuality*, published in 1905, and simultaneously a product of and contribution to the growth of sexual theory, Freud acknowledged the influence of nine writers: Krafft-Ebing, Albert Moll, P. J. Moebius, Havelock Ellis, Albert Schrenck-Notzing, Leopold Lowenfeld, Albert Eulenburg, Iwan Bloch, and Magnus Hirschfeldt (Freud 1953–74, vol. 7). To these could be added a host of other names out of the proliferating volumes of the time, from J. L. Casper and J. J. Moreau, to Cesare Lombroso and Auguste Forel, Valentin Magnan and Benjamin Tarnowsky, names dimly remembered today, some almost forgotten during their lifetimes, but significant influences nevertheless on the modern discourse of sexology – and of identity.

At the heart of their work was the firm belief that underlying the diversity of individual experiences and social effects was a complex natural process which needed to be understood in all its forms. This endeavour demanded in the first place a major effort at the classification and definition of sexual pathologies, giving rise to the exotic array of minute descriptions and taxonomic labelling so characteristic of the late nineteenth century. Krafft-Ebing's *Psychopathia Sexualis* announced itself as a 'medico-forensic study' of the 'abnormal' and proffered a catalogue of perversities from acquired sexual inversion to zoophilia. Urolagnia and coprolagnia, fetishism and kleptomania, exhibitionism and sado-masochism, frottage, chronic satyriasis, and nymphomania[1] made their clinical appearance via or in the wake of his pioneering cataloguing. Meanwhile, Iwan Bloch bravely stepped out to describe the strange sexual practices of all races in all ages. Charles Féré intrepidly explored sexual degeneration in man and animals. Albert Moll described the perversions of the sex instinct. Magnus Hirschfeld wrote voluminously on homosexuality and later on transvestism while Havelock Ellis's *Studies in the Psychology of Sex* offered a compendious encyclopaedia of the variations of sexual behaviour and beliefs (Weeks 1985: Chapter 4).

Secondly, this concentration on the 'perverse', the 'abnormal', cast new light on the 'normal', discreetly shrouded in respectable ideology but scientifically reaffirmed in clinical textbooks. Ellis began his life's work on the 'psychology of sex' by writing *Man and Woman*. First published in 1894, but subsequently reissued in much revised versions, it is a detailed study of the secondary, tertiary, and other characteristics of and differences between men and women. The study of the sexual instinct in the writings of others became an exploration both of the source of sexuality and of the relations between men and women (Ellis 1894). Krafft-Ebing's 'natural instinct' which 'with all conquering force and might demands fulfilment' (Krafft-Ebing 1931) is an image of male sexuality whose natural object was the opposite sex. Just as homosexuality was defined as a sexual condition peculiar to some people but not others in this period, so the concept of hetero-sexuality was invented to describe 'normality', a normality cir-cumscribed by a founding belief in the sharp distinctions between the sexes and the assumption that gender identity (to be a man or a woman) and sexual identity were necessarily linked through the naturalness of heterosexual object choice. All else fell into the vaguely written but powerful catalogue of perversity.

The scientific fervour of these early sexologists is undoubted, but their efforts cannot be detached from the wider currents of their time. Sexologists were something more than agents of anonymous social forces or even of male imperatives of sexual control as some recent feminists have argued (see Jackson in this volume). They were also something less than neutral observers of the passing sexual scene. One of the major roles of the sexologists was to translate into theoretical terms what were increasingly being perceived as concrete social problems. Problems concern-ing the social definition of childhood are transformed into a pro-longed debate over the existence, or non-existence, of child and adolescent sexuality. The question of female sexuality becomes focused on discussions about the origins of hysteria, the relation of the maternal to the sex instinct, and the social consequences of female periodicity. A concern with the changing relations between the genders produces a crop of speculations about bi-sexuality, transvestism, intersexuality, and the reproductive instinct. A growing precision in the legal pursuit of sexual ab-normality, with the abandonment of old ecclesiastical for new secular offences, leads to a controversy over the cause of homo-sexuality (hereditary taint, degeneration, seduction, or con-genital) and consequently over the efficacy of legal control. As Krafft-Ebing noted, the medical barrister 'finds out how sad the lack of our knowledge is in the domain of sexuality when he is called upon to express an opinion as to the responsibility of the accused whose life, liberty and honour are at stake' (Krafft-Ebing 1931: vii).

It was in particular through its relationship with the medical profession that sexology became respectable. A new thoroughness in the systematic exploration and understanding of the body in the nineteenth century in a very important sense made sexology possible by reshaping the questions that could be asked about the human (sexed) body and its internal processes. But the more dangerous side of this was that sexological insight could easily become subordinated to a medical norm. Many commentators in the nineteenth century, especially feminists, were noting the elevation of the medical profession into a new priestly caste, as the profession sought to consolidate itself, and as its principles and practices were utilized in social intervention, especially in relation to women. At best doctors, with few exceptions, generally acquiesced in stereotyped ideas of womanhood even if they were not militant in shaping them. At worst doctors actually intervened to shape female sexuality, through casework, organizing against women's access to higher education because of their supposed incapacity for intellectual work, supporting new forms of legal intervention and evidence, and campaigning against abortion and birth-control (L'Esperance 1977).

The production in sexological discourse of a body of knowledge that is apparently scientifically neutral (about women, about sexual variants, delinquents, or offenders) can become a useful resource for the production of normative definitions that limit and demarcate erotic behaviour. By the 1920s the traditional social purity organizations, deeply rooted as they were in evangelical Christian traditions, were prepared to embrace a selection of insights from Ellis and Freud (Weeks 1981: 212). Today even the moral Right finds it opportune to legitimize its religious crusades by reference to sexological findings. Sexology has never been straightforwardly outside or against relations of power; it has been deeply involved in them.

Sexology, then, is not simply descriptive. It is at times profoundly prescriptive, telling us what we ought to be like, what makes us truly ourselves and 'normal'. It is in this sense that the sexological account of sexual identity can be seen as an imposition, a crude tactic of power designed to obscure a real sexual diversity with the myth of a sexual destiny. This seems to be the argument of Michel Foucault in at least some of his writings. His edition of the tragic memoirs of the mid-nineteenth-century hermaphrodite, Herculin Barbin, is a paean to the 'happy limbo of a non-identity' and a warning of the dire consequences of insisting upon a true identity hidden behind the ambiguities of outward appearance: 'Biological theories of sexuality, juridical conceptions of the individual, forms of administrative control in modern nations, led little by little to rejecting the idea of a mixture of the two sexes in a single body, and consequently to limiting the free choice of indeterminate individuals' (Foucault 1980: viii). The seeking out of a 'true identity' is here seen as a threat and a challenge, because it is not freely chosen. It claims to be finding what we *really* are, or should be, and as a result identity becomes an imposition.

Identity as resistance

Yet at the same time, as Barry Adam (1978: 12) has put it, 'identity is differentiation': it is about affinities based on selection, self-actualization, and apparently choice. For the social theorists of the 1950s who first brought the question of 'identity' on to the agenda of the anguished liberal west – Erik Erikson, Erving Goffman, *et al*. (Gleason 1983) – personal identity roughly equalled individuality, a reality to be struggled for in the hazardous process of maturation or against the awesome weight of the social, rummaged out in the interstices of society, amongst the crevices forgotten or ignored by weighty social forces. For the 'sexual minorities' coming to a new sense of their separateness and individuality during the same period – male homosexuals and lesbians particularly – the finding of 'identity' was like discovering a map to explore a new country (D'Emilio 1983). As Plummer has put it, categorization and self-categorization, that is the process of identity formation, may control, restrict, and inhibit, but simultaneously they offer 'comfort, security and assuredness' (1981: 29). This is the paradox of the sexological endeavour. It not only sought to regulate through naming; it also provided the springboard for self-definition and individual and collective resistance.

The theoretical seeds of this counter-discourse – what Foucault has called a 'reverse affirmation' (Foucault 1979) – were sown within the sexological discourse itself. At the same time as he enthusiastically deployed the latest findings of the sexual science, Freud was working to undermine some of its founding assumptions. Though he never personally gave up the belief that a complex biological mechanism underlay the workings of the mind, his account of the dynamic unconscious and of the autonomy of psychic life served to challenge the fixity of all biologically given positions, the inevitability of sexual difference, and the essentiality of sexual identity (Coward 1983: Chapter 7). Identity for Freud was clearly not an inevitable product of inbuilt instincts; it was a struggle through which a tentative accommodation of conflicting drives and desires with the structures of language and reality was precariously achieved. If, *ab initio*, in some mythical point of origin, everyone was potentially bisexual and 'polymorphously perverse', if a sense of being masculine or feminine was only attained through complex psychic struggles, never preordained, and if the line between normal and perverse development was so fine that the distinction constantly breaks down in adult life, how could the neat demarcations of the sexologists be true? As Freud himself noted, homosexuality is a peculiarity of object-choice, not a constitutional, perverted instinct. The implication of this is that homosexuality is not absolutely separable from heterosexuality for 'one must remember that normal sexuality too depends upon a reduction in the choice of object'. Both are compromises from the range of possibilities rooted in the original, undifferentiated nature of the libido. It followed that: 'From the point of view of psycho-analysis the exclusive sexual interest felt by men for women is also a problem that needs elucidating and is not a self-evident fact based upon an attraction that is ultimately of a chemical nature' (Freud 1953–74, vol.7: 146). Looked at from the complexities of adult object-choice, achieved at the cost of sacrifice, renunciation, and pain, heterosexuality was no more naturally privileged than homosexuality.

Freud, of course, did not fully accept *that* implication. Even less so did many of his successors, who proceeded to erect on the subtleties of Freud's insights a dogmatic orthodoxy through which it became possible to argue that identity could only be satisfactorily achieved by adjustment to a pre-selected normality; all else was arrested development (Socarides 1978). But the radical insights of Freud have remained as a constant reminder of an alternative way of conceiving of sexual difference and sexual identity. It is at this point that contemporary feminism and the radical sexual movements seek to reappropriate Freud as a guide to a non-essentialist theory of identity (Mitchell and Rose 1982).

An alternative (though sometimes complementary) route to the same point has been through the sociological and anthropological investigations of social life. At the most general they showed that things had changed, that other times and other cultures lived their sexualities differently. More specifically, particular traditions of social investigation managed to normalize the peculiarities of sexual diversity and (from the contemporary western view) moral unorthodoxy. The sociological tradition initiated by George Herbert Mead, and culminating in the proliferating modern anatomies of minority sexual subcultures, sought to understand sexual diversity in its own terms and to suggest that the hazards of social scripting and the chances of contingency and drift played as much part in sexual identification as anatomy or destiny (Gagnon and Simon 1974). Almost at the same time the social anthropological tradition most famously represented by Margaret Mead offered vivid descriptions of other patterns of socialization and personal identity, with the suggestion that perhaps all was not well with western patterns of child rearing and family organization (Weeks 1985: Chapter 5).

The psychoanalytic and the sociological/anthropological discourses have their problematic elements, of course, but this is not the place to pursue them. The point that needs to be underlined here is that these two positions both sought to challenge the certainties of the 'sexual tradition' by asserting the tentative nature of sexual identification. Identity could never quite be seen as destiny again.

These fractures in the theoretical certainty of sexological accounts have been paralleled, as already suggested, by other developments on the terrain of individual lives and subcultural response. It is very tempting to write as if sexology *created* the sexual subjects it so enthusiastically attempted to describe, and in the radical critique of sexology that has developed over the past decade this is an ever-present temptation (Foucault 1979; Faderman 1981; Coveney *et al.* 1984). But the actual history is far more complex and the role of sexology more subtle than this would suggest. The example of homosexuality is a particularly useful one here again, partly because it was at the heart of sexological debates, partly because there are now flourishing schools of radical gay and lesbian history which throw new light on the actual developments.

From the latter it becomes clear that while erotic activity between men and men and women and women has existed in all times and all cultures, only in a few societies does a distinctive homosexual identity emerge. The evidence suggests that among women, almost into this century, close relationships were not clearly demarcated, either by women or by an otherwise inquisitive public opinion, into sexual or non-sexual, lesbian or heterosexual. The concepts just did not exist (Faderman 1981). Among men there probably did exist a growing sense of difference, with the early eighteenth century a key moment of differentiation, and there certainly existed an expanding subcultural network of meeting places and styles. Yet it is difficult to see clear signs of a distinctive homosexual life style and identity until the latter part of the nineteenth century (Weeks 1977; Bray 1982). Given this, the sexological 'discovery' of the homosexual during that period is obviously of crucial importance. It gives a name, an aetiology, and potentially the elements of an identity, marking off a special homosexual type of person, with distinctive desires, aptitudes, and even physiognomy. Inspired by the recognition of this sexological moment some historians have sought to argue that it was the categorizations that made 'the homosexual' and 'the lesbian' possible. Until sexology gave them the name there was only the half life of an amorphous sense of self. Thereafter, the homosexual belonged to a species (Foucault 1979).

On the other hand, there is abundant evidence that sexologists produced their definitions in order to understand phenomena presenting themselves before their initially slightly startled eyes: as patients, as clients before the courts or in the public print, as objects of scandal and derision. A more likely explanation of

sexological efforts is that they were trying to explain such manifestations, not create them. This is quite clear from Krafft-Ebing's
effusions on the subject and his aim to produce a 'medico-
forensic' study. Sexologists were, in fact, responding to social
developments providing the conditions for new identities which
were occurring through a different, if necessarily related, history. The definitions thus produced had, of course, powerful
effects. They led, as Katz (1982) graphically put it, to the 'medical
colonization' of a people. They established the boundaries
beyond which it has been very difficult to think. Homosexual
identities have been established within the parameters set by
sexological definition. But they have been established by living
and breathing men and women. What sexology did was indeed to
set up restrictive definitions, and to be regularly complicit with
the controlling ambitions of a variety of social practices. At the
same time it also put into language a host of definitions and
meanings which could be played with, challenged, negated, and
used. Sexology, usually against its intentions, contributed
through its definitions to the self-definition of those it sought to
identify.

The most obvious reason for the emphasis on identity as resistance is that for countless numbers of people it was their sexuality
that had been denied. Modern society is fractured by many
divisions, along lines of class, race, religion, ideology, status, and
age. These intersect with, and complicate, but do not cause, two
other major divisions, of gender and sexual preference. It is only at
certain times, in certain cultures, that these divisions become the
central foci of political controversy. Though feminism has swept
the west (and parts of the Third World) since the late 1960s, by and
large more specific questions of sexual choice have not become
major mobilizing issues. In countries like Britain and France active
gay movements have successfully inspired thousands of people,
but as political forces they have largely been subordinated to more
traditional progressive politics. Issues of class and ideology weigh
heavier than sexuality. But in the United States, where class
loyalties are less fixed, politics more coalition-minded, 'minority'
politics (especially the struggles of blacks) better established, and
social loyalties more fluid, sexuality *has* become a potent political
issue, and sexual communities have become bases for political
mobilization (D'Emilio 1983: Altman 1982).

This is not, however, merely another product of West Coast esotericism. A city like San Francisco has become a forcing house of sexual radicalism because, for a variety of historical reasons, it has been a refuge for those escaping the sexual ethics of moral America. San Francisco, Edmund White wittily argued, became 'a sort of gay finishing school, a place where neophytes can confirm their gay identity' (1980: 65–6). Women and men have mobilized around their sense of sexual identity in such a place because it was in their sexuality that they felt most powerfully invalidated.

The resulting preoccupation with identity among the sexually marginal cannot be explained as an effect of a peculiar personal obsession with sex. It has to be seen, more accurately, as a powerful resistance to the organizing principle of traditional sexual attitudes. It has been the sexual radicals who have most insistently politicized the question of sexual identity. But the agenda has been largely shaped by the importance assigned by our culture to 'correct' sexual behaviour.

But politicized sexual identities are not automatic responses to negative definitions. For their emergence, they need complex social and political conditions in order to produce a sense of community experience which makes for collective endeavour. Barry Adam has suggested that five conditions are necessary for this: the existence of large numbers in the same situation; geographical concentration; identifiable targets of opposition; sudden events or changes in social position; and an intellectual leadership with readily understood goals (Adam 1978: 123). Each of these has been present in the emergence of the most spectacularly successful of politicized sexual identities, the lesbian and gay identities, over the past twenty years. The growth of urban subcultures since World War II especially in North America, but also in Europe, the emergence of general currents of hostility, from McCarthyism to moral panics around the impact of 'permissiveness' and the sexual revolution, the growth of new social movements with radical sexual agendas, such as feminism and the lesbian and gay movements, not to mention the movements of the 'sexual fringe' following in their wake – each of these has helped to make for the emergence of 'the modern homosexual', now not so much a curiosity in the fading pages of sexology textbooks but the bearer of a fully blown social and human identity (D'Emilio 1983; Plummer 1981).

Identity as choice

One difficulty is that not all homosexually inclined people want to identify their minority status – or even see themselves as homosexual. Sexologists, at least since Kinsey, have pointed out that there is no necessary connection between sexual behaviour and sexual identity. According to Kinsey's best-known statistic, some 37 per cent of men had homosexual experiences to orgasm. But perhaps less than 4 per cent were exclusively homosexual – and even they did not necessarily express a homosexual identity, a concept of which, in any case, Kinsey disapproved (Kinsey, Pomeroy, and Martin 1948). Other surveys of homosexually inclined men have revealed a frequent 'flight from identity' with substantial numbers of people – up to a third in some earlier samples – wishing they could swallow a magic pill and not be homosexual (Adam 1978: 92).

Sexual identification is a strange thing. There are some people who identify as gay and participate in the gay community but do not experience or wish for homosexual activity. And there are homosexually active people who do not identify as gay. Many black homosexuals, for example, prefer to identify primarily as 'black' rather than 'gay' and to align themselves with black rather than gay political positions. Obviously, as Barry Dank has argued, 'the development of a homosexual identity is dependent on the meanings that the actor attaches to the concepts of homosexual and homosexuality' (1979: 130). These processes in turn depend on the person's environment and wider community. Many people, it has been argued, 'drift' into identity, battered by contingency rather than guided by will. Four characteristic stages have been identified by Plummer: 'sensitization', when the individual becomes aware of the possibility of being different; 'signification', when he or she attributes a developing meaning to these differences; 'subculturalization', the stage of recognizing oneself through involvement with others; and 'stabilization', the stage of full acceptance of one's feelings and way of life (Plummer 1975). There is no automatic progression through these stages; each transition is dependent as much on chance as on decision; and there is no necessary acceptance of the final destiny, of an open identity. Some choices are forced on individuals, whether through stigmatization and public obloquy or through political necessity. But the point that needs underlining is that *identity* is a choice. It is not *dictated* by internal imperatives.

The implication of this is that 'desire' is one thing, while subject position, that is identification with a particular social position and organizing sense of self, is another (Hocquenghem 1978). This means that labels such as 'gay' and 'lesbian' increasingly become *political* choices, and in that process the sexual connotations can all but disappear. This is clearest in recent debates about a lesbian identity. Among gay men the issue has fundamentally concerned sex, validating a denied sexuality. In debates on lesbianism, on the other hand, there have been heated exchanges about the necessary connection of a lesbian identity to sexual practices. Conventional wisdom and, even more stringently, sexological expertise, have defined lesbianism as a sexual category. But increasingly it has been proposed by feminists as primarily a political definition, in which sexuality plays a problematic role. As Lillian Faderman puts it, 'Women who identify themselves as lesbians generally do not view lesbianism as a sexual phenomenon first and foremost' (Faderman 1981: 142). It is instead a relationship in which two women's strongest emotions and affection are directed towards one another. It becomes a synonym for sisterhood, solidarity, and affection, and as such a fundamental attribute of feminism.

Recent lesbian-feminist writers have understandably largely rejected the social-science and sexological definitions of lesbianism. Traditionally female homosexuality has been seen almost exclusively in terms derived from the experience or study of males. Male homosexuality has invariably been more closely observed and researched than lesbianism, partly because of its greater public salience, partly because it challenged the dominant definitions of male sexuality, and partly because female sexuality has usually been studied only in so far as it was responsive to male sexuality, and lesbianism was hardly understandable in those terms. More recently, ethnographies of female homosexuality have tended to adopt research techniques honed in investigation of male behaviour, concentrating, for example, on 'coming out', contact patterns, sexual expression, and duration of relationships (Krieger 1982). The impact of this has been to conceptualize lesbianism, like male homosexuality, as a specific minority experience little different in its implications from male patterns. This has been criticized in turn by some lesbian-feminists as inevitably having the effect of establishing male homosexuality as the norm, while ignoring the implications of lesbianism for feminism.

The most powerful exponent of a 'political lesbian' position has been Adrienne Rich. In her influential essay 'Compulsory Heterosexuality and Lesbian Existence' she argues that a distinction has to be made between the 'lesbian continuum' and 'lesbian existence' (Rich 1980). The latter is equivalent to a lesbian identity but its character is not defined by sexual practice. It is the sense of self of women bonded primarily to women who are sexually and emotionally independent of men. In turn this is the expression of the 'lesbian continuum', the range through women's lives of woman-identified experience. Such experiences go beyond the possibility of genital sex, to embrace many forms of primary intensity, including the sharing of inner life, the bonding against male tyranny, practical and political support, marriage resistance, female support networks and communities. Such possibilities of bonding between women are denied by 'compulsory heterosexuality'. Rich speaks of 'the rendering invisible of the lesbian possibility, an engulfed continent which rises fragmentedly to view from time to time only to become submerged again' (Rich 1980: 647). 'Compulsory heterosexuality' is the key mechanism of control of women, ensuring in its tyranny of definition the perpetuation of male domination. Lesbianism is the point of resistance to this heterosexual dominance, its central antagonistic force.

Lesbianism is thus about the realization of the male-free potential of women, and in drawing on this essence, male definitions are cast aside. Rich sharply dissociates lesbianism from male homosexuality because of the latter's presumed relationship, *inter alia*, to pederasty, anonymous sex, and ageism. Lesbianism, on the other hand, she argues, is a profoundly *female* experience, like motherhood, and she looks forward to a powerful new female eroticism.

Against the passion and conviction of Rich's position three fundamental criticisms have been made (see Snitow, Stansell, and Thompson 1984: Section IV). In the first place it is based on a romantic naturalization of female bonds. It is not always clear whether Rich sees the 'lesbian continuum' as a powerful solidarity that is there but constantly suppressed, or as a potentiality that could be realized in a mythical future, but in either case it stretches towards an essentialism about femininity which can distort the complexities of the construction of women, and obscure the necessary politics. As Cora Kaplan has noted, in Rich's scenario, 'female heterosexuality is socially constructed and female homosexuality is natural. . . . Political lesbianism becomes more than a strategic position for feminism, it is a return to nature' (1983: 31). Nature is now benign, female and affectionate, sensual and creative, revolutionary and transcendent – and lesbian. But all the problems in naturalistic explanations of sex still come to the fore: its untheorized and untheorizable claims to truth, its transhistorical pretensions, and its strong moralism: this is how you must behave because nature tells us so. The result is a narrowing in political focus, and this is the second major objection. The view that attributes all women's oppression to 'compulsory heterosexuality' suggests that somehow women are always socially controlled by men. Women are, in consequence, inevitably presented as perpetual sufferers and victims, beyond the possibility of resistance.

Finally, the political lesbian position tends to deny the specifics of lesbian sexuality. Lesbian activists such as Pat Califia (1980) have suggested that there is a history of a specific lesbian eroticism which has been historically denied, and which has produced its own forms of struggle and institutionalization. According to Ann Ferguson, Rich's view:

'undermines the important historical development of an explicit identity connected to genital sexuality. My own view is that the development of such an identity, and with it the development of a sexuality valued and accepted in a community of peers, extended women's life options and degree of independence from men.'   (Ferguson 1981: 100)

For such feminists, the elevation of female sexuality in general into a semi-mystical bonding, where bodily contact and genital pleasure are secondary or even non-existent, denies the possibilities of female eroticism, including the real potentiality of lesbianism.

This is not the place to enter a full discussion of these differing positions. The point that requires emphasizing here is that like the gay male identity, the lesbian identity has a political as well as a social and personal implication. That means that there need be no necessary relationship between sexual practice and sexual identity. On the other hand the existence of a specific identity testifies to the historic denial of a particular form of female desire – and the struggle necessary to affirm it. As with the homosexual male, the lesbian identity – whatever its 'true' meaning – is historically contingent but seemingly inevitable; potentially limiting – but apparently politically essential.

Identity and relationships

Identity is not a destiny but a choice. But in a culture where homosexual desires, female or male, are still execrated and denied, the adoption of lesbian or gay identities inevitably constitutes a *political* choice. These identities are not expressions of secret essences. They are self-creations, but they are creations on ground not freely chosen but laid out by history. So homosexual identities illustrate the play of constraint and opportunity, necessity and freedom, power and pleasure. Sexual identities seem necessary in the contemporary world as starting-points for a politics around sexuality. But the form they take is not predetermined. In the end, therefore, they are not so much about who we really are, what our sex dictates. They are about what we want to be and could be. But this means they are also about the morality of acts and the quality of relations. We live in a world of proliferating 'sexual identities' as specific desires (paedophile, sado-masochistic, bisexual . . .) become the focus either for minute subdivisions of well-established notions (gayness or lesbianism) or spin off into wholly new ones. Can we therefore say that all identities are of equal value, and that minute subdivisions of desire, however apparently bizarre and esoteric, deserve social recognition on the basis of the *right* to erotic difference and sexual identity (Weeks 1985: Chapter 9).

Such questions have led to the development of what may be termed a 'relationship paradigm' as opposed to the traditional 'identity paradigm' as a way of thinking through some of the conceptual – and political – issues (De Cecco and Shively 1984). If, as many advocates of gay politics have suggested, identity is a constraint, a limitation on the flux of possibilities and the exploration of desires, if it is only a historical acquisition, then surely its assertion should be historically junked or at least modified (Minson 1981). The difficulty is to find a replacement that would equally satisfactorily provide a basis for personal coherence and social recognition. One possibility is to celebrate the flux, to indulge in a glorification of the 'polysexualities' to which, on a radical reading of the Freudian tradition, we are all heir (Semio-text(e) 1981). The unfortunate difficulty with this is that most individuals do not feel 'polymorphously perverse'. On the contrary they feel their sexual desires are fairly narrowly organized, whatever use they make of those desires in real life. Moreover, a social identity is no less real for being historically formed. Sexual identities are no longer arbitrary divisions of the field of possibilities; they are encoded in a complex web of social practices – legal, pedagogic, medical, moral, and personal. They cannot be willed away.

The aim of the 'relationship paradigm', in contrast, is not to ignore questions of identity but to displace them, by stressing instead the need to examine relationships. If this is done we can look again both at our sexual history and our sexual presence. Historically, we need no longer look for the controversial emergence of identities. Instead we can see the complicated net of relationships through which sexuality is always expressed, changing over time. Looked at from a contemporary point of view, we see not the culmination of a process of identity development but the formation of new types of relationships, validating hitherto execrated sexualities, in complex communities of interest around sex.

This is a very tempting position to adopt. In particular it potentially allows sexual thinking to move away from a 'morality of acts', where all debate is about the merits of this form of sexuality as opposed to that, to an 'ethics of choice', where the question becomes one of the quality of involvement and the freedom of relationships. This puts the whole debate on quite a new footing, allowing questions of power, diversity, and sexual pluralism to be brought in (Weeks 1985).

The difficulty with the 'relationship paradigm' is that it is offered as an alternative to questions of identity. This is a false antinomy. Identities are always 'relational' in the general sense that they only exist in relation to other potential identities. More crucially, identities must always be about relationships: to ourselves, precarious unities of conflicting desires and social commitments, 'composed of heterogeneous fragments of fossilized cultures' (Gramsci 1975: 213); and to others, who address us and call upon our recognition in diverse ways and through whom our sense of self is always negotiated. A sense of identity is essential for the establishment of relationships. As Foucault has argued, 'sex is not a fatality, it's a possibility for creative life' (Foucault 1984). For a variety of historical reasons that possibility is mediated through a recognition of identity. Identity may well be a historical fiction, a controlling myth, a limiting burden. But it is at the same time a necessary means of weaving our way through a hazard-strewn world and a complex web of social relations. Without it, it seems, the possibilities of sexual choice are not increased but diminished.

Note

1 Urolagnia refers to deriving pleasure from watching people urinate, coprolagnia from watching them defecate. Frottage means rubbing. Chronic satyriasis is the male equivalent of nymphomania, i.e. a state of constant sexual desire.

References

Adam, B. (1978) *The Survival of Domination: Inferiorization and Everyday Life*. New York: Elsevier.

Altman, D. (1982) *The Homosexualization of America, the Americanization of the Homosexual*. New York: St Martin's Press.

Bray, A. (1982) *Homosexuality in Renaissance England*. London: Gay Men's Press.

Califia, P. (1980) *Sapphistry: The Book of Lesbian Sexuality*. New York: Naiad Press.

Coveney, L., Jackson, M., Jeffreys, S., Kaye, L., and Mahony, P. (1984) *The Sexuality Papers: Male Sexuality and the Social Control of Women*. London: Hutchinson.

Coward, R. (1983) *Patriarchal Precedents. Sexuality and Social Relations*. London: Routledge & Kegan Paul.

Dank, B. (1979) Coming Out in the Gay World. In M. Levine (ed.) *Gay Men: The Sociology of Male Homosexuality*. New York: Harper & Row.

Darwin, C. (1871) *The Descent of Man, and Selection in Relation to Sex*. London: John Murray. 2 vols.

De Cecco, J. P. and Shively, M. G. (1984) From Sexual Identity to Sexual Relationships. *Journal of Homosexuality* 9 (2 and 3).

50   The Cultural Construction of Sexuality

D'Emilio, J. (1983) *Sexual Politics, Sexual Communities. The Making of a Homosexual Minority in the United States 1940–76*. Chicago and London: University of Chicago Press.

Ellenberger, H. F. (1970) *The Discovery of the Unconscious. The History and Evolution of Dynamic Psychiatry*. New York: Basic Books.

Ellis, H. H. (1894) *Man and Woman*. London: Walter Scott.

Faderman, L. (1981) *Surpassing the Love of Men. Romantic Friendship and Love between Women from the Renaissance to the Present*. London: Junction Books.

Ferguson, A. (1981) On 'Compulsory Heterosexuality and Lesbian Existence'. *Signs* 7 (1).

Foucault, M. (1979) *The History of Sexuality Vol. 1: An Introduction*. London: Allen Lane.

—— (1980) *Herculin Barbin. Being the Recently Discovered Memoirs of a Nineteenth Century French Hermaphrodite*. New York: Pantheon.

—— (1984) An Interview: Sex, Power and the Politics of Identity, by B. Gallagher and A. Wilson *The Advocate* 400.

Freud, S. (1953–74) *The Standard Edition of the Complete Psychological Works of Sigmund Freud*, ed. James Strachey. London: Hogarth Press.

Gagnon, J. H. and Simon, W. (1974) *Sexual Conduct. The Social Sources of Human Sexuality*. London: Hutchinson.

Gallop, J. (1982) *Feminism and Psychoanalysis. The Daughter's Seduction*. London: Macmillan.

Gleason, P. (1983) Identifying Identity: A Semantic History. *Journal of American History* 69 (4).

Gramsci, A. (1975) *Letters from Prison*, ed. L. Lawner. London: Lawrence & Wishart.

Hocquenghem, G. (1978) *Homosexual Desire*. London: Allison & Busby.

Kaplan, C. (1983) Wild Nights: Pleasure/Sexuality/Feminism. *Formations of Pleasure*. London: Routledge & Kegan Paul.

Katz, J. N. (1982) *Gay/Lesbian Almanac*. New York: Crowell.

Kinsey, A. C., Pomeroy, W. B., and Martin, C. E. (1948) *Sexual Behaviour in the Human Male*. Philadelphia and London: W. B. Saunders.

Krafft-Ebing, R. von (1931) *Psychopathia Sexualis*. Brooklyn: Physicians and Surgeons Book Co.

Krieger, S. (1982) Lesbian Identity and Community: Recent Social Science Literature. *Signs* 8 (1).

L'Esperance, J. (1977) Doctors and Women in Nineteenth Century Society: Sexuality and Role. In J. Woodward and D. Richards (eds) *Health Care and Popular Medicine in Nineteenth Century England*. London: Croom Helm.

Minson, J. (1981) The Assertion of Homosexuality. *m/f* 5–6.

Mitchell, J. and Rose, J. (eds) (1982) *Jacques Lacan and the Ecole Freudienne: Feminine Sexuality*. London: Macmillan.

Plummer, K. (1975) *Sexual Stigma*. London: Routledge & Kegan Paul.

Plummer, K. (ed.) (1981) *The Making of the Modern Homosexual*. London: Hutchinson.

Rich, A. (1980) Compulsory Heterosexuality and Lesbian Existence. *Signs* 5 (4).

Semiotext(e) (1981) Polysexuality. *Semiotext(e)* IV (1).

Snitow, A., Stansell, C., and Thompson, S. (eds) (1984) *Desire: The Politics of Sexuality*. London: Virago.

Socarides, C. W. (1978) *Homosexuality*. New York: Jason Aranson.

Weeks, J. (1977) *Coming Out: Homosexual Politics in Britain from the Nineteenth Century to the Present*. London: Quartet.

—— (1981) *Sex, Politics and Society. The Regulation of Sexuality since 1800*. London: Longman.

—— (1985) *Sexuality and its Discontents. Meanings, Myths and Modern Sexualities*. London: Routledge & Kegan Paul.

White, E. (1980) *States of Desire*. New York: Dutton.

Wilson, E. (1983) I'll Climb the Stairway to Heaven: Lesbianism in the Seventies. In S. Cartledge and J. Ryan (eds) *Sex and Love: New Thoughts on Old Contradictions*. London: The Women's Press.

2 'Facts of life' or the eroticization of women's oppression? Sexology and the social construction of heterosexuality

Margaret Jackson

My research into sexology stemmed initially from my involvement in the Women's Liberation Movement, and especially in the campaigning group Women Against Violence Against Women. I was a member of a group which was interested in analysing male sexuality and its function in the social control of women, and I took on the task of investigating the role of sexologists in legitimizing prevalent myths about male sexuality, for example the myth that men rape women because they are overcome by uncontrollable sexual urges. As I ploughed through the sexological literature of the early and late twentieth century it became clear to me that sexology was about much more than legitimizing myths; it was also about constructing a model of sexuality which purported to be objective and scientific but in fact reflected and promoted the interests of men in a sexually divided society. Although I had long ago abandoned belief in simplistic notions of sexual liberation, and had learned, like other feminists, to see the 'sexual revolution' for what it really was, namely a means of increasing and legitimating male right of sexual access to women, I was surprised at the degree of anti-feminism contained in the sexologists' writings. I had gained the impression, from reading feminist and Marxist analyses of the work of early twentieth-century sexologists and sex reformers such as Havelock Ellis and Stella Browne, that these pioneers of sexual enlightenment had been decidedly pro-feminist (Rowbotham 1977; Rowbotham and Weeks 1977); and I had read several articles by American radical feminists drawing attention to the feminist implications of the work of Masters and Johnson (e.g. Koedt 1970). But the more sexology I read, the more convinced I became that its theories and recommendations, if put into practice, could only work against the interests of women and reinforce male supremacy.

Feminism, sexuality, and sexology at the turn of the century

It is generally agreed that the three major landmarks of twentieth-century sexology are represented by the work of Havelock Ellis (from the turn of the century to the late 1930s), Alfred Kinsey (from World War II up to the 1950s) and William Masters and Virginia Johnson (from the 1960s onwards). According to most historians and biographers, it is largely due to these researchers that sex in the twentieth century has been 'modernized' (Robinson 1976), and many people – especially women – liberated from Victorian sexual repression (Brecher 1970). Havelock Ellis is regarded as especially significant because of his key role in establishing sexology as a science and laying the foundations of modern sex research. In his own time he achieved world-wide recognition as the leading authority on sex, and his influence on the popular sex manuals of the 1920s and 1930s and even of the post-war years was enormous.[1]

Ellis's ideas did not emerge in a social or political vacuum. Quite apart from the factors in his personal life which may have impelled him towards the study of sexual behaviour, such as his difficulties in sexual relationships with women and his urolagnia,[2] he was thinking and writing at a time when sexuality was very much an area of debate and struggle. Rosalind Coward (1983) has discussed the nineteenth-century debates around marriage, the family, and the origins of patriarchy, debates which, according to Coward, were sparked off in the 1860s within anthropology and had an important influence on Marxist theory and psychoanalysis and on subsequent attempts to analyse sexuality from these perspectives. Ellis, too, was heavily influenced by anthropology, which constituted one of his main sources; his *Studies in the Psychology of Sex* (in seven volumes) are full of references to and lengthy quotations from contemporary anthropologists, many of whom, such as Malinowski and Westermarck, he knew personally and were involved with him in the World League for Sexual Reform. As Coward points out, evidence of the existence of non-patriarchal societies existed before the 1860s, but it was not until then that it became an important issue and the matriarchalists and patriarchalists began to fight it out. The patriarchalists, drawing heavily on Darwin and evolutionary theory, pointed to evidence of patriarchal patterns in animal life and argued that patriarchy was natural; the matriarchalists, on the other hand, argued for the historical primacy of matriarchy and denied that human societies were necessarily based on animal patterns. Central to this debate was the question of 'the natural', especially with regard to sexual relations.

It hardly seems coincidental that the same period – roughly from the 1860s to the 1920s – witnessed a wave of feminist activity and struggle that – as far as is known – had never before been seen in this country. Historians have focused their attention mainly on the struggle for the vote, and, to a lesser extent, on campaigns such as those for access to higher education and the medical profession, neglecting other equally important and interrelated aspects of feminism at that time. Of particular relevance to this discussion are feminist campaigns around sexuality, which began in the 1860s with Josephine Butler's campaign to repeal the Contagious Diseases Acts, and continued in various forms up to and beyond World War I. Campaigns were organized against the whole spectrum of male violence against and sexual exploitation of women, including wife-beating and murder, organized prostitution, rape in marriage, sexual abuse of children, and all kinds of what would now be called sexual harassment (Jeffreys 1982). Although not all those involved in these campaigns were feminists, and the feminists themselves were not always in agreement over the precise nature of the issues and the best strategies to use (as is still the case today, of course), it is clear that what was absolutely central to all the campaigns was, first, a challenge to the double standard of sexual morality and, second, a critique of the ideology and practice of male sexuality. Above all feminists challenged the prevailing belief that men were victims of sexual urges over which they had no control; on the contrary, far from viewing male sexuality as natural, they regarded it as a weapon of male power, a means by which men were able to exercise control over women and keep them in their place. Some feminists were so determined to fight this aspect of male power that they advocated what amounted to a sex strike against men as a means of resistance. Lucy Re-Bartlett, for example, writing in 1912 in the context of opposition to organized international prostitution and the sexual abuse of children, declared: 'In the hearts of many women today is rising a cry somewhat like this: I will know no man, and bear no child until this apathy is broken through – these wrongs be righted. . . . It is the "silent strike" and it is going on all over the world' (Re-Bartlett 1912). What this represented, in effect, was a challenge not only to marriage and motherhood, but to the institution of heterosexuality itself, though the feminists of the day did not use our terminology. Judging by the high proportion of spinsters involved in the campaigns, especially in the most militant society, the Women's Social and Political Union (led by the Pankhursts), the call did not fall on deaf ears.

I suggest that it is in this sexual-political context that Ellis's work, and the development of sexology as a science, must be analysed. Contemporary feminists were fighting for political, economic, and *sexual* emancipation which, for the majority, was *not* reducible to 'free love' or a single moral standard on male terms;[3] on the contrary, in demanding an end to the use of male sexuality as a tool of male supremacy, what they were fighting *for* was what western feminists today would call *female sexual autonomy*: the right to define and control our own sexuality, free from male sexual exploitation and coercion. Some feminists, moreover, in addition to their involvement in the campaigns, wrote books and articles in which they criticized 'normal' heterosexual intercourse, arguing not only that most women neither enjoyed nor needed it, but that it was a positive danger to women's health. Their criticisms represented not merely an attack on male selfishness and brutality in heterosexual relations but an attempt to redefine female sexuality, male sexuality, and heterosexuality and to construct alternative models.[4] The development of sexology undermined these attempts, by declaring that those aspects of male sexuality and heterosexuality which feminists viewed as social and political were in fact *natural*, and by constructing a 'scientific' model of sexuality on that basis. What I am suggesting is that, in effect, Ellis and his contemporaries (including not only sexologists but biologists, anthropologists and other scientists) were attempting, consciously or unconsciously, to defend male interests against feminist attacks by depoliticizing sexuality; in other words, by removing it from the sexual-political arena and

consigning it to the sphere of 'the natural', the exclusive preserve
of the (male) scientist, they helped to protect it from feminist
challenge.

HAVELOCK ELLIS AND THE EROTICIZATION OF WOMEN'S OPPRESSION

Above all, it has been my analysis of Ellis's work which has led
me to make this claim, and space permits only a brief summary
here.[5] In many respects his ideas can be seen as a direct response
to feminism, a response which he sometimes made quite explicit.
At one point in his *Studies*, for example, he expressed his concern
at the apparently increasing tendency of women to reject their
maternal function, and accused feminists of turning women
away from 'the laws of their own nature'. In the main, however,
his response was much more indirect and subtle. He frankly
conceded that most men were selfish, inconsiderate, and even
brutal lovers, but attributed this to their ignorance and lack of
education in the 'art of love', comparing the average husband to
an orang-utan trying to play the violin. He even presented himself as a champion of female sexual pleasure, apparently endors-
ing women's demands for what *he* termed their 'erotic rights'. It
is partly for this reason that some feminists and socialists, then as
now, have interpreted his ideas as progressive (the other main
reason being his contribution to the liberalization of attitudes
towards male homosexuality). Precisely what he meant by the
erotic rights of women, however, can only be understood in the
context of his model of heterosexuality, a model in which the
concept of female sexual autonomy had absolutely no place.

Ellis argued that sexual intercourse between men and women
was based on animal courtship, which he defined as the pursuit
and conquest of the female by the male. This, he claimed, existed
throughout the animal kingdom and was therefore *natural* – a
biological fact of life. The female's role in courtship, according to
this model, is that of the hunted animal who lures on her pursuer,
not with the aim of escaping, but in order to be finally caught; the
male's role is to capture the female, overcoming her resistance by
force if necessary. Female resistance is, in any case, not 'real', but
all part of the 'game', and designed to increase male sexual
arousal; indeed, Ellis considered that 'normal feminine modesty'

originated from this primitive fear of the hunted animal, and that
'the woman who is lacking in this kind of fear is lacking, also, in
sexual attractiveness to the normal and average man' (1913: I, 1).
For Ellis, then, every act of heterosexual intercourse was essentially a re-enactment of primitive, animal courtship; the male
sexual urge was essentially an urge to conquer, and the female
sexual urge an urge to be conquered: 'The sexual impulse in
woman is fettered by an inhibition which has to be conquered
. . . her wooer in every act of courtship has the enjoyment of conquering afresh an oft-won woman' (1913: I, 3). Thus the close
association between male sexuality, power, and violence was a
biological necessity and therefore inevitable: 'to exert power . . .
is one of our most primary impulses, and it always tends to be
manifested in the attitude of a man towards the woman he loves'
(Ellis 1913: III, 82). Similarly, since the function of female resistance is to increase male arousal (and ultimately to ensure,
according to the 'law' of natural selection, that only the best and
most vigorous males succeed in passing on their genes), there
must be an equally close association between female sexual
pleasure and pain. This Ellis was determined to prove, and
devoted many pages to documenting 'evidence', culled mainly
from anthropological and criminological sources, that women
'really enjoy' being raped, beaten, and sexually humiliated and
brutalized. He concluded that in women pain and sexual
pleasure were virtually indistinguishable: 'the normal manifestations of a woman's sexual pleasure are exceedingly like pain'
(1913: III, 84), brushing feminist objections aside by referring, in
one very revealing paragraph, to 'facts', 'fundamental instincts',
and the 'laws of nature':

'I am well aware that in thus asserting a certain tendency in
women to delight in suffering pain – however careful and
qualified the position I have taken – many estimable people
will cry out that I am degrading a whole sex and generally
supporting the "subjection of women". But the day for
academic discussion concerning the "subjection of women"
has gone by. The tendency I have sought to make clear is too
well established by the experience of normal and typical
women – however numerous the exceptions may be – to be
called into question. I would point out to those who would

deprecate the influence of such facts in relation to social progress that nothing is gained by regarding women as simply men of smaller growth. They are not so: they have the laws of their own nature; their development must be along their own lines, and not along masculine lines. It is as true now as in Bacon's day that we only learn to command nature by obeying her. . . . We can neither attain a sane view of life nor a sane social legislation of life unless we possess a just and accurate knowledge of the fundamental instincts upon which life is built.'   (Ellis 1913: III, 103)

It is not difficult to see how such a model of heterosexuality, presented as scientific fact, might severely undermine the feminist critique of male sexuality and 'normal' heterosexual relations. Most feminist campaigners made it perfectly clear that they did not believe that men were naturally violent or sexually aggressive; on the contrary, they saw male sexuality as an aspect of male power rather than male biology, and believed that it could be changed – indeed, logically they *had* to believe that men could change, otherwise what would have been the point of campaigning? Ellis, by arguing that male dominance and female submission were biologically determined and inherent in heterosexual relations – and, moreover, essential to female sexual pleasure – gave scientific legitimation to precisely that model of sexuality which feminists were challenging; he thereby helped to render it immune from feminist attack. If it was natural, how could it possibly be bad? And how could it possibly be changed? The 'art of love' advocated by Ellis, and enthusiastically promoted by post-war marriage manuals, consisted in teaching man how to arouse in woman 'an emotional condition which leads her to surrender' (1913: III, 69); in other words women had to learn that male sexual demands were natural and inevitable, that they could only achieve sexual pleasure by 'consenting' to be conquered and 'enjoying' their submission to the male. So much for women's 'erotic rights'! At least when they were 'gritting their teeth and thinking of England' they probably had a fairly clear idea of what was being done to them, even if they were powerless to prevent it. This attempted eroticization of their oppression could only obscure the real power relations between the sexes.

'Facts of Life': marriage manuals between the wars

'The wife must be *taught*, not only how to behave in coitus, but, above all, how and what to feel in this unique act!'
(Van de Velde 1928: 232, emphasis in original)

The inter-war period witnessed the birth of the modern sex manual, written with the explicit aim of teaching women how to enjoy sexual intercourse within marriage. It was chiefly by this means that the ideas of Ellis and other sexologists were disseminated; very few members of the general public had direct access to sexological literature at this time since both sales and borrowing from libraries were restricted to specified persons such as doctors, lawyers, and *bona fide* researchers. Even if they had been freely available, very few people would have had either the time or the patience to wade through the huge tomes of extremely dense and largely incomprehensible scientific descriptions and explanations of sexual behaviour.

If the new sexual knowledge was to reach 'ordinary' people, universally regarded by the scientists as woefully ignorant and in urgent need of sexual enlightenment, then it had to be presented in a form and a language which they could understand. The need to popularize the new science thus gave rise to a new kind of 'expert', with the status and credentials to allow them to translate abstract theories into concrete and practical advice which 'ordinary' people could follow. The medical profession was well placed to take on this role, and it was from its ranks that the vast majority of new 'sex experts' was recruited. While some of them had a background in the relatively new disciplines of psychology and psychoanalysis, most specialized in gynaecology and were also involved in the birth-control movement. This intervention of the medical profession into the field of sexual relations, mediating between scientists and ignorant laypersons, can thus be seen as an extension of the medicalization of reproduction and motherhood which had already been established by the early twentieth century (Ehrenreich and English 1979; Oakley 1976).

The explicit rationale of the inter-war marriage manual (and sex education literature in general) was the prevention and cure of sexual maladjustment, which was seen not only as the primary cause of marital unhappiness and instability, but as a threat to the social order itself. Almost without exception there would be a foreword or preface, often written by a clergyman or magistrate, in which concern was expressed at the allegedly rising divorce rate and the need to preserve the institution of marriage.[6] The texts themselves had a strongly evangelical tone, often referring to heterosexual intercourse as a 'sacrament', and preaching a new gospel of personal happiness and fulfilment through the achievement of mutual sexual harmony in marriage.[7] The task of the experts was to teach husbands and wives the sexual techniques which would enable them to achieve this, thereby restoring stability to marriage and thus to the social order. As one gynaecologist and sex reformer expressed it:

> 'Marriage being the mainstay of modern society, its widespread disruption involves not only individual happiness but also the security of our social order. . . . If we succeed through practical advice in increasing marital happiness . . . we shall feel that we have fulfilled our mission, namely, to tighten dangerously relaxed conjugal ties.'   (Haire 1934: 179–80)

Since sexual disharmony was seen as the root cause of all marital discord it was possible to deflect criticisms of marriage as an institution and to side-step questions of the power relations between the sexes; indeed most of the 'experts' assumed that women's emancipation had already been achieved (occasionally hinting that it might even have gone too far). The only remaining obstacle to sexual equality lay, apparently, in the sphere of sexual fulfilment: this was the *only* one of women's rights which the experts unanimously endorsed and which they set out wholeheartedly to promote.

As we have seen, Ellis's concept of women's erotic rights was based on a complete denial of female sexual autonomy; for him the 'art of love' meant orchestrating female sexual pleasure in such a way as to transform submission to the male into an 'erotic' experience for women (as it already was for men). Ellis himself, however, gave very little in the way of explicit advice on sexual technique; it was left to the doctors to translate the basic principles established by Ellis into practice, and to teach women – more precisely, to teach *men* how to teach their wives – how to participate actively and enthusiastically in their own sexual slavery. Marriage manuals (and sex education literature generally) were extremely didactic and prescriptive: they insisted that the education and practical advice they offered was grounded in scientific fact, the implication being that no sane or rational person would challenge or contradict it. Ellis's concept of courtship was accepted and taught as axiomatic, and the imagery of 'The Chase' and 'Man, the Hunter' encapsulated the central theme, which was that in every act of sexual intercourse the woman needed to be 'wooed and won'. Margaret Sanger, an intimate friend of Havelock Ellis, asserted, for example: 'Nature and tradition have decreed that man shall be the wooer, the pursuer, the huntsman. Man is the aggressor . . . adventurous, primitive man does not value highly an easy capture' (1926: 61).

Leonora Eyles declared in similar vein: 'Every woman likes a man to be, at times, something of the caveman; she likes surprise; she likes to run away and be captured and made love to' (1923: 96).

Estelle Cole, who also ran sex education classes for young girls, urged women to remember 'that man is a hunter by nature. He likes to chase his game. His pleasure lies in the pursuit. With capture and possession there often comes loss of interest; so that the wise woman restrains herself at such passionate moments, in order that he may be kept eager in his pursuit' (1938: 53).

This 'natural' difference between female and male sexuality meant that mutual sexual adjustment would be difficult to achieve, and the marriage manuals exhorted husbands to be patient and considerate, assuring them that the long-term rewards would be far greater than any pleasure they might gain from selfish and clumsy attempts at immediate gratification. Women were 'slow' to be aroused and needed to be made 'ready' for coitus; considerable time and, above all, regular practice would be needed in order to establish mutual – and preferably simultaneous – orgasm. For, as Ellis had declared: 'a lock not only requires a key to fit it, but should be entered only at the right moment, and, under the best conditions, may only be adjusted to the key by considerable use' (Ellis 1913: III, 235).

It was musical imagery, however, which tended to predominate, sometimes with monotonous regularity. While the clumsy, inept husband was symbolized by an orang-utan trying to play the violin, woman was variously described as a harp or other delicate instrument who, provided that her husband studied the book of rules, would eventually reward him with melodious tunes:

> ' "woman is a harp who only yields her secrets of melody to the master who knows how to handle her" . . . the husband must study the harp and the art of music . . . this is the book of rules for his earnest and reverent study . . . his reward comes when the harp itself is transformed into an artist in melody, entrancing the initiator.'   (Van de Velde 1928: 214)

Most of the marriage manuals were written with a predominantly male readership in mind, and some were explicitly addressed to husbands, since it was they whom the experts charged with the responsibility for initiating and directing their wives' sexual education and orchestrating their sexual pleasure. Ellis's dictum that 'she is, on the physical side, inevitably the instrument in love; it must be his hand and his bow which evoke the music' (1913: VI, 539) was taken so literally by Van de Velde that the pages of *Ideal Marriage* are littered with words like 'prelude' and 'leitmotiv', and husbands were instructed how to stimulate their wives to 'concert pitch' by playing on the clitoris!

Van de Velde's *Ideal Marriage* was extremely influential. It was first published in English in 1928 and rapidly became regarded as the 'Bible' of sex manuals, a status which it continued to enjoy right up to the 1970s. Van de Velde, a Dutch gynaecologist, was hailed by a recent historian of sex research as the man who 'taught a generation how to copulate' (Brecher 1970). Of all the texts of the inter-war period it is the most thoroughly medical in its approach and it appears that most other writers used it as their principal source after Ellis and the other sexologists. The 1977 paperback edition informs us that the book has been reprinted, with revisions, thirty-eight times, that over 1,000,000 copies have been sold, and that it is still 'the book doctors recommend'. One of the most striking characteristics of this text, and of the many others modelled on it, was the way that it warned husbands of the need to be considerate and sensitive to their wives, especially in the early days of marriage, while emphasizing at the same time the pain and violence supposedly inherent in sexual intercourse. Van de Velde included a lengthy discussion of Ellis's concept of courtship and the biologically inevitable association between love and pain, concluding:

> 'What both man and woman, driven by obscure primitive urges, wish to feel in the sexual act, is the essential force of *maleness*, which expresses itself in a sort of violent and absolute *possession* of the woman. And so both of them can and do exult in a certain degree of male aggression and dominance – whether actual or apparent – which proclaims this essential force.'   (Van de Velde 1928: 139, emphasis in original)

He admitted that the infliction of pain on a woman as a prelude to or a part of coitus reflected the man's pleasure in manifesting power over her, but argued, following Ellis, that since this was an outcome and survival of the primitive process of courtship, it must be 'an almost or quite normal constituent of the sexual impulse in man' (1928: 138). Other texts, too, underlined the inherently violent nature of the sexual act, emphasizing, for instance, that most women wanted to be deeply, even 'savagely' penetrated, 'even if that penetration should imply suffering' (Haire 1934: 379). Some women, they insisted, could not have orgasms unless they were beaten and brutalized.

One aspect of sexual intercourse which received much attention was the number and variety of positions in coitus, and which ones were to be recommended. Here the experts found themselves in a dilemma: on the one hand logic seemed to demand that they recommend those positions which afforded women most pleasure, since one of the main motivations for writing marriage manuals at all was to enable women to achieve orgasms from coitus; on the other hand they felt unable to recommend those positions because they were the ones in which the 'natural' roles of the sexes were reversed, i.e. positions which rendered the man almost totally passive, with the woman active and in control. Both Van de Velde and Haire, for instance, claimed that women were now recognized as active sexual beings and were entitled to take the sexual initiative occasionally, but strongly advised that the only positions which should be regularly adopted were those which enabled the man 'to entirely play the active part allotted to him', and warned that too great a degree of female activity and male passivity was 'directly contrary to the natural relationship of the sexes, and must bring unfavourable consequences if it becomes habitual' (Van de Velde 1928: 198).[8]

As my selection of examples has indicated, by no means all the authors of marriage manuals and sex advice literature were male; on the contrary, given that the medical and scientific professions during the first half of the twentieth century were even more male-dominated than they are now, the proportion of female authors does seem surprisingly high. What is disturbing, from a feminist perspective, is that despite certain differences in approach and emphasis, most of them appear to have accepted quite uncritically the model of sexuality and heterosexual relations established by the sexologists, and to have been just as enthusiastic about promoting it as the male sex reformers and educators. It was Stella Browne, for instance, who translated *Ideal Marriage* into English and thus made a major contribution to the promotion of the male supremacist model of sexuality upon which it is based. Stella Browne was a socialist feminist who was active in the campaign for birth-control and abortion during the 1920s and 1930s and had been much involved with the sex reform movement since before World War I. At the height of the suffrage campaign she had launched a vitriolic attack on those feminists who were challenging male sexuality and arguing that marriage and sexual intercourse were dangerous to women's health. Writing in *The Freewoman* in 1912 she had dismissed such feminists as 'sexually defiant and disappointed women, impervious to facts and logic and deeply ignorant of life', and insisted that celibate spinsterhood was unnatural.[9]

Why were so many women, including some feminists, so uncritical of this sexology, and so heavily involved in promoting such a male-defined sexual ideology? To understand and explain this phenomenon would be a research project in itself, but some light may be shed on it by a brief consideration of the work of Marie Stopes, whose *Married Love*, published ten years before *Ideal Marriage*, was the first and best-known of all modern English sex manuals.

MARIE STOPES: 'SEX STARVATION'

Marie Stopes aroused the wrath of the medical establishment because, though a doctor of science (an extremely rare qualification for a woman at that time), she had no medical training whatever and was therefore considered unfit to meddle in matters of human sexuality and reproduction. Yet her activities as a sex reformer and birth controller in the 1920s probably had more popular impact, at least initially, than all the others combined. *Married Love* (1918) sold over 2,000 copies in the first fortnight and over 400,000 by the end of 1923, and its popularity continued until well after World War II; by 1955 it had gone through numerous reprints and twenty-eight editions, and had been translated into fourteen languages (Hall 1978). It was also considerably shorter and much more readable than its main rival, *Ideal Marriage*, which did not appear until ten years later; also, because of its author's notoriety, it probably reached a far wider audience than the sales figures indicate. Stopes was a prolific writer, and in 1928 she published a sequel, *Enduring Passion*, which also sold well, and was followed by numerous other books, articles, and pamphlets expressing her views on sex, marriage, and birth control.

Stopes's sexual ideology deserves detailed analysis,[10] but here I can only highlight what I believe to be its most outstanding characteristic, namely its contradictory nature. Of all the marriage manuals of the period, *Married Love* was undoubtedly the most feminist, in the sense that it expressed its author's deep commitment to female sexual autonomy, and was heavily critical, in a manner reminiscent of pre-war feminists, of the ideology and practice of male sexuality; at the same time, however, Stopes utterly failed to challenge the male supremacist, 'scientific' model of sexuality which in and of itself denied female sexual autonomy and legitimated the exercise of male sexuality as a tool of male power. Indeed, I suggest that it was the feminist aspects of Stopes's writings that aroused the wrath of the medical establishment, as much as her lack of medical expertise; for not only did she insist that men had no right to use women for their own sexual gratification, asserting quite unequivocally that sexual coercion of the wife by the husband constituted rape; she also had the audacity to assert that since female sexual desire waxed and waned according to each woman's own biological rhythm, men should – and could – exercise self-restraint and adapt themselves to their wives' sexual needs. This amounted in essence to a demand that control of heterosexual activity within marriage pass from the male to the female, a very radical demand indeed, and one which the male sex experts were not prepared to countenance.[11] They were prepared to accept that some women were slower to be aroused at certain times of the month, but merely advised husbands to 'woo' them more ardently and indulge in more prolonged foreplay.

In other respects, however, Marie Stopes's sexual ideology was profoundly reactionary; in common with her contemporaries she exalted the 'thrills of the chase' and man's innate hunting instincts, and contradicted her own commitment to female sexual autonomy by vehemently condemning lesbianism, attacking 'prudes', and emphasizing that women's orgasms should only be given by their husbands. She seemed obsessed with the need to 'prove' the naturalness of both heterosexuality and coitus, claiming that women deprived of regular and satisfying coitus were *literally* sex-starved, in the sense that they lacked the chemical substances supplied by male secretions (which their bodies absorbed if they remained long enough in the 'post-coital embrace'). She even went so far as to recommend that women thus deprived should dose themselves with daily capsules containing prostatic extracts! Furthermore, by 1928 her criticisms of male sexuality had so far evaporated as to allow her to attribute many sex crimes to men's 'insatiable' sexual desires, caused by a similar lack of physiological 'nourishment'. Such views (by no means unique to Stopes) implicitly depoliticized sexuality, in particular the feminist argument that male sexuality was a manifestation of male power, and gave strong reinforcement to the male supremacist model of sexuality established by the sexologists and other 'experts'. It comes as no surprise, therefore, to learn that Stopes acquired almost all her sexual knowledge from reading books by sexologists, and that foremost among them was Ellis's *Studies* (see Hall 1978: 102).

The point of showing that some women, too, accepted this model and were actively involved in promoting such ideas and practices is not to dismiss them as deluded or to attack them as anti-feminists, but to suggest how pervasive the ideology was and also how powerful science was (and still is) as a legitimizing force. It also illustrates, I think, the contradictions and dangers inherent in attempts by women to gain access to male privileges without challenging the more fundamental structures upon which male power rests; it is extremely difficult for women to achieve equality with men within the scientific and medical establishments, for example, without in the process internalizing the male values with which those professions are saturated. Helena Wright, a gynaecologist who worked in one of the earliest birth-control clinics and remained actively involved in 'family planning' right up to the 1970s, provides another interesting illustration of the same phenomenon.

EDUCATING THE VAGINA

Helena Wright was a contemporary of Marie Stopes and knew her quite well. In 1930 she published her own sex manual, which was to a large extent a 'Reader's Digest' version of Van de Velde's *Ideal Marriage*, and was followed by a sequel in 1947. In recent years her writings have attracted the interest of some feminists because of the attention she paid to the role of the clitoris in female sexual arousal and orgasm (Campbell 1980; Ruehl 1983). It has been claimed that Wright, alone among her contemporaries, recognized that the female orgasm was located in the clitoris and that this led her to 'reject sexual intercourse as the best sexual practice for women' (Ruehl 1983: 23). In my view the latter half of this claim is entirely false, though I admit that there is considerable confusion and ambiguity in Wright's texts. She was well aware, on the basis of both her own and her patients' experience, that many women not only did not achieve orgasm from coitus, but did not experience any pleasure whatever from penile penetration; she was fond of quoting one typical response from a patient: 'Doctor, have I got to put up with this? I can't bear it [penis] pumping in and out!'[12] Yet all normal women, she acknowledged, were capable of experiencing acute clitoral sensation, including orgasm, if the appropriate rhythmical friction were applied. Her solution to this puzzle was that in most women the vagina *did* have an equal – or even greater – potential for sexual pleasure, but that it took considerable time and patience to establish. Taking a leaf out of Van de Velde's book, she said that it was not merely women but their vaginas which needed to be taught how and what to feel: In her own words:

'Nearly all women find vaginal sensation through, as it were, the gateway of clitoris sensation. . . . For the full experience of

the orgasm or sexual climax, intense feeling must generally be present in both places.'
(Wright 1930: 72)

'It looks as if the sensory nerve endings in the vagina need practice and experience before they acquire full sensitivity . . . the vagina appears to learn best and most quickly after successful experience with the clitoris has been established. The clitoris can, therefore, be regarded as a kind of teacher for the vagina.'
(Wright 1947: 71–2)

Wright made it quite clear that ultimately clitoral sensation was only a means to an end: vaginal orgasm by means of penile penetration. This was the real goal, and every wife should 'maintain an optimistic attitude and never give up hope', if necessary seeking 'expert' help (1947: 77). During an interview with her, I questioned her closely on this matter and she reiterated emphatically the need to *educate* the vagina, adding, moreover, that it was 'unfair' to deny penetration to men. In reply to my objection that some women had tried really hard but still could not enjoy penetration she was only able to suggest that in some women the vagina was 'dead'.

WOMEN AND FRIGIDITY: RESISTING NATURE OR MALE POWER?

Despite the tremendous efforts expended by the experts (the vast majority of whom, it must be remembered, were male) to educate women – and their vaginas – to yield their 'secrets of melody' to the hand of the master, many of them obstinately refused to be 'wooed into compliance' (Van de Velde 1928). The 'problem' of frigidity, which the 'art of love' had been designed to overcome, appered to become more and more intractable as the 1920s wore on; marriage manuals and sex educators devoted more and more space to it, whole volumes were written about it, and the reader is left with the impression that female sexual 'anaesthesia' was reaching epidemic proportions. Although frigidity was usually defined simply as aversion to coitus, or failure to achieve orgasm from coitus, most experts were clearly aware that the problem was far more deep-seated than such simple definitions implied. They repeatedly emphasized that although woman, like man, was biologically endowed with a sexual instinct, in women, unlike men, it did not emerge spontaneously but had to be 'awakened' – by a man. Furthermore, the awakening of a woman's sexual instinct did not depend solely on her husband's skill and patience: she had to be *willing* to have it awakened. If she were not, no amount of artistry on the part of the husband, guided by the experts, could succeed. Frigidity, then, was seen not just as a consequence of an unfortunate lack of sexual desire but as a form of *resistance*, a refusal not merely to comply with male sexual demands, but to accept the 'facts of life'.[13]

One writer who expressed this view quite explicitly was Walter Gallichan,[14] who wrote a number of books on women, sex, and marriage, with such revealing titles as *Modern Woman and How to Manage Her*, *The Poison of Prudery*, and *Sexual Apathy and Coldness in Women* (1927), the latter betraying a heavy indebtedness to Ellis and also to the growing influence of psychoanalysis. What is particularly interesting about this book is the explicit connection made between 'frigidity' and feminism: 'the cold natured woman is often an active supporter of reformative organizations, female emancipation crusades, purity campaigns, and societies for the suppression of vice . . . [she is] lacking understanding of the fundamental facts of life' (Gallichan 1927: 1).

He quoted approvingly from an acknowledged psychoanalytic expert, Wilhelm Stekel, who argued that 'the cold woman suffers from an inhibitory force, which is hidden, and expresses itself as *"I will not"*' (quoted in Gallichan 1927), and that the increase in frigidity in modern times was to be interpreted as 'distinctly a social manifestation', specifically as 'a phase in woman's struggle for equal rights'. Gallichan attributed an alarming number of social ills to 'the prude' and 'the frigide' (the terms were used more or less synonymously) and maintained that it was vital that this 'sexphobia' be overcome: 'The hysterical frigide must be taught to face the realities of Nature, and to abandon the false perceptions of the "horridness" of sexuality' (Gallichan 1927). Unfortunately, however, such women were 'extremely resistant': 'Their resistance to the acceptance of the facts of the love of the sexes is frequently so stubborn that no kind of instruction appears possible in their case' (Gallichan 1927). They were also extremely dangerous, as they regarded themselves as a 'superior order of womanhood' and more often than not passed on their sexphobia to their daughters! At the same time, Gallichan was at pains to include approving references to those feminists such as Olive Schreiner who were not prudish or frigid but were 'well-balanced' and understood the 'beauty and sacredness of sex'.[15] Like most male advocates of women's rights he was very selective about which rights he would support. He divided feminists into those who proclaimed the joys of heterosexual sex and were therefore 'truly' emancipated, and those who refused to do so and were consequently dismissed or attacked as man-haters, spinsters, prudes, and lesbians – not only frigid, but neurotic, hysterical, and often 'secretly obsessed' with sex.

From this very brief survey of marriage manuals and sex education literature between the wars it is difficult to see in what sense 'sex reform' could be said to be in women's interests. To be sure, women were now permitted to have sexual feelings and to experience sexual pleasure, but strictly on male terms. Female sexuality was defined and controlled in such a way as to destroy any potential autonomy and to harness it in the service of men. It was defined as passive in a far more fundamental sense than is usually implied: it was not merely that women were 'slow' to become aroused, or that they needed to be made 'ready' for coitus, or 'given' orgasms, but rather that female sexuality was seen as having no independent existence of its own. A woman's sexual instinct could only be awakened by, and satisfied by, a man, thus rendering women sexually dependent on men at precisely that point in history when they were beginning to achieve a significant degree of political and economic independence. No wonder the male experts became so hysterical about frigidity; lesbians could be conveniently explained away by being defined as 'congenital inverts', members of a third sex, so 'masculine' that they did not really count as women and thus posed no serious threat to male power.[16] 'Frigid' women, on the other hand, were 'real' women who refused to accept the facts of life, or yield to the hand of the master; in thus resisting (perhaps intuitively) the erosion of their autonomy, and the attempts to eroticize their oppression, they were deeply threatening to male supremacy. No wonder such strenuous efforts have been, and still are being, made to cure them.

Exactly why female sexuality needed to be awakened by a man was never explained; nor was it seen as a problem in need of explanation. Some writers accounted for the 'ever-ready' nature of male sexuality in terms of the need to ensure the continuation of the species (Gallichan 1927), but most merely asserted that the difference between female and male sexuality was natural and left it at that. The notion of an instinct which has to be awakened is very puzzling, if not paradoxical. A more glaring contradiction, however, lies in the notion of an instinct which has to be *learned*; yet all the experts were agreed that women had to learn, not merely to enjoy heterosexual intercourse, but to desire it. Nobody seems to have asked: if heterosexual attraction – specifically the desire for coitus – is natural and instinctive, why does it need to be taught? And why only to women? Could it possibly be because, as Stekel (1926) succinctly observed: 'To be roused by a man means acknowledging oneself as conquered'?

The scientific model of sexuality: male sexuality universalized

These, then, were the 'facts of life' as taught to generations of women and men, based on the scientific model of sexuality established by Ellis and his contemporary sexologists. The effect of the intervention of the medical profession in this field was not only to popularize and promote the model but to add its own legitimating power to that of science, thus cementing the model more securely and rendering it even more immune to feminist challenge. To teach not only that heterosexuality is natural, but that a particular form of heterosexual practice which defines and institutionalizes male domination and female submission is natural and inevitable, cannot but have adverse implications for feminism and for female sexual autonomy, especially when presented in the guise of sexual liberation. When seen in relation to other features of the inter-war years, such as the drive to persuade women to leave the labour market and the renewed emphasis on motherhood (see for example, Dyehouse (1976, 1978), Lewis (1980), Littlewood (1985)), this attempt to restructure heterosexual relations and reinforce women's sexual as well as economic dependence on men constitutes, at the very least, a significant contribution to the decline of western feminism during this historical period.

The influence of the early twentieth-century sexologists and sex reformers did not end with the beginning of World War II. The more popular sex manuals continued to be read well into the second half of the twentieth century, and new ones, based on the same naturalist and essentialist assumptions, were written (see, for example Chesser (1966), Stone and Stone (1952)). The subsequent research of Kinsey and Masters and Johnson, though based on very different methodologies, has led to further refinements and modifications of the model, but its essential characteristics remain the same.[17] They may be briefly summarized as follows:

1. Sexual desire is a basic, biological urge, drive, or instinct which demands satisfaction, or, to use Kinsey's term, 'outlet';[18] in men the urge is usually considered to be much stronger than in women (though not all sexologists are agreed on this).

2. If the (male) sexual drive is denied legitimate outlets, it will find satisfaction in illegitimate ones; this is one of the main findings of Kinsey's *Sexual Behaviour in the Human Male* (1948), and was his favourite explanation for rape, the sexual abuse of girls, and other 'sex crimes' and sexual deviations.

3. Alternatively, repression of sexual desire may lead to physical or mental illness, and especially 'neurosis' in women; it is in this aspect of sexuality that the influence of psychoanalysis has been particularly strong, and even those sex researchers most hostile to psychoanalysis in general have accepted the repression-neurosis connection (albeit a crude, over-simplified version thereof).

4. The need for sex is as basic as the need for food; throughout the literature this analogy between sexual desire and hunger is repeatedly made, with the implication that the consequences of 'sex starvation' are extremely harmful.

5. The 'sex' that we all allegedly need is 'intercourse', i.e. copulation or coitus, to use the precise technical term; it is important to use the technical term, I believe, because the meaning of 'intercourse' is very broad (as in 'social intercourse') and could in theory be taken to mean any kind of sexual activity or interaction. In practice, however, its meaning is quite specific, and refers to the penetration of the vagina by the penis; thus 'having sex' is in everyday speech as well as the sexological literature synonymous with coitus.

These are the underlying assumptions of the scientific model of sexuality and the 'facts of life' that we in western societies still learn to accept as 'common sense'. The model not only reflects and legitimates the male supremacist myth that the male sexual urge *must* be satisfied; it defines the very nature of 'sex' in male terms. Thus although women are now regarded as sexual beings in their own right, female sexuality too has been shaped according to this androcentric model. In other words, male sexuality has been universalized and now serves as the model of *human* sexuality. Furthermore, by equating human sexual desire with a coital imperative, i.e. a biological drive to copulate, 'sex' is ultimately reduced to a reproductive function, with the obvious implication that the only really 'natural' form of sexual relationship is heterosexual.[19]

THE PRIMACY OF THE PENIS

The implications of this for female sexual autonomy are enormous, both in terms of our freedom to choose the sex of our potential partners, and our freedom to define our own sexual needs and desires, especially within heterosexual relationships. Even the most cursory glance at contemporary sex manuals makes it clear that all forms of sexual expression other than coitus are seen as 'foreplay', optional extras, or substitutes for 'the real thing'. Masters and Johnson, whose research and writings have provided the scientific basis for such popular works as Alex Comfort's *The Joy of Sex*,[20] describe female sexual response as essentially 'an invitation to mount' (Masters and Johnson 1966: 69) and the penis as the primary organ of sexual pleasure for *both* sexes: 'The functional role of the penis is that of providing an organic means for physiologic and psychologic increment and release of both male and female sexual tension' (1966: 188).

The emphasis throughout their writing, their own sex therapy programme, and the countless other sex therapy programmes based on their techniques, is on curing male sexual inadequacy (impotence) and female frigidity. Since frigidity is defined in terms of failure to achieve orgasm from coitus, and male sexual inadequacy in terms of failure to achieve or sustain erection adequate to full and prolonged penetration, these preoccupations in themselves underline the primacy of the penis in this model of sexuality.

That the failure of a man to penetrate a woman with his penis should be described in both scientific and everyday language as 'impotence' is perhaps not insignificant in terms of understanding heterosexuality and its relationship to male power. 'Impotent' means powerless, and carries the implication that a man who is unable to penetrate a woman is also unable to exercise power over her; his penis is, or should be, a 'tool' of male power ('tool' being slang for penis) and his failure to use it as such is, under male supremacy, a double disgrace, since he not only suffers a personal loss of status and power in relation to a particular woman but also, as it were, lets the side down. (Men's well-known obsession with the size of their penises is another indication of their significance as weapons and symbols of male power.) Many feminists have pointed out that whether or not penetration is essential to male sexual pleasure, it is certainly *not* essential to female sexual pleasure; in fact it often interferes with female sexual pleasure. The feminist debate on the nature of the female orgasm which took place during the 1970s relied heavily on the clinical findings of Masters and Johnson, which appeared to settle the issue once and for all by showing that all female orgasms originated in the clitoris; also that most women are much more likely to achieve orgasm from masturbation than from coitus.[21] While many feminists (e.g. Koedt 1970) interpreted this as confirming their own experience that penile penetration is irrelevant to female sexual pleasure, Masters and Johnson went to great lengths to demonstrate that this was *not* the case by emphasizing the function of penile thrusting in indirectly stimulating the clitoris, and by advocating the kind of sexual techniques specifically designed to ensure that female orgasms *are* achieved by means of coitus.[22]

Feminism, naturalism, and heterosexuality

I have tried to argue that the scientific model of sexuality constructed by sexologists is one which both reflects male supremacist values and promotes the interests of men by defining sex in male terms and thus facilitating the sexual-political control of women by men within the institution of heterosexuality and by means of specific heterosexual practices. I have suggested that the increasing sexualization of western women which has taken place since the nineteenth century should not be seen as 'liberating' but rather as an attempt to eroticize women's oppression, thereby concealing the real power relations between the sexes and making a significant contribution to the maintenance and reproduction of male supremacy. It is beyond the scope of this paper to assess how far the attempt to cement the institutions of heterosexuality and marriage through a 'bond of pleasure' (Masters and Johnson 1975) has been successful. The very existence of the contemporary Women's Liberation Movement suggests that the attempt has not, to say the least, been entirely successful.

At the same time, however, the continuing confusions and divisions among and between feminists and women of all kinds around issues of sexuality and its relationship to male power give cause for considerable concern to all those seriously committed to the cause of women's liberation; most of these confusions are directly or indirectly attributable to the interventions of science and medicine into the sexual-political arena. By highlighting the naturalist and essentialist assumptions on which sexology and its model of sexuality are based I have tried to reveal their antifeminist implications, and have suggested that it is possible to view these as a response to the threat posed by feminism to the system of male supremacy and especially to one of its most central institutions, the institution of heterosexuality. I suggest that Havelock Ellis and his contemporaries and successors did not simply *fail* to question these naturalist and essentialist assumptions, nor were they simply blinkered by patriarchal values; rather they responded to feminist attempts to question them by defending and reinforcing those assumptions and by using them as the foundation on which to build a scientific model of sexuality.[23]

Lest I be accused of postulating a 'conspiracy theory' in accounting for the model in this way, I should add that I do not imagine that sexologists and other 'experts' sat round a table plotting how to use sex to overthrow feminism, and I am well aware that the picture I have painted is in many respects oversimple. My principal aim in this paper has been to sketch an analysis of one particular area of struggle between the sexes which I believe has hitherto been neglected and misunderstood; and to suggest that defining certain kinds of sexual practices and institutions as *natural*, rather than as social and political, meant removing sexuality to a large extent from the political arena and placing it under the protection of science (especially medical science).

Naturalism has always been a formidable anti-feminist weapon. Even today, when many of the allegedly 'natural' differences between the sexes have been shown by feminists to be socially constructed, many people still cling firmly to naturalist beliefs. One example is the belief that prostitution will always exist in order to provide sexual release for those men who are unable to achieve it through marriage or friendship – after all, it's only 'human' nature, isn't it? Indeed, it seems as though the more some barriers to sexual equality get torn down, the more important it becomes (to those who want to maintain male power) to reinforce those which remain, by ensuring that the most crucial naturalist myths become more deeply entrenched. One of the most crucial is surely the belief or assumption that heterosexuality is natural: despite, or perhaps because of, a slight liberalization of attitudes towards lesbians and gay men, anyone who dares to challenge this assumption is likely to face responses ranging from blank incredulity to outright hostility – 'Well if it wasn't natural, human beings would just die out, wouldn't they?'

Heterosexist assumptions are unfortunately not confined to anti- or non-feminists. Heterosexual feminists, too, must bear some responsibility for the failure to challenge such assumptions sufficiently rigorously, and to examine critically their own naturalism. Lesbian feminists such as Adrienne Rich have pointed out that much otherwise excellent feminist scholarship and theorizing are seriously flawed by the failure to acknowledge or examine the institutionalization of heterosexuality and its enforcement as a means of assuring male right of physical, economic, and emotional access to women (Rich 1980). Rich adds that feminist research and theory that contribute to lesbian invisibility or marginality are actually working against the liberation and empowerment of women as a group. I should like to expand that point by arguing that any research and theory which takes heterosexuality for granted also reinforces the belief that heterosexuality is natural and thus contributes to its maintenance as an institution and hence to the maintenance of male supremacy.[24] For despite the fact that most women probably experience heterosexuality as natural, or possibly as a positive choice, I would argue that it is the key institution in and through which male power is produced and maintained. Numerous studies by feminists have shown how women are exploited and controlled in marriage, in the family, in the labour market, by the state, and by means of male violence; underpinning all these institutions, and the sanctions which enforce male dominance within them, is the institution of hetero-sexuality, a system of social relations – hetero-relations – in which male domination and female subordination are institution-alized and sexualized.

Some feminists have made a distinction between coercive and non-coercive heterosexuality, implying that it is only the former which should be subjected to criticism, and that heterosexuality *per se* is not intrinsically oppressive to women.[25] I would argue that not only is it impossible to make such a simple distinction, but that under male supremacy there can be no such thing as 'heterosexuality *per se*'. No human sexual behaviour or practice can be divorced from the socio-political context in which it takes place and the system of social relations in which it is embedded. To assume or assert that it can be is to fall into the trap of natural-ism and essentialism. The extent to which it is possible to trans-form institutions from within is of course an open question and I do not wish to enter into that particular debate here. What I do wish to emphasize is that although individual women, and differ-ent groups and classes of women, will experience heterosexuality as more or less coercive according to their specific circumstances, in terms of the production and reproduction of male supremacy it is absolutely crucial that the vast majority be structured into the system of hetero-relations which lies at the very base of that supremacy. The means by which the social structuring of hetero-sexuality takes place are many and varied, and include direct physical force and economic pressures and sanctions, as well as the more subtle and insidious forms of ideological coercion; obviously the precise combination of means employed will vary historically, cross-culturally, and according to other specific social conditions. My own research into sexology is an attempt to explore just *one* aspect of this process, in one culture, and at one specific historical period, and will, I hope, make a modest contri-bution towards the development of a theory of heterosexuality and its relationship to male power. What I hope I have conveyed

here is the crucial importance of resisting and challenging
naturalist and essentialist beliefs and assumptions about heterosexuality which only obscure the real power relations between
the sexes and which have been constructed (though not necessarily consciously) precisely for that purpose. The rejection of
naturalism is a prerequisite both for the development of a theory
of heterosexuality and for resistance to further attempts to
depoliticize sexuality and hetero-relations; it is also a vital
weapon in the struggle against the eroticization of women's
oppression.

Notes

1 Although Freud was, and still is, much better known, I do not think
  his influence on sexual education or mainstream sexual theorizing
  has been nearly as great as Ellis's.
2 'Urolagnia' refers to the phenomenon of men deriving sexual
  pleasure from watching women urinate.
3 As Jeffreys (1982) has pointed out, feminists at the turn of the century
  were deeply divided over this issue, and before World War I a minority
  did indeed appear to advocate a single moral standard on male terms.
4 Two examples are Elizabeth Wolstenholme-Elmy and Frances
  Swiney, though the latter, a fervent matriarchalist, represented a
  strand of feminist thinking which seems of limited usefulness in
  bringing about social change, since it too is based on naturalist and
  essentialist assumptions. For further details see Jeffreys (1982, 1985).
5 For a more detailed analysis see Jackson (1983).
6 During the 1930s there developed a 'moral panic' about juvenile
  delinquency, and some 'experts' argued that sexual maladjustment in
  marriage was a significant factor; at least one London magistrates
  court regularly referred the parents of juvenile offenders for sexual
  counselling (Griffith 1937).
7 'A New Gospel' was in fact the title of a pamphlet which Marie Stopes
  addressed to the Anglican bishops, in which she claimed that God
  had spoken personally to her as his prophet, commanding her to pass
  on his revelation of the divine nature of sexual union between man
  and woman as an end in itself and not merely as a means to procreation (Hall 1978).
8 The 'unfavourable consequences' were left unspecified, but it was
  clearly implied that certain practices would upset the balance of
  power between the sexes and probably result in the husband's
  impotence.
9 The Freewoman 7 March, 1912. For further details, see Jeffreys (1982).
10 Ruth Hall's biography (1978) is in many respects an excellent source
  but is unfortunately marred by an uncritical acceptance of the

ideology of sexual 'liberation'. My own analysis of Stopes's sexual ideology will be presented as part of my Ph.D. thesis.

11 To cite only two examples, both Van de Velde and Haire published scathing attacks on Stopes, dismissing her as a dangerous crank.

12 I interviewed Helena Wright shortly before her death, and although I was unable to record the interview on tape, I was able to write down verbatim some of her remarks, of which this is one.

13 Havelock Ellis himself used the term 'resistance' in connection with frigidity; and it will be remembered that according to Ellis the function of 'courtship' was to overcome female resistance.

14 Gallichan was married to a well-known feminist who wrote under the name of Mrs Gascoigne-Hartley.

15 He included in this category Edith Lees, the wife of Havelock Ellis. One wonders whether he knew she was a lesbian; certainly there is no indication in his writings that he did.

16 For a detailed discussion of how sexologists defined lesbianism at this time, see Faderman (1981).

17 For a more detailed analysis, see Jackson (1984).

18 This is often referred to as the 'hydraulic model' of sexuality (e.g. Robinson 1976).

19 Recent work by feminists has shown how sex education in schools today is based on similar assumptions (e.g. Jackson 1978; Rance 1978).

20 The subtitle, 'A Gourmet Guide to Lovemaking', recalls the analogy between sex and hunger.

21 In fact Kinsey had already shown this in 1953.

22 For further discussion of the implications of the work of the Kinsey Institute and of Masters and Johnson (including the relationship between sex and violence) see Jackson (1984).

23 It must be admitted that much feminist analysis, in both the 'last wave' and the 'present wave' of western feminism, is flawed by the failure to challenge naturalism and essentialism. To explore the reasons for this would require another article.

24 For a recent and particularly striking example, see the article by the German feminist, Barbara Sichtermann, published in *New Socialist* January 1986. Subtitled 'Feminism and Sexual Desire' the discussion is based on the implicit assumption that the only kind of 'sex' is and always will be heterosexual, and the 'objects' of female sexual desire and pleasure necessarily male.

25 See, for example, Lynne Segal's review of 'The Sexuality Papers' (Coveney *et al.* 1984) in *City Limits* 19–25 October, 1984; also various contributors to Snitow *et al.* (1984) and Vance (1984).

References

Bland, L. (1981) It's Only Human Nature?: Sociobiology and Sex Differences. *Schooling and Culture* 10: 6–10.
Bleier, R. (1984) *Science and Gender*. London: Pergamon Press.

80   The Cultural Construction of Sexuality

Brecher, E. M. (1970) *The Sex Researchers*. London: André Deutsch.

Campbell, B. (1980) Feminist Sexual Politics. *Feminist Review* 5: 1–18.

Chesser, E. (1966) *Love Without Fear*. London: Arrow.

Cole, E. (1938) *Education for Marriage*. London: Duckworth.

Comfort, A. (1975) *The Joy of Sex: A Gourmet Guide to Lovemaking*. London: Quartet Books.

Coveney, L., Jackson, M., Jeffreys, S., Kaye, L., and Mahony, P. (1984) *The Sexuality Papers: Male Sexuality and the Social Control of Women*. London: Hutchinson.

Coward, R. (1983) *Patriarchal Precedents*. London: Routledge & Kegan Paul.

Dyehouse, C. (1976) Social Darwinistic Ideas and the Development of Women's Education in England, 1880–1920. *History of Education* 5: 41–58.

—— (1978) Towards a 'Feminine' Curriculum for English Schoolgirls: the Demands of Ideology 1870–1963. *Women's Studies International Quarterly* 1 (4): 297–330.

Ehrenreich, B. and English, D. (1979) *For Her Own Good: 150 Years of the Experts' Advice to Women*. London: Pluto Press.

Ellis, H. (1913) *Studies in the Psychology of Sex*. Vols I–VI. Philadelphia, PA: F. A. Davis.

Eyles, L. (1923) *Family Love*. London: Andrew Melrose.

Faderman, L. (1981) *Surpassing the Love of Men: Romantic Friendship and Love between Women from the Renaissance to the Present*. London: Junction Books.

Gallichan, W. (1909) *Modern Woman and How to Manage Her*. London: T. Werner Laurie.

—— (1927) *Sexual Apathy and Coldness in Women*. London: T. Werner Laurie.

—— (1929) *The Poison of Prudery*. London: T. Werner Laurie.

Griffith, E. (1937) *Modern Marriage and Birth Control*. London: Gollancz.

Haire, N. (ed.) (1934) *Encyclopaedia of Sexual Knowledge*. London: Encyclopaedia Press.

Hall, R. (1978) *Marie Stopes*. London: Virago.

Jackson, M. (1983) Sexual Liberation or Social Control? *Women's Studies International Forum* 6 (1): 1–17. (Reprinted in Coveney *et al.* 1984.)

—— (1984) Sex Research and the Construction of Sexuality: a Tool of Male Supremacy? *Women's Studies International Forum* 7 (1): 43–51. (Reprinted in Coveney *et al.* 1984.)

Jackson, S. (1978) How to Make Babies: Sexism in Sex Education. *Women's Studies International Quarterly* 1 (4): 341–52.

Jeffreys, S. (1982) 'Free from All Uninvited Touch of Man': Women's Campaigns around Sexuality 1880–1914. *Women's Studies International Forum* 5 (6): 629–45.

—— (1985) *The Spinster and Her Enemies*. London: Pandora Press.

Kinsey, A., Pomeroy, W. B., and Martin, C. E. (1948) *Sexual Behaviour in the Human Male*. Philadelphia and London: W. B. Saunders.

—— (1953) *Sexual Behaviour in the Human Female*. Philadelphia: W. B. Saunders.

Koedt, A. (1970) The Myth of the Vaginal Orgasm. Reprinted by Know, Inc. from *Notes from the Second Year*.

Lewis, J. (1975) Beyond Suffrage: English Feminism in the 1920s. *Maryland Historian* VI: 1–17.

—— (1980) *The Politics of Motherhood*. London: Croom Helm.

Littlewood, M. (1985) Makers of Men: the Anti-feminist Backlash of the National Association of Schoolmasters in the 1920s and 30s. *Trouble and Strife* 5: 23–9.

Masters, W. and Johnson, V. (1966) *Human Sexual Response*. New York: Little, Brown, & Co.

—— (1975) *The Pleasure Bond*. New York: Little, Brown, & Co.

Oakley, A. (1976) Wisewoman and Medicine Man: Changes in the Management of Childbirth. In J. Mitchell and A. Oakley (eds) *The Rights and Wrongs of Women*. Harmondsworth: Penguin.

Rance, S. (1978) Going All the Way. *Spare Rib* 75 (October).

Re-Bartlett, L. (1912) *Sex and Sanctity*. London: Longmans.

Reed, E. (1978) *Sexism and Science*. New York: Pathfinder Press.

Rhodes, D. and McNeill, S. (1985) *Women Against Violence Against Women*. London: Onlywomen Press.

Rich, A. (1980) Compulsory Heterosexuality and Lesbian Existence. *Signs* 5 (4): 631–60.

Robinson, P. (1976) *The Modernization of Sex*. New York: Harper & Row.

Rowbotham, S. (1977) *A New World for Women: Stella Browne – Socialist Feminist*. London: Pluto Press.

Rowbotham, S. and Weeks, J. (1977) *Socialism and the New Life; The Personal and Sexual Politics of Edward Carpenter and Havelock Ellis*. London: Pluto Press.

Ruehl, S. (1983) *The Changing Experience of Women: Unit 4: Sexuality*. Milton Keynes: Open University Press.

Sanger, M. (1926) *Happiness in Marriage*. New York: Brentano.

Sichtermann, B. (1986) Histories of the Orgasm. *New Socialist* 34.

Snitow, A., Stansell, C., and Thompson, S. (eds) (1984) *Desire: the Politics of Sexuality*. London: Virago.

Stekel, W. (1926) *Frigidity in Woman in Relation to her Love Life*. New York: Liveright.

Stone, H. and Stone, A. (1952) *A Marriage Manual*. London: Gollancz.

Stopes, M. (1918) *Married Love*. London: Putnam.

—— (1928) *Enduring Passion*. London: Putnam.

Vance, C. S. (ed.) (1984) *Pleasure and Danger: Exploring Female Sexuality*. London: Routledge & Kegan Paul.

Van de Velde, T. H. (1928) *Ideal Marriage: its Physiology and Technique*. London: Heinemann.

Wright, H. (1930) *The Sex Factor in Marriage*. London: Williams & Northgate.

—— (1947) *More About the Sex Factor in Marriage*. London: Williams & Northgate.

3 Reason, desire, and male sexuality

Victor J. Seidler

Reason, madness, and masculinity

In Western Europe since the period of the Enlightenment in the seventeenth century, men have assumed a strong connection between their rationality and their sense of masculine identity. They have learned to appropriate rationality as if it were an exclusively male quality denied to others, especially women. This is embedded in the very experience of language and it has become an integral part of the ways in which men blind themselves to the experience of women and children. Rationality has become a critical basis for male superiority within social life. It affects how men, especially heterosexual men, listen to others and what they are ready to hear. Since 'rationality' is identified with knowledge, it is denied to women. Emotions and feelings are likewise denied as genuine sources of knowledge within the culture. Rather, they are associated predominantly with weakness and femininity, and so as antithetical to the 'strengths' with which boys learn their sense of masculine identity. If men's difficulties with emotions and feelings have become more visible and recognizable recently, especially with the challenges of feminism, little work has been done to show the philosophical and historical sources of masculine identity.

In this context, Foucault's work offers important insights. In this article, I discuss first his earlier work on madness, and later that on the history of sexuality. I seek to show, however, that there are limitations to his analysis, not least because of his failure to grapple with gender.

MADNESS AND MASCULINITY

When Foucault writes of 'madness', it is a strength that he does not do so from the standpoint of reason, since he refuses to see

reason as a constant, unchanging reality. Whereas both Newton-
ian physics and Cartesian rationalism had worked for the establishment of the sovereignty of reason (MacIntyre 1981), Foucault
showed that this involved an act of exclusion of anything that constituted a threat to its rule. It is clear from his preface that Foucault
already saw this exclusion as itself a cultural form of madness: 'We
have yet to write the history of that other form of madness, by
which men, in an act of sovereign reason, confine their neighbour,
and communicate and recognize each other through the merciless
language of non-madness' (Foucault 1967: 11).

If he had also recognized how reason was to be connected to a
redefinition of masculinity, he could have explored the limited
terms in which men, as a gender, were also to come to 'communicate and recognize each other'. This could have profoundly
affected his later studies of sexuality, since the relation between
masculinity and reason would have been seen as a part of the
sexual relations of power between men and women. But it would
have also meant conceiving issues of power and desire in sexual
relations in radically different terms from the ones which he in
fact used.[1]

Possibly what has been most significant in the treatment
accorded to the 'insane' over the last 300 years is not an increase
in scientificity but, as Sheridan states, 'the continuing allegiance
paid to "reason" and the complete failure to listen either to one's
own "necessary" madness or to those labelled "mad"' (Sheridan
1980: 14). Consequently, at the beginning of *Madness and Civilization* Foucault states as one of his aims: 'The language of psychiatry, which is a monologue of reason about madness, could be
established only on the basis of such a silence. I have not tried to
write the history of that language, but rather the archaeology of
that silence' (Foucault 1967: 12–13).

In order to do this, he has to go back to a time before modern
rationalism and science, when madness was still an undifferentiated experience, before, in fact, reason and madness were
relegated to separate and exclusive realms. As Sheridan makes
clear in his study of Foucault, 'In exploring that "uncomfortable
region" we must, of course, renounce as far as possible the attitudes, techniques, vocabulary inherited from that division'
(1980: 14). We have to learn, as had Foucault himself, not to
speak the language of exclusion. This awareness in relation to

madness did not, however, alert Foucault to the metaphysics of language as universal that had been so readily assimilated into his ideas of language as a discursive practice.[2] In part this omission weakens his later influential writings on sexuality, especially his failure to recognize how men and women grow up with a different experience of sexuality. Feminism has challenged the ways in which women are objectified as sexual objects, maintaining that these indicate much more than the language in which men grow up to think of women, significant as this can be. Such objectification is an aspect of a relationship of power which profoundly affects the freedom and autonomy of women.[3]

Foucault's investigations dispense with a concept of experience because he is inveighing against a notion of the history of ideas which would characterize 'madness' as a constant, unchanging 'experience'. He recognizes that the experience of madness has been historically transformed with the advent of modern rationalism. Madness is no longer, as it once was, connected to the significance of dreams, fantasies, and imagination, giving access to a deeper wisdom. For example, it is possible to show that, in folly and madness, Shakespeare's Lear finds the wisdom he never knew as king and which, in his own way, the Fool had possessed all along. But after the mid-seventeenth century, this kind of free communication between folly/madness and reason disappeared as reason came to dominate and exclude all forms of unreason. Folly and the fool were no longer a major preoccupation in literature and art as they had been from the mid-fifteenth century. In English, as Sheridan has noted, 'folly' disappeared from the exalted language of philosophers and moralists altogether. Folly could no longer defend itself by claiming that it was closer to happiness and truth than reason, or that it was closer to reason than reason itself (Ignatieff 1984).

For Descartes, as for modern philosophy, madness belonged with dreams and all forms of error. As Sheridan has put it, 'The experience, so familiar to the Renaissance, of an unreasonable Reason and a reasonable Unreason, is now precluded' (1980: 23). Madness was firmly excluded from the centre of intellectual life, demoted as it was to the purely negative, dependent status of Unreason. During this 'Classical age', as Foucault calls it, the tragic, illuminating experience of madness was banished from the light of day. It was left to haunt people's dreams until Freud was able to give it some voice within a redefined rationalist project of psychoanalysis. Since this was also the period in which masculinity came to have a special identification with reason, we can expect it to have inherited this same 'unbalance', even if it has been carefully concealed as a form of inherited superiority. Since the Enlightenment, masculinity has been identified with reason, while concealing a sexuality closer to the 'beast' and the 'animal' (Midgely 1978, 1983). This remained part of a hidden threat of violence that reason was deemed powerless to control.

MASCULINITY AND REASON

With the development of rationalism, philosophy came increasingly to be seen as a mirror to be held up to the world of nature (Rorty 1979). People learnt to think of themselves as free to the extent that their behaviour was governed by an autonomous will. To the extent that human bodies were part of the empirical world, they needed to be governed by laws. Cartesian dualism had fundamentally *fragmented* people's experience of themselves, and divided it between two separate and independent spheres. Since classical epistemology has concentrated on the knowledge of objects, not persons, very little exploration of the nature of self-knowledge has been attempted in philosophical writing since Bacon, Locke, and Descartes prepared the ground for the new science (Cavell 1969).

As men have been closely identified with this rationalist tradition, they have often remained strangely ignorant of themselves, while rarely appreciating how this ignorance forms the character of their experience and relationships. It is as if they are left with little access to personal experience, so it can hardly be surprising if they feel drawn to intellectualist traditions, such as structuralism, which would seek to banish that very category of experience.[4]

Knowledge has become increasingly viewed as a commodity which can be accumulated and stored. It becomes a means of self-assertion within a competitive society in which men have constantly to prove their worth in relation to others. In this way language comes to be separated from communication and listening to others. For men, language often seems universal and objective, as if it were always a matter of following an impersonal set of reasons. Men, confident in the superiority of the impersonal modes of argument they have inherited, become deaf to the different terms in which women often conceive issues (Gilligan 1982).

This is an issue Foucault could more easily recognize in the situation of madness than he could ever do for relations between the sexes. Nevertheless his recognition that a common language asserts a relationship of dominance which silences the insights of madness remains potentially crucial:

> 'In the serene world of mental illness, modern man no longer communicates with the madman: on the one hand, the man of reason delegates the physician to madness, thereby authorizing a relation only through the abstract universality of disease. . . . As for a common language, there is no such thing; or rather, there is no such thing any longer; the constitution of madness as mental illness, at the end of the eighteenth century, affords the evidence of a broken dialogue, posits the separation as already effected, and thrusts into oblivion all those stammered, imperfect words without fixed syntax in which the exchange between madness and reason was made.'   (Foucault 1967: 12)

Within a rationalist tradition, it was emotions and desires which were seen as threatening. Kant was adamant that feelings must be treated as 'inclinations' which could so easily tempt people from the path of reason and morality (Blum 1981). Within a Kantian moral tradition, then, as long as people act in accordance with their desires and feelings, their behaviour is being externally determined and is thereby unfree. Such a sense of freedom as essentially 'inner', still an intrinsic part of a Protestant culture, has only served to confirm the greater freedom and autonomy of men. They are thought to be able to act out of a sense of duty, since they are supposedly more able to control the influence of feelings and desires. In this sense men have been taken to be the free sex, and women only able to achieve their freedom through accepting their subordination to men.[5]

Such a view also begins to explain the depths to which men can feel *threatened* by emotions and feelings. Not only do these imperil a masculine sense of superiority to women, but also begin to question the very sources of masculine identity itself. The Kantian inheritance helps to institutionalize an inner connection between masculine identity and a sense of self-control as a form of *dominance* over one's emotional life. This is how Kant conceived his sense of moral maturity, since he envisaged that gradually men's emotions and feelings would become attenuated and have a weaker hold upon their behaviour. Gradually reason would assert its sovereignty over conduct as people, especially men, learned to act out of a sense of duty.

We need to be clear that we are dealing with masculinity as a social and historical process as we learn to reveal the ways in which forms of contemporary masculinity are still marked by this inheritance. The problem is that masculinity is so often treated as an ontological category which is fixed because of the power which men share in relation to women. The alternative view, which would see masculinity as a social role defined by the expectations of others, tends to assume it is easier for men to change than it has proved to be. This is partly because of the institutional and social power men share, but it is also related to the forms of inherited masculine identity which have so rarely been theorized.

Just as madness was perceived by the eighteenth century as a relapse into animality, so it has been a male identification with reason that has supposedly allowed an escape from a state of servitude in which reason is enslaved to the passions (Hirschman 1977). Male sexuality therefore becomes a sign of an animality that we have not been able to leave behind us. It is women, defined as sexual creatures by Rousseau, who have subsequently been seen as constantly tempting men away from the path of reason and morality. It is as if women are to be blamed for reminding men of their sexuality. But this also becomes part of a history of men forsaking responsibility for male sexuality since, once aroused, sexuality is supposedly beyond the control of reason. It threatens the very sense of self-control that defines men's rationality. It can have no part in civilized lives or in defining a sense of masculine identity.[6] It is a threat to the very existence of 'men of reason'. If men could have had a choice, they would have perhaps eradicated sexual desire completely, were it not for the importance of children to the survival of male identity after death and hence to masculine dreams of immortality, as well as to the continuation of the species.

Rousseau argued that the consequences of her sex are inevitably much greater for a woman than maleness is for a man. 'The male is only a male at certain times, the female is a female all her life or at least throughout her youth' (Rousseau 1959–69: 697). Rousseau admits that woman does not spend her whole life bearing children, but 'that is her proper purpose' (Rousseau 1959–69: 698). As far as Rousseau was concerned, a 'woman is made to please and to be subjected to man' and 'it is according to nature for the woman to obey the man' (Rousseau 1959–69: 693, 766).

Okin points out in her discussion of Rousseau that

> 'it was women who were accused of having nurtured carefully the emotional side of love and of playing up its importance, so as to establish their dominance over men. The blame for the guilt and fear experienced in relation to sexuality was laid on the female sex, as the arouser of the passions.'
>
> (Okin 1980: 150)

Rousseau never denied that men and women have similar sexual needs, but he did assume that the male will be aroused only if the female makes herself especially pleasing to him by luring him with her bashfulness or resistance. The mutuality and spontaneity of the original state of nature described in his *Discourse on Inequality* vanish in the *Letter to d'Alembert*, where he argues that the man must necessarily be the pursuer. As Okin points out, it is because Rousseau seems to have a dubious faith in the natural potential for sexual arousal in the male that he concluded that whereas it is not essential for the man to please the woman beyond displaying his strength, woman, on the other hand, is specially made to please the man. If women did not veil their desires with shame or at least feign resistance, 'the passions, ever languishing in a boring freedom, would have never been excited' (Rousseau 1968: 84).

In *Émile*, Rousseau gives a different account of human sexuality in which both sexes have been endowed with 'unlimited passions', but he has given reason to men, and modesty to women, in order to restrain them. Here female resistance becomes essential, as Okin has noted, 'not in order to entice and arouse the male, but as a curb to the boundless desires of both sexes' (Okin 1980: 117). These conflicting accounts of sexuality are at the root of the conflicting demands that Rousseau makes of women and that ultimately lead to the tragedy of Sophie in *Émile* and of Julie in *La Nouvelle Héloïse*. As Okin says, 'Women must, on the one hand, allure, and on the other hand, control and restrain; they must be sensuous, lovable and passionate, but on the other hand scrupulously chaste' (1980: 118).

A CHRISTIAN INHERITANCE

In many ways Rousseau gave a secular expression to earlier, deeply entrenched Christian views of sexuality. This is something Foucault increasingly appreciated as he came to look at the ideas of sexuality in early Christianity. In his later writings, Foucault maintained that Christianity had not invented its own code of sexual behaviour, but rather that Christianity had accepted an already existing code, reinforced it, and given it a much larger and more widespread strength than it had before. As the discussion between Foucault and Sennett on 'Sexuality and Solitude' makes clear, if the important change was not in the sexual code itself, it was 'at least in the relationships everyone has to his (her) own sexual activity. Christianity proposed a new type of experience of oneself as a sexual being' (Foucault and Sennett 1981: 174). To illuminate this, Foucault also looks to Augustine's texts *The City of God* and *Contra Julian*. Foucault accepts Augustine's account of the 'sexual act' as at once familiar to his times while also a rather horrifying description. He quotes Augustine as saying that the whole body is shaken by terrible jerks, and one loses control of oneself; thus it practically paralyses all power of deliberate thought. As far as Foucault is concerned, 'The surprising point is not that Augustine would give such a classical description of the sexual act, but the fact that, having made such a horrible description, he then admits that sexual relations could have taken place in Paradise before the Fall' (Foucault and Sennett 1981: 175).

Foucault seems to share this sense of sexuality, at least in the form we have inherited it, as a kind of necessary evil. The rationalist vision of control, and its dismissal of the experience of women, seem to haunt the text. He rushes to assure the reader that if sexual relations took place in paradise it would not be the kind of sexuality we could recognize. Rather it would express the very vision of control that was so close to the aspirations of the Enlightenment, the identification of masculinity with reason:

'Of course, sex in Paradise could not have the epileptic form which we unfortunately know now. Before the Fall, Adam's body, every part of it, was perfectly obedient to the soul and the will. If Adam wanted to procreate in Paradise, he could do it in the same way and with the same control as he could, for instance, sow seeds in the earth. He was not involuntarily excited. Every part of his body was like the fingers, which one can control in all their gestures. Sex was a kind of hand gently sowing the seed.'   (Foucault and Sennett 1981: 175–76)

Here we seem to have a rationalist dream of paradise. This is the vision of self-control carried into the realm of sexual relations. But unlike Foucault's writings on madness, in which the imbalance and distortion are rendered visible, the repression and denial seem now part of a legitimated dream that Foucault appears powerless to challenge.

At least it helps him to explain our inherited forms of sexuality, if not the sexual body itself, as a *punishment*. It was because Adam had tried to escape God's will and wanted to acquire a will of his own that 'As a punishment of this revolt and as a consequence of this will to will independently from God, Adam lost control of himself' (Foucault and Sennett 1981: 176). So it was that 'His body, and parts of his body, stopped obeying his commands, revolted against him, and the sexual parts of his body were the first to rise up in this disobedience.' As Foucault concludes, 'Sex in erection is the image of man revolted against God. The arrogance of sex is the punishment and consequence of the arrogance of man' (Foucault and Sennett 1981: 176).

This view is important for Foucault because he considers that it bears witness to the new type of relationship which Christianity established between sex and subjectivity. It is a significant transformation since the problem of sexuality was no longer a problem of relationships to other people, 'but the problem of the relationship of oneself to oneself, or, more precisely, the relationship between one's will and involuntary assertions' (Foucault and Sennett 1981: 176). We inherit the problem of the relationship to oneself as a relationship between one's will and involuntary assertions. So the issue of libido, which is what Augustine calls the principle of autonomous movement of sexual organs, becomes an internal component of the will itself. This defines the spiritual struggle, in Foucault's terms, as an indefinite task of attempting to separate the will from the libido in which it has become enmeshed, 'in turning our eyes continually downwards or inwards in order to decipher, among the movements of the soul, which ones come from the libido' (Foucault and Sennett 1981: 177). This means that men are constantly scrutinizing themselves as libidinal beings. As Foucault puts it, 'Shall we say that after Augustine we experience our sex in the head?' (Foucault and Sennett 1981: 177).

This leaves us with a potentially revealing insight into dominant forms of male sexuality, though it is difficult to explore unless issues of control – or what Foucault calls 'mastership' – are also challenged. Issues of sexuality are potentially threatening because they challenge the ideals of control which a rationalist culture has continued. Just as emotions and feelings are treated as mental phenomena, so are sexual desires. This is part of the denigration of the body and somatic experience that has been such a pervasive aspect of western cultural inheritance (Reich 1961; Boadella 1976). The body is to be feared because it threatens to disturb and upset the kind of control so closely identified with masculinity.

SEXUALITY AND SELF

An essential part of the Protestant inheritance of Luther and Calvin was the idea that thoughts are significant since they have been given the power to reveal the continued existence of an evil and animal nature. People could only live a moral life by a radical separation from their natures which continually pulled them back to a world of unfreedom (Fromm 1956). Kant formulated this most clearly in his distinction between the 'empirical world' of desire and inclination, and the 'intelligible world' of the autonomous will. Following this dichotomy, men gradually learn to act out of a sense of duty. They learn to silence the voice of nature and desire within themselves. This is part of a more general relation between culture and nature in which reason is assigned to culture and so defines our humanity as a form of superiority in relation to nature which is conceived as constraining and determinate. Sexuality is assigned in this hierarchical scheme of things to nature.

If Foucault was very aware of how the Classical age had seen madness in terms of animality, he was also aware of an important strain in the late eighteenth century which, influenced by Rousseau, was to identify the possibility of madness not with animality but with a human society, an environment, that repressed man's natural animality. But these images of repression of a 'natural animality' could barely be recognized within the theoretical language in which Foucault's early work on sexuality was expressed. He still remained powerless to articulate the crucial insights of his earlier study of madness, though by the time he came to write his *History of Sexuality* he had struggled to free himself from the framework of discursive practices.

We inherit a tradition in which sexuality is often defined in terms of desire rather than activity, and Sennett helpfully reminds us that the privilege accorded to desire is a Christian heritage. He argues that both medical and Christian texts share the notion that examining what one desires rather than what one does is what really constitutes self-knowledge. Both Sennett and Foucault criticize the idea, inherited from the last century and still current, 'that by understanding our sexuality we will understand what is distinctive and individual about ourselves' (Foucault and Sennett 1981: 182).

Sennett maintains, for example, that it is difficult, if not impossible, to deduce from private sexual desires a person's capacity for loyalty, courage, or truthfulness with others (Foucault and Sennett 1981: 183). He suggests that sexuality has become the medium through which people seek to define their personalities, and above all the means by which people seek to be conscious of themselves (Foucault and Sennett 1981: 165). Elsewhere he refers to sexuality as 'an index of self-consciousness' or to the 'idea of having an identity composed of one's sexuality' (Foucault and Sennett 1981: 167). He finds such ideas particularly disturbing because, in his view, the inflation of sexuality to a measure of psychological truth helps to disorientate the kind of self-knowledge that a liberal tradition has prided itself on, namely the freedom individuals supposedly have to choose their own lives.

Both Foucault and Sennett thus object to a tendency that has become influential since the 1960s to fix people according to their sexual identities, without really grasping, I think, why this has been so meaningful to women and gays in struggle against particular forms of sexual oppression.

Their newly discovered liberalism is precisely what feminist conceptions of sexual equality have set out to challenge, having experienced how liberal equality has served to legitimate the subordination and oppression of women. It is because women have sought to exist as people in their own right, rather than in relation to men and children, that they have questioned structures of power in personal and domestic relations. This has involved a transformation not only of the language in which women's experience can be recognized, but also a change in material relations of power and subordination. This has meant appreciating the *significance* and *power* of a sexual identity which liberal theory has always treated as contingent and incidental. It is because women and gays have discovered that their sexuality has fundamentally formed their experience that sexual identity has assumed such an importance in people's definition of themselves. This is not a point simply about the discourses that have been made available in modern society, but about the organization of power, identity, and oppression. If Foucault has helped us understand from a distance how such theoretical categories can mislead, he has unfortunately failed to grasp the significance and power they have had within contemporary movements of sexual liberation: Foucault's critique remains trapped within a fundamentally rationalist tradition.

Repression, the body, and male sexuality

THE BODY AND REPRESSION

Foucault and Sennett have both been concerned to understand late Enlightenment and Victorian fears that a person alone with his or her own sexuality appears to be alone with a very dangerous force. They realize that these fears express ideas about the relation between mind and body, speech and desire, discourse and political domination. But even though Foucault and Sennett recognize that this highly charged psychological value put on sexuality is a legacy of Victorian wisdom which is still with us (even if we would flatter ourselves otherwise), they find it hard to explain its continuing hold. They are left with statements of regret but with little substantial sense of the ongoing power of these notions. It is as if we are to transform ourselves through these insights alone, learning to replace one form of discourse by another. It is as if we can wish away the difficulties and tensions of our sexual experience, through learning to give up the language of repression.[7]

If we are to grasp how dominant forms of male sexuality are still experienced within Augustinian terms, we need to understand how they have been historically modulated and redefined. If we are to know, following Foucault, that since Augustine we have experienced our sex primarily in our heads, we need also to grasp how the Cartesian split between mind and body gives this fragmentation a secular form. It was Descartes who conceived the human body as a machine organized according to mechanical laws. The body, in western culture, is radically separated from a sense of personal identity; the latter is defined in purely mental terms as a matter of consciousness. This reiterates a Christian tradition which had often denigrated the body as a source of spiritual knowledge. The male body in the Cartesian tradition was to be used as an instrument, rather than as something through which individuality could be expressed. Men were to be estranged from their bodies as they were from a natural world they had learned to fear and distrust. Men could only assert their humanity by mastery over the physical world, and by learning to dominate their passions and desires. It is this inherited notion of self-control *as dominance* that has been so closely identified with modern forms of masculinity. This is something Foucault fails to grasp, since his writing on sexuality leaves sex strangely disembodied, disconnected from the lived experience of men and women.[8]

But paradoxically it was the very rationalism that Foucault explores in his investigations of madness which was such an integral part of redefining and reorganizing relationships of power between men and women. Since nature was conceived by the scientific revolution of the seventeenth century as dead matter to be moulded to the designs of men, so women, being closer to nature, had also to be dominated. As masculinity became increasingly identified in an emerging rationalist tradition with culture, women were gradually and brutally reduced to the status of a denigrated nature, and so could even be burned as witches.

This deep, if often unrecognized, contradiction within our inherited moral culture has been brought into focus by Susan Griffin in her book *Pornography and Silence*. She recognizes that our culture is inherently split and that in the negation of nature, people have been set against themselves. She sees our culture as one which seeks to deny the natural in itself. But this is to deny central aspects of our experience which will continually seek to reassert themselves in forms we barely recognize.

As discussed earlier in this paper, the denigration of dreams, emotions, and bodily experience as genuine sources of knowledge was recognized by Foucault as an integral part of the creation of modern forms of madness. It was also at the core of Freud's understanding of the place of sexual repression in modern culture.[9]

Freud had himself responded to an enquiry from Jones on the true historical source of repression, saying 'every *internal* barrier of repression is the historical result of an *external* obstruction. Thus, the opposition is incorporated within; the history of mankind is deposited in the present-day inborn tendencies to repression' (Ernest Jones 1953: 455). Building on his work, Marcuse's *Eros and Civilisation* shows that Freud's repressive organizations of the instincts 'are not inherent in the "nature" of the instincts but emerge from the specific historical conditions under which the instincts develop' (Marcuse 1955: 187). This area is a rich source of historical genealogy that could have appealed to Foucault, were he not, in so much of his writings, trapped in his idea that individuality is itself constituted through discourse. This leaves no space for developing a critical language able to identify the tension between what individuals need and desire for themselves and what the discourses of society would represent for them.[10] There is evidence in Foucault's latest work on sexuality that he was struggling to establish such a space. He was original enough to worry less about consistency than have those who have blindly followed him.

Freud has built his theory of psychosexual development around the need of the male child to separate himself from his mother and from the feminine within himself, to identify with his father, and so to resolve the Oedipus complex. He saw the development of the superego, and so of conscience and morality, as the heir to the Oedipus complex. In this deeper sense, Freud remains within a Kantian tradition, and psychoanalysis itself remains informed in its deeper structure by the connection between reason, masculinity, and morality. Having tied the formation of the superego or conscience to castration anxiety, Freud considered women to be deprived by nature of the impetus for a clear-cut Oedipal resolution. Consequently women's superego and sense of morality were compromised: they were never 'so inexorable, so impersonal, so independent of its emotional origins as we require it to be in men'. This allows Freud to conclude that women 'show less sense of justice . . . that they are more often influenced in their judgements by feelings of affection or hostility' (Freud 1925: 257–58).

Since women have been deemed closer to nature, it has often been feminism that has forced a reassessment of our relationship to nature. Susan Griffin sees the natural as positive, as that sense of ourselves as temporal, conscious, and emotional beings who have a material reality. Bodily existence is not regarded as the functioning of a machine, but is continuous with our emotionality. Our attempts to deny ourselves as material and emotional beings is itself a consequence of a masculine identity defined in terms of a disembodied conception of reason. This helps produce the projection of what Griffin calls a 'pornographic consciousness' which pits culture against nature. She sees the genesis of this consciousness, where an imagined reality displaces material reality, in a child's attempt to fantasize the presence of a mother who has withdrawn or separated, as a way in which the child reassures itself that it has power in the world.

It is this *displacement* which seems crucial in grasping particular forms of male sexuality. As men have learnt to identify with their reason, they have also learnt to be *estranged* from their bodies, to regard them as having no part in their identities or experience. This can place men outside and beyond their own lived experience, as if destined to observe their lives from outside. Men can achieve tasks they have set themselves, but often they are deaf to their own emotions, feelings, and desires. If the only centre men have is in their heads, it is hardly surprising that sexuality becomes primarily a mental experience for them.

Within the dominant sense of masculine identity that rationalism has prepared, sexuality remains a troubling contradiction. It demands the very surrender and spontaneity which men have grown up to be suspicious of. It is only through turning sex into performance, and separating it from intimacy and personal contact, that they can still see it as an issue of control. Griffin argues that the objectified woman in the pornographic image represents not women in their actuality, but that part of the masculine self which remains attached to feelings of need, emotionality, and dependency. This is what little boys are required by culture to crush in themselves, in return for the prestige, power, and status that accompany the achievement of masculine identity.

INTIMACY AND SEPARATION

It is the nature of this displacement from emotional lives and needs for dependency which has so deeply formed masculine sexuality. Often it is closeness and intimacy which are feared; men experience any compromise of their independence, defined as self-sufficiency, as a threat to their very sense of male identity. Nancy Chodorow in her book *The Reproduction of Mothering* has challenged the tacit assumption which renders male identity as the norm, in an attempt to attribute differences between the sexes not to anatomy but rather to the fact that women, universally, are largely responsible for early child care. This gives girls a more continuous experience of relationships, since they do not have to separate themselves from their mothers to achieve their sense of sexual identity. As a result 'feminine personality comes to define itself in relation and connection to other people more than masculine personality does' (Chodorow 1978: 43–4).

Female identity formation takes place in a context of ongoing relationships since mothers tend to experience their daughters as more like, and continuous with, themselves. Girls also, in learning to be female, see themselves as like their mothers, thus fusing the experience of attachment with the process of identity formation. In contrast, mothers view their sons as male opposites, and boys, in defining themselves as masculine, separate their mothers from themselves and so cut themselves off from the qualities they learn to regard as 'feminine'; in this way, males curtail 'their primary love and sense of empathic tie' (Chodorow 1978: 47).

Chodorow replaces Freud's negative description of female psychology with a positive sense that girls emerge with a stronger basis for experiencing another's needs or feelings as their own. So it is that girls emerge from this period with a basis of 'empathy' built into their primary definition of self in a way that boys do not. This helps to explain how male gender identity is threatened by intimacy and dependency, while female gender identity is more often threatened by separation. But this can also illuminate the tensions and anxieties for men within sexual relationships and the separation they often make between sexuality and intimacy. For boys, but not for girls, 'issues of differentiation have become entwined with sexual issues' (Chodorow 1978: 166–67). It becomes harder for men to give themselves up to a sexuality which involves blending and melting into the rhythms of sexual contact. Men can easily feel threatened by any experience which threatens their differentiation, such as a sexual contact which often involves a regression to pre-Oedipal relational modes.

This, then, is part of the difficulty men often have with relationships. It can make it difficult for men to support others, since they readily assume they should be able to pull themselves together as an act of will. The masculine resolution of the Oedipus complex leaves men with a sense of reason as an independent faculty and source of morality which has lost connection with its emotional origins.[11] They are constantly working out the correct thing to do, often out of touch with the emotional realities of their relationships. If a relationship ends, they are more likely to blame their partners than to take responsibility for themselves. Often they will not mourn the loss and separation, thinking, in utilitarian terms, that this will not bring the person back. Yet it is hard to understand why men seem to feel so threatened when they get close to others, knowing at another level that this is precisely what they want.

Language, desire, and identity

DESIRE AND CONTROL

Within Freud's psychoanalytic grasp of male sexuality, fathers are experienced as competitors for the love of mothers. A fear of castration is what secures the transition through the Oedipus complex, as men learn to crush their feelings of need, dependency, and emotionality to achieve a masculine identity. It is not simply that these feelings and emotions threaten the sense of masculine identity, but that the denial of these feelings and desires *establishes* the very sense of male identity. Masculinity has to be constantly reasserted in the continuous denial of 'femininity' or 'feminine qualities'. It was Jung, not Freud, who saw the acknowledgement and then the integration of these feminine aspects as an integral part of our development as human beings (Jung 1962). As long as a sense of masculinity is built upon the systematic denial of 'feminine' qualities, men are left in a continuous and endless struggle with themselves, in constant anxiety and fear of the revelations of their natures. They think they can control these fears within themselves, but they do so by projecting them, according to Griffin (1981), on to women, homosexuals, Jews, and blacks.

Within the psychoanalytic framework, it can be hard for men to acknowledge their feelings of love and need for their fathers. In this sense, psychoanalytic theory has often reproduced traditional assumptions which leave it to women to provide nurture, love, and caring. Supposedly, men are not to feel anger and resentment at the absence of their fathers, since this leaves them more of their mothers' time and undivided attention. Even if they want to acknowledge the distinctive contribution of fathering, they need a new understanding of its form and significance in the development of gender identity.

Nancy Chodorow certainly helps to analyse the abstract and discontinuous relationship boys often have with their fathers. Since boys from an early age are taught to deny their needs and dependency, they often learn to destroy these feelings within themselves. But this can also threaten the 'control' that boys are constantly struggling to assert, since boys seem to have so little control over their relationship with fathers. This can encourage boys to create this control within an imaginary realm, since they cannot experience it in a living relation. They fantasize the relation they want to have, so as not to feel the pain of separation. This has a peculiar significance, since it provides the ground upon which their gender identity is to be built. It can make them less aware of the dynamics of personal and sexual relationships since they so easily assume that things are what we would like them to be. In later life this can help to explain why so many men are shocked when women eventually decide, after many hints and warnings, to leave them. It is as if they have lived in a world of their own, hardly conscious of the seriousness of the frustration and difficulties their partners have endured. This adds bitterness to divorce, since men so often claim that they had no idea things were so wrong. They cannot grasp why women often refuse to give the relationship another try, since they do not know the process which brought such women to make the decision in the first place.

At another level, psychoanalysis has been crucial in helping people to appreciate the lengths to which we all go in *avoiding* the reality of our experience. We constantly blame others for our misery and we do everything to evade responsibility for our own lives. It remains crucial to rethink issues of individual and social responsibility which prevailing traditions of political thought, be they liberal or Marxist, seem incapable of illuminating.

This denial of personal responsibility was part of Freud's antipathy towards revolutionary politics, making him suggest that instead we rethink our expectations of politics. Such a critique can be of help in thinking about the nature of human needs in a culture which has repressed sexuality. Freud was centrally concerned with awakening people to the human costs of modern culture. This was part of his insistence on talking of repression, since he saw the negation of sexuality as producing misery and unhappiness in the name of virtue and morality. A use of Freudian insights can help to show that, as men learn to deny their emotionality, need, and dependency, these parts of themselves do not go away, but find different and disguised forms within which to assert themselves.

Foucault thus leads us astray when he suggests that all human needs are constituted as well as articulated in language. There is in fact an ongoing tension between the language in which we can articulate, identify, and recognize needs, and the *quality* of everyday experience.[12] The proliferation of discourses concerning sexuality, significant as it may be, is not itself evidence for a concern with the quality of sexual and personal relations. It can as easily be evidence for a denial of genuine forms of sexual expression. But Foucault cannot recognize compulsive activities as expressions of need, any more than he can question pornography as the basis of a society we want to live in.

Susan Griffin thinks of pornography as a particularly graphic depiction of men's need to reassure themselves that sexuality is controllable. It offers control without the threat of intimacy. But it is ultimately fruitless in that the image of a woman, in arousing desire, continually reminds men of that very part of themselves they have forsaken. Hence the monotonous regularity with which 'Over and over again, that part of our beings which can feel in both body and mind is ritually murdered' (Griffin 1981: 83). It is partly because men are brought up to replace material reality with their rationalizations and efforts of imagination that it becomes hard to discern and discriminate between different forms of satisfaction. This becomes part of the repetitious rituals of pornography.

Griffin is clear that, in opposition to the idea that our desires are infinite, it is in the nature of material needs that they are satiable. The delusionary need to deny the existence of a part of ourselves has a reality which is in principle insatiable. It will find its own forms of expression, however difficult it is for us to recognize them. This potentially restores the central insight of Freud's idea of repression to feminist theory. It can also help us to appreciate the discussions of human needs which the Frankfurt School initiated without ever really finding an adequate means of developing them. Marcuse, for example, was critical of hedonism's abstract conception of the subjective side of happiness, of its inability to distinguish between true and false wants, interests, and enjoyments:

> 'Pleasure in the abasement of another as well as self-abnegation under a stronger will, pleasure in the manifold surrogates for sexuality, in meaningless sacrifices, in the heroism of war are false pleasures, because the drives and needs that fulfill themselves in them make men less free, blinder, and more wretched than they have to be.'   (Marcuse 1968: 190)

Griffin attempts to work with a similar insight when she offers an explanation of why particular sexual practices, such as pornography, are constituted as objects of pleasure. She discusses the extremely ambivalent nature of this pleasure, showing that 'pornography . . . shocks us away from feeling' (Griffin 1981: 83). It offers men power and control as the image is silenced so that it cannot question and answer back. Griffin shows how the pornographic image becomes part of the way men construct their reality so that women are objectified. This is itself an act of violence; 'The models of pornography as they appear on the page lose their actuality as women, they acquire a two-dimensional quality which goes beyond mere posture and enters into an absence of meaning' (Griffin 1981: 233).

SEXUALITY AND POWER

Foucault's *A History of Sexuality* discusses the 'hysterization of women's bodies' without being able to connect this to the sexual relations of power between men and women. He suggests that the theory of power which has traditionally underpinned our questioning about sex is a juridico-discursive model which encourages asking the wrong questions. This model conceives power to be essentially negative: it only forbids. It operates through taboos and prohibitions, and therefore does not allow that power can be *affirmative*, operating through the constitution of pleasure. But this sense of power as affirmative could be conceived of in terms of personal power, giving people more control and experience of their capacities and potentialities. Some feminists have thought of this affirmative power as more closely connected to women's experience, while power as prohibition, in which power is always at the expense of others, is conceived of as a masculine form of power.

Foucault challenges the idea that through abandoning the taboos on sexuality, by resisting a power essentially external to our sexuality, we can achieve freedom. He thinks that the very idea that this constitutes freedom is itself an effect of power. It is because we think of power as a pure limit set on freedom that we cannot grasp that the fact that sex is pleasurable is also an 'effect of power':

> 'By creating the imaginary element that is "sex", the deployment of sexuality established one of its most essential internal operating principles: the desire for sex – the desire to have, to have access to it, to discover it, to liberate it, to articulate it in discourse, to formulate it in truth. It constituted "sex" itself as something desirable.'   (Foucault 1980a: 86)

With this theory of power, Foucault thinks he can avoid the binary alternatives involved in the juridico-discursive model which lead 'either to a promise of liberation if power is seen as having only an external hold on desire, or, if it is constituent of desire, to the affirmation: you are always already trapped' (Foucault 1980a: 83).

If Foucault shows how to escape from this false opposition, he still leaves people powerless to make discriminations in their sexual experience and with a false sense of freedom that anything goes. He does not help illuminate the difficulties in personal and sexual relations or the problems people face in changing themselves. At the same time he unwittingly fosters the idea prevalent in the 1960s of sex as a commodity which should be freely available. Nor does he differentiate between the implication of this idea for the sexual experience of men and women. This lack in his work reproduces the very masculine conception of sex as a commodity which would free it from concern with commitment, vulnerability, and caring in personal relations.

Similar to Foucault's ungendered conception of sex, we find an equally undifferentiated notion of power. Although Foucault questions the idea of power as centred in state institutions, his definition makes it hard to situate sexuality within gender relations of power. For Foucault 'Power is everywhere; not because it embraces everything, but because it comes from everywhere' (Foucault 1980a: 93). Again Foucault is doing useful work in helping question notions of power we have implicitly taken for granted, but he is not making his own view clear. As he says, 'power is not an institution, and not a structure; neither is it a certain strength we are endowed with; it is the name that one attributes to a complex strategical situation in a particular society' (Foucault 1980b: 93). But this makes it difficult to illuminate the particular relation of power between men and women and between heterosexuals and homosexuals, even if it does disturb the notion that men are always powerful in every area of life, and women always powerless. Though Foucault insists on the heterogeneity of power, this is simply a heterogeneity of forms and strategies.

If we think of power as having certain effects, such as the production of certain objects of desire, we see these objects constituted in discourses which are neither true nor false in themselves. We cannot criticize certain forms of sexual relations as exploitative, nor can we discern changes in our sexual relations as an enrichment or growth. Nor can we think about how relations of power operate within the sexual relations of men and women.

As Gilligan (1982: 68) has expressed it, 'For centuries, women's sexuality anchored them in passivity, in a receptive rather than an active stance, where the events of conception and childbirth could be controlled by a withholding in which their own sexual needs were either denied or sacrificed'.

Since Foucault thinks of 'sex' and 'sexuality' as if these are defined by particular discourses available at any given moment in time, there is little grasp of the *different relation* which men and women can have to sexuality. History is acknowledged, formally and abstractly, only as a history of discourses which constitute particular forms of subjectivity. There is no way of investigating how people's sexual experience is formed within particular relations of power and subordination. Since he has dispensed with the language of the subject, Foucault cannot consider the different consequences this can have for men and women, for crushing their particular capacities, abilities, and emotional lives. He cannot consider, for instance, relations between experience, identity, and power. It also makes it difficult to discriminate, as Emma Goldman was seeking to do in her lecture 'False Fundamentals of Free Love', between promiscuity and the free choice of committed love. While working on her lecture, she wrote illuminatingly to her lover of ten years Ben Reitman: 'Your love is all sex with nothing but indifference left when that is gratified. . . . My love is sex, but it is devotion, care, anxiety, patience, friendship, it is all' (Falk 1984). She had been forced to rethink her ideas of free love because of the pain caused by his frequent affairs. Redefining a relationship between love, freedom, and autonomy has also been important for women in the Women's Liberation Movement in the 1970s (Rowbotham 1983).

LANGUAGE, DESIRE, AND IDENTITY

Like relativism, Foucault's post-structuralism undermines the grounds for a judgement and critique of existing relations. We are left with a 'positive history' of discourses concerning sexuality, but without the power to discern and identify male dominance and female subordination. Unlike the work of the Frankfurt School, Foucault offers no way of making central in social theory a concern with the justice of existing relations. This crucial ground of contesting existing social relations is forsaken since the language of oppression and repression has been rendered meaningless. But this theoretically disempowers us, even if it leaves us feeling secure in our linguistic radicalism, with a clear sense of the discourses invoked by the existing structures of power and subordination. Even though Foucault separates himself from a sense of power as domination, he is left bereft of ways of articulating the pain and indignity of subordination. He cannot grasp that repression could be a different experience for men and for women. Even if we can acknowledge, along with Foucault, that what is being repressed is not a uniform sexual force or a coherent entity located outside the forces that repress it, we still need to investigate relations between sexuality, power, and identity. This is centrally connected to the sense of ourselves as autonomous and authentic beings. To affirm that sex is negated or repressed is to recognize a fundamental fragmentation in men's inherited sense of identity, a sense in which they are set against themselves. So often the language used to talk about sexuality makes no distinction between an authentic sexuality which appreciates the richness of bodily experience without fetishizing it, and a sense of sex as commodity through which men do violence to their potentiality as human beings.

Conclusion

Foucault's *A History of Sexuality* has certainly been useful in helping to rethink the concept of repression and the tacit conceptions of sexuality it can leave us with. But rather than rework this notion, it is characteristic of his rationalistic method to want to replace it completely. The hope seems to be that if a different discourse is involved, the problems Freud and Reich were concerned to illuminate will somehow disappear (Reich 1961; Sharaf 1983). But what is lost is the possibility of illuminating tensions and contradictions within the experience of sexuality. There will be a failure to grasp tensions written into a masculine sexuality, where male identity has been connected to reason. It will be harder to acknowledge that the process through which sex comes to be constituted as 'an object of desire' is the process through which women are subordinated as somehow closer to nature. The historical antagonism between reason and desire, which has sought to deny our existence as natural beings, is unwittingly

reproduced in the talk of discourses as constituting our experience. Foucault leaves us with the idea that reality is in principle
identical with the structures through which we talk about it.
Since he has banished any tension between our language and an
experience it struggles to articulate, we are left powerless to
appreciate Griffin's insight that structures of thought can specifically *silence* reality, making it possible for people to *avoid* the
truth about themselves. Since there is no 'reality' or 'nature' that
can exist independently of the discourse in which we can articulate them, we are left bereft of terms of criticism. We are also left
powerless to illuminate the inhibition, oppression, and sexual
misery in a culture which would treat sex as a commodity.

Foucault assumes that to talk of repression is unavoidably to
invoke an idea of 'natural' sexuality that has waited in silence
ready to be awakened in its pristine state, and therefore to
commit ourselves to some conception of 'free' or 'liberated'
sexuality, meaning a sexual expression that is untouched by
relations of power. But this is a vision of Foucault's construction
that has little to do with illuminating the kind of problems Freud
and Reich were arguing over, even if it does help to dispense with
any appeals to nature. Foucault's theory follows a structuralist
tradition which debases such notions as 'humanism', 'biologism',
and 'essentialism' even before it learns to grasp what is at issue.
Griffin, on the other hand, has understood the antipathy towards
'nature' where this has been used to legitimate and reinforce the
subordination of women. But she has also shown the deeper
cultural sources of the temptation to think that this means that we
should dispense with ideas of nature completely. She is aware of
how both Freud and Reich used the idea of a 'natural sexuality' to
reinforce a heterosexual norm. But she is also critically aware of
the danger of thinking we have solved deep cultural issues of sexuality through simply labelling ideas as 'biologistic' or 'naturalistic'. These categorical distinctions which have been such a
strong part of a structuralist inheritance have often made our
thinking more superficial and abstract than it need be.

If Foucault tempts us into agreeing with him that a proliferation
of discourses relating to sexuality shows that we mistakenly
think of the Victorian period as a time of sexual repression, he
only begins to illuminate the difficulties in discourse analysis.
Since he leaves us thinking that social practices are constituted

through discrete discourses, we are left unable to illuminate a tension between the ways people talk about sex and the quality of their sexual experience. This is something individuals have to explore for themselves, albeit in a social context in which women have traditionally been forced to silence and repress their own sexualities. We certainly cannot assume that a proliferation of discourses around sexuality is any evidence for a refutation of the reality of sexual repression. If we believe Freud, we can suppose that people might well talk in order to escape making an emotional contact with the reality of their experience. We learn to be suspicious of those who do all the talking. This raises difficult questions about the relation of language to experience, questions which tend to be silenced with the declaration that since discourse is a material process, there is nothing beyond it to which we can appeal.

From a reading of Foucault, it is also difficult to grasp the significance of sexuality for a sense of personal identity. Indeed, we can begin to grasp it only in the context of the history of sexual repression and the subordination of women and gays. It is hardly surprising that this remains such a puzzle for both Foucault and Sennett. If theory is to help illuminate our grasp of social and historical reality, it should not be allowed to replace this reality. It is because an experience of subordination and oppression has largely gone unacknowledged that issues of sexual identity have become so significant to people since the 1960s. In denying or privatizing one's sexuality, a person was often learning to be ashamed of who he or she was. Hence the personal importance of declaring the public significance of a sexual identity which the culture has denied or negated. If this has helped many people to accept the reality of sexual repression, it has also forced the development of an understanding of the differentiated sexual experience of men and women, and the rejection of an ungendered conception of 'sex' and 'sexuality', such as we find in the work of Foucault.

In the seminar organized by Foucault and Sennett, we are told that 'sexuality has become too important, that it has become charged with tasks of self-definition and self-knowledge it can't and shouldn't perform' (Foucault and Sennett 1981: 168). There is a note of desperation in Sennett's words as he resists 'this yoking of sexuality to subjectivity' (Foucault and Sennett 1981: 189).

This shows the difficulties they have in appreciating attempts, however sketchy or exaggerated, to develop a more embodied language. These moves, however tentative, question the very rationalism which Foucault's post-structuralism defends. But we can learn to listen to our bodies without thinking that we must consequently ignore mental forms of knowledge. Certainly such listening will challenge rationalist conceptions of personal identity, but then this sense of a coherent, pre-given identity is often very significantly challenged by Foucault himself. The point worth devoting attention to is the difficulty Foucault and Sennett seem to have in learning from historical experience. They are too ready to trivialize through exaggeration. Learning to reinstate and value a language of the body is bound to be stumbling and uncertain, since it challenges such cherished rationalist notions. It looks towards a different form of theory, but one that can, it is to be hoped, illuminate tensions in our sexual experience and identities.

We should certainly remember that we cannot conclude that 'if something isn't felt it isn't true' (Foucault and Sennett 1981: 168), but this does not diminish the importance of listening to and learning from our bodily feelings. If our inherited identification of truth with reason is thereby questioned, we also know that this identification was an integral part of the original denial of emotions and feelings as genuine sources of knowledge. This knowledge marks an important shift in the relation between truth, identity, power, and experience, though not in the terms that Foucault imagined. It might well mark a significant shift in our inherited philosophical and moral tradition that sexual politics and therapy have helped to create. If this is a new vision struggling to be born out of a desire for more honest and open personal and sexual relations, we should learn to be more welcoming of it.

As we learn to place reason and desire in a different relation to each other, we might discover a language of male sexuality which is less instrumental and brings us into closer relation with ourselves and our partners. This is an urgent need which both heterosexual and gay men are learning to express.

Notes

I would like to thank the Masculinity Research Group at Goldsmiths' College, University of London, for encouragement with this writing, also Pat Caplan, Bob Connell, Caroline Ramazanoglu, and Janet Ransom.

Anna Ickowitz and our son Daniel have helped shape an experience out of which these ideas have grown.

1   I don't want to draw attention to Foucault's work on madness simply to contrast it favourably with his later work on sexuality. I want to bring out the significance of his insights for grasping tensions inherent within dominant forms of masculinity in western culture.

2   Foucault came to recognize some of the inherent difficulties in his more theoretical studies such as *The Order of Things*. He learnt, especially through his work with prisoners while writing *Discipline and Punish*, of the ways a generalized notion of discursive practice can blind you to the workings of relationships of power. He learnt how dominant institutional discourses which would constitute subjectivity were continually being subverted. A careful reading of the writings gathered in *Knowledge/Power* can help to illuminate significant transitions in his writings.

3   In the end this amounts to a significant weakness in Dale Spender's pioneering study *Man-Made Language*. Though showing the significance of language in sustaining relationships of power, it tends to see language as some kind of net against which reality is placed. Wittgenstein's *Philosophical Investigations* challenges this vision of language as autonomous and so potentially provides a deeper challenge to Cartesian rationalism and its relation to masculinity.

4   It has been part of the potential theoretical significance of feminism to restore to us a sense of the contradictions within lived experience. These are contradictions not simply at the level of our consciousness but in the organization of our everyday lives. This is an insight which a structuralist tradition has continually undermined legitimizing as it does a distancing from self and lived experience that resonates particularly with dominant forms of masculinity. See my article 'Trusting Ourselves; Human Needs, Marxism and Sexual Politics' (Seidler 1980).

5   This view was shared by both Kant and Rousseau. It reflects upon the kind of rationalism we take for granted within liberal political theory and its inadequacy to sustain fuller conceptions of freedom and democracy. See my *Kant, Respect and Injustice: The Limits of Liberal Moral Theory* (Seidler 1986).

6   This is more fully discussed in my article 'Fear and Intimacy' which appears in Metcalf and Humphries (1984).

7   If this was not Foucault's hope it has been the lesson that many have drawn. Our grasp of important issues has been weakened as we have learnt to think of issues of sexual repression as issues of language.

8   These aren't connections which can easily be made. They lead us back into questioning some of the assumptions of his work which had seemed so fruitful, especially in his study *Discipline and Punish*.

9   See Freud's *Civilisation and Its Discontents* which needs to be placed in historical context if we are to be aware of the differences that come to separate Freud from Reich.

110   The Cultural Construction of Sexuality

10 A useful account which demonstrates how issues of sexuality have
    been side-stepped as part of a critique of Freud's theory of instincts is
    given in Harry Guntrip's *Psychoanalytic Theory, Therapy and the Self*.
    It is in a shared opposition to instinctual theories that structuralist
    and object relations theories come together.
11 It is an enduring strength of Freud continually to make us think about
    the emotional sources of our moral theories. He was critical of Jung
    and Binswanger who seemed to sublimate psychoanalysis into
    religion and morality by ignoring its psychic and erotic base. But this
    remains a difficult issue.
12 This tension between language and experience has generally been
    foreclosed within a structuralist tradition which assumes we must be
    appealing to a pre-theoretical conception of experience. This estab-
    lishes a false opposition which blinds us to the issues at hand. Again
    feminist theory could find support in Wittgenstein's later writings.

References

Adorno, T. (1968) Sociology and Psychology. *New Left Review* 47.
Blum, L. (1981) *Friendship, Altruism and Morality*. London: Routledge &
    Kegan Paul.
Boadella, D. (1976) *In the Wake of Reich*. London: Coventure.
Cassirer, E. (1970) *Rousseau, Kant, Goethe*. Princeton, NJ: Princeton
    University Press.
Cavell, S. (1969) *Must We Mean What We Say?* New York: Scribners.
Chodorow, N. (1978) *The Reproduction of Mothering*. Berkeley, Calif.:
    University of California Press.
Clarke, S., Seidler, V. J., Lovell, T., McDonnell, K., and Robins, K. (1981)
    One Dimensional Marxism. London: Allison & Busby.
Easlea, B. (1982) *Science and Sexual Oppression*. London: Weidenfeld &
    Nicolson.
Falk, C. (1984) *Love, Anarchy and Emma Goldman*. New York: Harper &
    Row.
Foucault, M. (1967) *Madness and Civilization*. Trans. R. Howard. London:
    Tavistock.
—— (1970) *The Order of Things*. London: Tavistock.
—— (1975) *Discipline and Punish*. London: Allen Lane.
—— (1980a) *The History of Sexuality*. Harmondsworth: Penguin.
—— (1980b) *Knowledge/Power*. Ed. C. Gordon. Brighton: Harvester
    Press.
Foucault, M. and Sennett, R. (1981) Sexuality and Solitude. In *Anthology 1*.
    London: Junction Books.
Freud, S. (1905) *Three Essays on the Theory of Sexuality*. Standard Edition,
    Vol. 7. London: Hogarth Press.
—— (1925) *Some Psychical Consequences of the Anatomical Distinction
    between the Sexes*. Standard Edition, Vol. 19. London: Hogarth Press.
—— (1929) *Civilisation and Its Discontents*. New York: Norton, 1962.
Fromm, E. (1956) *The Fear of Freedom*. London: Routledge & Kegan Paul.

Gilligan, C. (1982) *In a Different Voice*. Harvard: Harvard University Press.

Griffin, S. (1981) *Pornography and Silence*. London: The Women's Press.

Guntrip, H. (1971) *Psychoanalytic Theory, Therapy and the Self*. New York: Basic Books.

Harding, S. and Hintikka, M. (1983) *Discovering Reality*. Dordrecht, Holland/London: D. Reidel.

Hirschman, A. (1977) *The Passions and the Interests*. Princeton, NJ: Princeton University Press.

Horney, K. (1937) *The Neurotic Personality of Our Time*. New York: Norton, 1964.

Ignatieff, M. (1984) *The Needs of Strangers*. London: Chatto.

Jacoby, R. (1975) *Social Amnesia*. Hassocks: Harvester Press.

Jones, E. (1953) *The Life and Works of Sigmund Freud*. Harmondsworth: Penguin, 1978.

Jung, C. (1962) *Memories, Dreams and Reflections*. London: Fontana.

Lichtman, R. (1982) *The Production of Desire*. New York: The Free Press.

Lloyd, G. (1984) *The Man of Reason*. London: Methuen.

Lukacs, G. (1971) *History and Class Consciousness*. London: Merlin Press.

MacCormack, C. and Strathern, M. (1980) *Nature, Culture and Gender*. Cambridge: Cambridge University Press.

MacIntyre, A. (1981) *After Virtue*. London: Duckworth.

MacPherson, C. B. (1962) *The Theory of Possessive Individualism*. London: Oxford University Press.

Marcuse, H. (1955) *Eros and Civilisation*. New York: Vintage Books.

—— (1968) *Negations*. London: Allen Lane.

Metcalf, A. and Humphries, M. (1984) *The Sexuality of Men*. London: Pluto Press.

Midgely, M. (1978) *Beast and Man*. Brighton: Harvester Press.

—— (1983) *Animals and Why They Matter*. Harmondsworth: Penguin.

Mitchell, J. (1974) *Psychoanalysis and Feminism*. Harmondsworth: Penguin.

Okin, S. Moller (1980) *Women in Western Political Thought*. London: Virago.

Reich, W. (1961) *The Function of the Orgasm*. New York: Farrar, Straus, & Giroux.

Rorty, R. (1979) *Philosophy and the Mirror of Nature*. Princeton, NJ: Princeton University Press.

Rousseau, J.-J. (1959–69) *Oeuvres Completes, Vols 1–4*. Paris: Pleiade Edition.

—— (1968) *Letter to d'Alembert*. Trans. Allan Bloom. Cornell University Press.

Rowbotham, S. (1983) *Dreams and Dilemmas*. London: Virago.

Seidler, V. J. (1980) Trusting Ourselves; Human Needs, Marxism and Sexual Politics. In S. Clarke, V. J. Seidler, *et al.* (eds) *One Dimensional Marxism*. London: Allison & Busby.

—— (1986) *Kant, Respect and Injustice: The Limits of Liberal Moral Theory*. London: Routledge & Kegan Paul.

112   The Cultural Construction of Sexuality

Sharaf, M. (1983) *Fury on Earth: A Biography of Wilhelm Reich*. New York: St Martins/Marek.
Sheridan, A. (1980) *Michel Foucault, The Will to Truth*. London: Tavistock.
Spender, D. (1982) *Man-Made Language*. London: Routledge & Kegan Paul.
Wittgenstein, L. (1963) *Philosophical Investigations*. Oxford: Basil Blackwell.
—— (1975) *On Certainty*. Oxford: Basil Blackwell.

4 A note on gender iconography: the vagina

Shirley Ardener

In January 1977 when I agreed to give one of four lectures on gender at the Warneford Hospital, Oxford, I said that I would choose my exact topic after attending the first paper, which was entitled 'Sexual Selection'. This paper turned out to be concerned with the penis and included a consideration, illustrated by slides, of penile length. I therefore decided that the empty theoretical slot to be filled would have to be a complementary offering concerning the vagina. In my introduction to the paper I then presented I noted that it differed from Dr Short's in being 'less concerned with quantity and more with quality; less concerned with measurement than ideology; and less concerned with function and more with meaning'. This chapter derives in some measure from that presentation. However, while it draws attention to an aspect of gender symbolism – that associated with the female pudenda – which may have been relatively neglected compared to that of the more familiar male, phallic imagery, the theme of my paper is the replacement of male honour by shame and female shame by honour, and the use of the body and of vulgarity in making these transformations.

The manner in which we clothe or leave unclothed different parts of the body has long interested social anthropologists and other commentators. It has been recognized that, as Polhemus sums it up, the body has an iconography of signs and symbols; body imagery is 'part of man's existence as a social animal' (1973). It differentiates very efficiently both between social groups and within social groups, and, as Mary Douglas (1966) has pointed out, threats to social boundaries between groups and between individuals can produce increased concern with the

boundaries of the body. Distinguishing our bodies is important
and, as Goffman (1956) noted, in our society, rules regarding the
keeping of one's distance are multitudinous and strong. They
'tend to focus around certain matters, such as physical places and
properties defined as the recipient's own, the body's sexual
equipment, etc.' (Goffman 1956: 482). The body's 'sheath', that is
skin and, at a little remove, the clothes that cover the skin, can
function, Goffman thinks, as the least of all possible personal
spaces, and also the purest kind of egocentric territoriality. 'Of
course', he writes, 'different parts of the body are accorded
different concern – indeed this differential concern tells us in
part how the body will be divided up into segments conceptually'. He notes that across different cultures, the body will be
differently segmented ritually.

Iona Mayer (1975) has discussed the role of 'prudery' in maintaining hierarchical social institutions. She states that:

> 'any assertion of status distinction demands a tight handling of
> the body. Every manifestation of the physical body simply as
> such will tend to draw attention to the common animal nature,
> or if not that, the personal peculiarities, which are both inimi-
> cal to the discriminating sense of "who is who" in strictly social
> terms.'[1]

Goffman stresses the importance of seeing that the self is in part a
ceremonial thing, a sacred object which must be treated with
proper ritual care and in turn must be presented in a proper light
to others. He speaks of the 'ritual game of having a self' and of the
'ceremonial grounds of selfhood' (1956: 497). Goffman points out
that even

> 'infractions such as profanity and violence which, from the
> point of view of the actor, may appear to be a product of blind
> impulse, or have a special symbolic meaning, from the point of
> view of society at large and its ceremonial idiom, are not
> random. Rather they are exactly calculated to convey complete
> disrespect and contempt through symbolic means.'

He is thinking particularly of mental patients who throw faeces
at attendants – 'a use of our ceremonial idiom that is as exquisite
in its way as is a bow from the waist done with grace and a flour-
ish' (Goffman 1956: 496). Here I aim to show how women have

employed 'ritual games' and gestures, not randomly, but in an idiom which reverberates across time and space, to defend their corporate identity.

I

When I lived in Cameroon my attention was drawn to a complex of thought and action in the traditions of the Bakweri people. I found that, on certain infrequent occasions in the past, Bakweri women would demonstrate in ways which might be considered vulgar or obscene and of which they would certainly disapprove in their everyday life – paradoxically in order to affirm their pride.[2] The Bakweri distinguish a category which they label *titi ikoli*. *Ikoli* has the independent meaning of 'thousand'; *titi* is a childish word for 'vulva'. Bakweri explain the expression in different ways: *titi ikoli* is 'beautiful'; it is also 'valuable'; the word also 'refers to an insult'. The combination comprehends the following main association: 'a woman's underparts' and insults to these; and 'women's secrets' and the revealing of these. At the same time it is associated with certain types of mandatory female sanctions which follow upon these insults.

These insults may take various forms but that most typically envisaged is the accusation that the sexual parts of women smell. A Bakweri woman so insulted before a witness must call out *all* the other women of the village. Converging upon the offender dressed in vines, they demand immediate recantation and a recompense of a pig, plus something extra for the woman who has been directly insulted. The women then surround him and sing songs which are often obscene by allusion, and accompany them by vulgar gestures. An example of another kind of song is *'Titi ikoli* is not a thing for insults, beautiful, beautiful'. All the men beat a hasty retreat (since they will be ashamed to stay and watch while their wives, sisters, sisters-in-law, and old women join the dance) except the culprit, but he will try to hide his eyes. Finally the women share the pig between themselves.

During the late colonial period women had largely replaced these traditional direct sanctions by the use of formal judicial procedures. The Bakweri courts regarded insults of this kind as extremely serious and fines were very heavy compared to those

imposed in other types of defamation case. There are many
migrants from other parts of Cameroon in the Bakweri area who
are also sensitive to these kinds of offences, and one of the cases
from court records in the 1950s (which I have presented elsewhere in more detail (S. Ardener 1975a)) was brought by a
woman from an inland group.

The Balong are another Cameroonian people who live in four
villages sharing a boundary with the Bakweri. Balong women too
would, according to tradition, come out on the pathways *en masse*
in defence of their gender group. It was said that if a man insults
his wife's lower parts 'it is like insulting all women, and all the
women will be angry'. If an offending man refuses to compensate
the women, 'they will take all their clothes off. They will shame
him and sing songs'. Significantly, all the women of the village
will be affected, including the newly born female children. The
term used for this phenomenon (*ndoŋ*) is probably derived from a
root meaning 'beautiful'.

Three hundred miles up-country a very different people, the
Kom, have a traditional practice called *anlu*, described by Ritzenthaler as a

'disciplinary technique employed by women for particular
offences. These included the beating or insulting (by uttering
such obscenities as "Your vagina is rotten") of a parent; beating
of a pregnant woman; incest; seizing of a person's sex organs
during a fight; the pregnancy of a nursing mother within two
years after the birth of the child; and the abusing of old
women.'   (Ritzenthaler 1960: 151)

A Kom man, son of an important woman leader, described the
practice of *anlu*: the women of the village gather before dawn,
garbed in vines and bits of men's clothing, with their faces
painted, ready to carry out the ritual:

'The women pour into the compound of the offender singing
and dancing and, it being early in the morning, there would be
enough excreta and urine to turn the compound and houses
into a public latrine. No person looks human in that wild
crowd, nor do their actions suggest sane thinking. Vulgar parts
of the body are exhibited as the chant rises in weird depth.'
                                      (Nkwain 1963)

The offender is ostracized until he repents and is ritually purified in a stream by the women.

Thus the Kom can be seen to have a pattern of female militancy not unlike that of the Bakweri and Balong. Revenge is taken on an offender by corporate action, and typically he is disgraced by the exhibiting of parts of the body normally hidden by women, as well as in other ways. The traditional picture is of such militancy being aroused by offences against women relating to their gender or sexual characteristics.

I have material from many other parts of Africa in which women, for example among the Azande, 'tear off their grass covering from over the genitals and rush naked after the intruder, shouting obscene insults at him' (Evans-Pritchard 1929: 320, 1956: 87–8); or among the Kikuyu, deliberately exhibit 'the private parts towards the thing or person cursed' (Lambert 1956: 99); or among the Pokot, sometimes shame the offender by dancing 'around him and put their naked vulvas in his face' (Edgerton and Conant 1964).

This is by no means simply an African phenomenon, however. I have also collected data from various parts of the world where the underparts of women are publicly exhibited, including, for example, Sri Lanka, France, and the United States (for cases of 'mooning' in the United States, see S. Ardener 1974), which I have no space to deal with here. Regarding the Bakweri case, however, we may ask how we are to interpret the meaning of *titi ikoli*. Why, for example, is this offence regarded as the mandatory concern of all women, regardless of age, status, and origin, rather than being merely an individual, personal matter, like most other offences concerned with defamation? Why this particular and rare form of militancy and rule enforcement, so apparently out of keeping with their conventional modes of deportment?

I have ventured to suggest elsewhere that *titi ikoli* concerned 'the dignity of a concept which Bakweri women consider to be valuable and beautiful – the dignity of their corporate sexual identity, of which the symbol is part of their unique sexual anatomy – the vaginal area' (S. Ardener 1975a). When this symbol was insulted, Bakweri women traditionally manipulated the dominant conventions, and instead of conforming to the requirement of propriety which required their 'underparts' to be hidden, they deliberately drew attention to them. They thereby shamed the offender according to his own logic, but at the same time transformed the discourse, reversing his negative to their positive values. They proclaimed their pride, and made their hidden secrets a dominant and public emblem. They reclaimed the honour of their gender. Thus may alternative meanings be given to existing signs, or may those meanings considered to be misused be reappropriated (S. Ardener 1975b).

II

I would like to turn now to some case material separated widely in time and space from that we have been considering. I am indebted to Froma Zeitlin (1982) for drawing my attention to some data from classical Greek studies. Certain references in her paper on cultic models of the female in the rites of Dionysus and Demeter are pertinent to my theme here. Dealing with early classical sources is fraught with difficulty, especially, of course, for a non-specialist in this field like myself,[3] but it would appear that there are elements in the Demetrian cults which offer resonances to some of the material I have just summarized.

The story of Demeter and the rape of Persephone, as presented by the Homeric myth, is well known in outline: Demeter's daughter Persephone is kidnapped by Hades with the consent of Zeus, when she is gathering flowers. Demeter is distraught and, disguised as an old woman, wanders the world looking for her daughter. She eventually becomes nurse to the baby son of the king of Eleusis. Entering his palace she resumes divine form for a moment. She sits down on a stool 'in silent sorrow' until the maid Iambe makes her laugh. Iambe seems to have shocked Demeter out of her grief by vulgar speech or jests. Demeter, who has hitherto refused to drink wine, then breaks her fast and accepts a simple mixture of barley and water. Prevented from making her baby charge immortal by placing him in the fire, Demeter angrily causes famine in the land, until Zeus agrees that Persephone should spend two-thirds of the year with her mother and the rest underground with Hades (see Richardson 1974: 1–3).

The important women's festival of the Thesmophoria re-enacts the myths associated with Demeter and also with Kore who (along with the swineherd Eubuleus and his pigs) was swallowed up, like Persephone, by the earth. The first day of the rituals seems to be mainly concerned with the myth of Kore, together with echoes of Persephone's abduction. On the second day the women sit on the ground reliving the grief of Demeter at the loss of her daughter, exchanging ritual obscenities (*aischrología*), thereby alluding to the role of Iambe. The next and last day of the Thesmophoria is a joyous one. Zeitlin sums up:

> 'The days of the Thesmophoria, during which the women actually occupied the male space of power and authority near the Acropolis, also saw a cessation of the normal business of political and economic life (at least on the second day), as though the society of women functioned as an alternative reality to that of everyday life, a temporary surrender to the natural sacrality of life at its source, incarnated in the female body and correlated with the founding myth of Demeter and Persephone.'
>
> (Zeitlin 1982: 139)

We may note that Kore (the 'virgin') is sometimes identified with Persephone. Zeitlin writes that:

> 'On the level of myth, the *aischrología*, the ritual obscenities which the women hurl at one another, reenacts the role of Iambe in the Homeric Hymn, who made Demeter laugh when she sat in mourning and fasted after the abduction of her daughter (202–04). On the level of ritual, however, those obscenities are in their double signification properly renamed *árrhēta* (or *apórrēta*), for that "which cannot be spoken" can refer either to religious secrets which may not be disclosed or to obscenity, that which is "unspeakable" because it violates the social norms. This double meaning is comprehensible in view of the thematic of the festival as an expectant interiority; an opening up of its potentiality; an intensification, as it were, of the receptacle, the reservoir of fertility that is woman.'
>
> (Zeitlin 1982: 144)

I have speculated elsewhere on some of the language used by Germaine Greer in her pioneering work *The Female Eunuch* (1970):

> 'Greer speaks (though not approvingly) of those in the [modern feminist] movement who "mock and taunt" men. This she may

not, herself, do, but does not the mode by which she presents her case itself sometimes appear to be a verbal display of vulgar parts? "The key to the strategy of liberation", she says, "lies in exposing the situation, and the simplest way to do it is to outrage the pundits and the experts by sheer impudence of speech and gesture . . ." (1970: 328). *Titi ikoli* indeed!'

(S. Ardener 1975b: 49)

As Rickles (1950) noted, Freud, in discussing the relation of wit to the unconscious, has pointed out that a smutty joke is in effect a denudation of the person to whom it is told. The listener is forced to form a mental picture inspired by the words that are used, visualizing either some part of the body or a sexual situation, and is aware that the teller is visualizing the same thing. 'There is no doubt', Freud concludes, 'that the original motive of the smutty joke was the pleasure of seeing the sexual displayed' (Rickles 1950). Zeitlin also sees the link between verbal and behavioural obscenities: 'Ritual obscenity is, in a sense, a form of exposure, of uttering the secret and unspeakable which shame and scruple have hidden away. . . . This ritual exposure can, in fact, take two forms, that of verbal obscenity and that of *anasyrma*, the act of revealing the genitals' (Zeitlin 1982: 144).

In the Greek sources Iambe has her counterpart in Baubo who replaces her in some recensions as having jolted Demeter into laughter and back into social life (by accepting a drink); she did so, however, not like Iambe by *verbal* vulgarities, but by *anasyrma* (exposure of the genitals), the physical manifestation of them. Zeitlin writes that, while Baubo, as far as is known, does not have a place in the common Thesmophoria festivals, the 'analogue of her action may well be in the women's use of piglets, a well-known gloss for the vulva, and of cakes fashioned in the form of genitalia' (1982) which are important on the first day.

The reasons for Baubo's gesture are debated by Graf. A version of the story gives Baubo as the baby's mother and states that she was angry with Demeter because she threw the baby in the fire and killed him. One authority, Clement, seems to have indicated that Baubo was aggrieved with Demeter; from another, Arnobius (who translated Clement), it seems that she wished to cheer her up (Graf 1974: 195). I cannot claim to be able to interpret the sources, since my knowledge of the Greek texts is deficient.

I would, however, like to speculate on Baubo's gesture in the
light of my assessment of similar gestures in other parts of the
world by other, non-mythical, women. It seems to me that the
verbal and gestural obscenities of Iambe, Baubo, and their Greek
imitators at the Thesmophoria are capable of two meanings (at
least).

First I would see hostility and anger as one important aspect. I
would like to consider the possibility that Iambe and Baubo are
making gestures towards the defilers of Persephone – of the kind
that the Bakweri and Kom women (for example) make – both on
behalf of Demeter and of *all* women. By this gesture they are
affirming the support and interest of other women in this case of
sexual insult (rape), which, like the insults dealt with through the
rituals of *titi ikoli*, *ndoŋ*, and *anlu*, are seen to demean the social
identity of the whole female gender group. Demeter's change of
spirits following this show of solidarity is therefore understandable.

In Prienne, in Turkey, excavations of ancient Greek sites have
revealed some representations of pigs and some unusual
figurines which are known to Greek scholars as Baubo statuettes
(see *Figure 4.1*). The latter consist of legs, vulva, and head; some
of these torso-less figurines have arms (see Wiegand and
Schrader 1904: 161). These cult objects have been described by
Zeitlin: 'their iconic representation makes explicit this connection of face and genitals in a bizarre anticipation of Magritte's
grotesque "Le Viol"' (1982: 145). The strange relation of head on
genitals prompts Zeitlin to see a relationship between the mouth
and the vulva:

> 'if the aim of the ritual jest is to produce laughter, we might
> consider that laughter opens the mouth in a mimetic represen-
> tation of that other orifice below, the vulva, an interpretation
> that is supported by the probable etymology of Baubo as the
> bark of a dog, the latter animal being another term applied to
> the female pudenda.'   (1982: 144)

She draws attention to the ambiguity of the Gorgon's image, with
its gaping mouth:

> 'Even without Freud's observations on the head of the Medusa,
> the various spheres of reference to which the Gorgon belongs

Figure 4.1   Baubo statuettes

suggest her identity as a "genitalized" head. Her apotropaic function in war magic is beyond question when heraldically displayed on shields or on the aegis of Athena in order to terrify and drive away the enemy.[4] In this context, the gesture of women in besieged cities who repel the enemy by an act of *anasyrma* (Plutarch, *de Virt. mul.* 5, 9) is analogous in its intention to the role of the Gorgon. . . . The women's *anasyrma*, in turn, terrifies the enemy by exposing its secrets to those who may not see them.'   (Zeitlin 1982: 145)

This brings us to the *second* 'meaning' of this verbal or actual exhibitionism. Zeitlin rightly points out that in a different context from that just described – that is, in a female fertility rite conducted

by women in secrecy (she means, I think, the Thesmophoria) –
the effect of the exposure of the genitals or verbal obscenity is
reflexive, 'directed away from and then back to the source, the
female herself' (1982: 145). There is, as I have indicated earlier, a
positive valuation which can be proclaimed. Thus I do not think
that we need to seek only one meaning in this symbolism; it is not
a case of either/or. The whole point is that the actors can have it
both ways. They can by their revelations shock the witnesses,
towards whom the act is hostile, and they can at the same time
proclaim the honour of that which is exposed. They can (rightly)
profess that it is all in the eye of the beholder. I have already
demonstrated elsewhere (S. Ardener 1983) how the Doukhobors
of Canada adopted the nude parade and employed it to the same
dual effect. So was it, I venture to suggest, with the Greeks.

III

I would now like to turn to some ethnography from Britain and
America, relating mainly to the 1960s and 1970s, when a number
of women likewise attempted to break certain cultural taboos
and pejorative stereotypes by turning them on their heads, by
changing the signs from negative to positive. Germaine Greer, for
example, arrived at a position close to that of the Bakweri when
she recognized the value of body symbolism and sought its
reinstatement: 'The vagina', she complained, 'is obliterated from
the imagery of femininity in the same way that signs of independence and vigour in the rest of her body are suppressed' (Greer
1970: 15).

Now I should say here that all along I have been discussing, and
Germaine Greer is referring to, a symbolic sexual body, rather
than the western, medical body. The classification of these two
systems is, of course, not identical. The boundaries of 'the vagina'
in the symbolic body seem to extend further than in the medical
body to include, for instance, the vulva.[5] Indeed, this seems to be
the primary reference in many cases. The vagina of the medical
body seems only to be the hidden recesses of the wider category
label 'vagina' in the sexual body, and it is interesting that it is this
hidden recess that seems the most potent symbol. The womb,
incidentally, *is* distinguished in the sexual body, and its symbolic

force seems to be quite different. I have drawn attention to the fact that significantly *titi ikoli* does not appear to be concerned with fertility (S. Ardener 1975b: 47). Zeitlin supports the general view that the Demeter cult of the Thesmophoria (especially that part relating to the rotting pigs (vaginas) which are buried and then retrieved from the earth during the first rites associated with Kore) is to do with female fecundity, women participants extolling their dominant role in procreation. She notes, however, that this 'role is paradoxically more clearly defined by the cultic chastity, which seems to separate sexuality and fertility even as it separates male and female spaces' (1982: 146). A further blurring of the boundaries of the category comprising 'underparts' would include the buttocks and anal area.

If the vagina has been, as Greer says, relatively invisible in the expression of culture, for many women it has also been literally unseen. As Simone de Beauvoir wrote: 'The feminine sex organ is mysterious even to the woman herself. . . . Woman does not recognise herself in it and this explains in large part why she does not recognise its desires as hers' (1953). Linda Dove noted in *Spare Rib* that sometimes it seems that doctors and lovers have had more access to our bodies than we have. In the 1960s and 1970s some women in England, America, and elsewhere began to attempt to redress the situation. The women's magazines started to provide copious detailed diagrams of the internal and external sexual parts of women, presumably reacting at least partly to popular demand. Further, women began to gather in small groups in order to conduct practical explorations of female anatomy for educational purposes, to 'demystify' their bodies (e.g. Dove 1977). A film, described as consisting exclusively of thirty-eight women's vaginas, was produced, apparently as an attempt to 'understand and portray our relationship to our bodies'. In making her film *The Big Chakra*, Anne Severson stated that she hoped to 'creatively release energy in order for women to move on up the cerebrospinal ladder'. She designed a 'flyer' with a red rose in the centre, 'a good symbol for the vagina – spiritual unfolding, femininity, fecundity', inviting women to be in a film about 'women's parts'. 'This phrase seemed evasive but I was still uneasy', she reported. She says that when she was filming, over and over again, 'women who came into the room where I was shooting expressed their anxiety about the most intimate part of their bodies. The "invisible ideal" I began to call it'. Reactions to Severson's film were mixed. At one extreme, friends of a prostitute who had exposed herself for the cameras whistled and applauded, but, at another, a lot of people 'have seen the film and gotten angry'. Crowds at the 1972 Edinburgh Festival were annoyed and when it was shown at the Ann Arbour Film Festival several hundred walked out. One woman who favoured the film was so enraged by this response, 'especially since some of those leaving were making rude and irreverent comments', that she chased them up the aisles, bashing them with her bag. Later she explained to Severson: 'I would kill for your film', thus giving an indication of the intense emotion this focus on the vagina had engendered (*Spare Rib* 1974: 8–9).

Firestone wrote that women

'have no means of coming to an understanding of what their experience *is* or even that it is different from male experience. The tool for representing, for objectifying one's experience in order to deal with it, culture, is so saturated with male bias that women almost never have a chance to see themselves culturally through their own eyes. So that finally, signals from their direct experience that conflict with the prevailing (male) culture are denied and repressed.'   (1972: 149)

Firestone sought 'an exploration of the strictly female reality', from which will be developed an 'authentic female art', a task which, she stressed, is not to be regarded as reactionary but rather as progressive.

By 1972, when Firestone was making her plea, however, some female artists were already applying themselves to this task. Lee Bontecon, in an *Untitled* 1961 painting, centred her abstract round a large oval shape across which was a kind of zipper. Petersen and Wilson describe this work:

'The sense of vulnerability, of being a target and needing armour, paradoxical images, based at least somewhat on the primitive folk art motif of the teethed vagina and the psychological archetype of the devouring mother, the teeth mother. It takes a woman artist to think of installing zippers in a chastity belt!'   (Petersen and Wilson 1979: 129)

Figure 4.2 'Fantasy Rejection Drawing' from 'The Rejection Quintet' by Judy Chicago, 1974

Another feminist artist, Hannah Wilkes, noted that in the early 1960s, she was scared to show her work around: 'you were put down if you were doing female genitalia'. In 1966 she exhibited a lot of small terracotta boxes. 'The shapes were very sexy, like little tiny genitalia.[6] But nobody noticed them.' (This seems to confirm the contention that until very recently the vagina was effectively 'invisible' in public.) Wilkes found that 'being an artist is difficult, an unbelievable risk, and to make a female sexual statement is even riskier'. However, by the 1970s, her work was receiving attention. Wilkes's images are explicit. She has developed forms from folds of red latex hangings, held together by metal snappers, representing vaginas. 'My art is a very female thing', she states, 'it is about multi-layered forms, and it's organic like flowers' (1974: 57).

Figure 4.3   Centre panel from 'Sacred Heart' by Judy Chicago, 1975–76

Judy Chicago also began experimenting with body symbols, both male and female, in the 1960s. One of the first of these paintings 'held a double vagina/heart form, with a broken heart below and a frozen phallus above'. It represented the death of her father and her husband. In 1975 she wrote: 'When I showed these paintings to the two painting instructors on my thesis committee they became irate. . . . They threatened to withdraw their support if I continued to make works like these. One sputtered out something about not being able to show the paintings to his family' (Chicago 1982: 34).

Chicago 'became intimidated and began to hide [her] subject matter' (1982: 34–5) eventually producing

'closed forms transmuted into doughnuts, stars and revolving mounds representing cunts. (I use the word "cunt" deliberately, for it embodies society's contempt for women. In turning the word around, I hope to turn society's definition of the female around and make it positive, instead of negative.) I chose that format to express what it was like to be organized around a central core, my vagina, that which made me a woman . . . because I had a cunt, I was despised by society.[7] By making an image of the sensation of orgasm, I was trying to affirm my own femaleness and my own power and thus implicitly challenge male superiority.'   (1982: 55)

Some of these works and her later *Pasadena Lifesavers* (described by Parker and Pollock as sharing 'the same optical colour mixture and rippled format, reminiscent of the style practised in Los Angeles in the 1960s' (1981: 130)) were so abstract that the organic symbolism was not always detected. Echoing Wilkes, Chicago reported that although some, like Miriam Shapiro, could 'read' her art in the way she expected,

> 'On the other hand, a male artist friend of mine had told me: "Judy I could look at these paintings for twenty years and it would never occur to me that they were cunts". The idea that my forms were cunts was an over-simplification, obviously, but at that time, even a greatly simplified perception seemed better than no perception at all of the relationship between my femaleness and my art. . . . I wanted . . . to speak to people, to tell them that women possessed all aspects of human personality, that society's conception of the female was distorted and that other values in the culture that grew out of that distortion were also questionable. Fundamental to my work was an attempt to challenge the values of the society, but either my work was not speaking, society didn't know how to hear it, or both.'   (Chicago 1982: 64)

While Chicago and others were working in the United States, another American, Suzanne Santoro, who worked in Rome, was changing her style. Her early work had been heavy sculptures, made of sheet metal and the like, but after having become involved in a feminist group, she decided to take a cast of herself and she was amazed by the structural solidity, the very precise construction and form, of her hidden recesses. She went on to photograph other female genitals and published the pictures in her book *Towards New Expression* (1974) juxtaposing them with matching photographs of flowers and shells. The photos are said to be a refined examination of structure, desexualized, each isolated in the centre of a blank page. She carefully points out that the juxtaposition of flowers, shells, and genitals is not intended to confirm the old identification of women with nature as against culture. She stated:

> 'For most feminists vaginal imagery signifies a rejection of images by men of women, and an exploration and affirmation of their own identity. It attacks the idea of women's genitals as mysterious, hidden and threatening, and attempts to throw off a resulting shame and secrecy. I just wanted to make the point that I had found structural identities, not symbolic identities.'
>
> (Parker 1977: 44)

Suzanne Santoro also sees demystification as a prerequisite for sexual self-expression which, she believes, leads to greater self-knowledge in other areas of our lives: 'Expression begins with self assertion and the awareness of the difference between ourselves and others' (Parker 1977: 44).

Niki de Saint-Phalle produced large standing or prancing females: her *Black Venus* (1967) is embellished with a large heart- or vagina-shaped motif from between her legs and covering her stomach. At an exhibition in Stockholm she presented a large reclining figure within whose inner space visitors could walk about; the entrance was through a vaginal opening.

In New York in 1973 there were dozens of shows of women's erotic art, and there have subsequently been more there and elsewhere. Dorothy Seiberling (1974: 55) suggests that since, for women, 'repressing erotic subject matter was in fact repressing their own natures, the removal of taboos may unleash a remarkable creative energy among the female artists of our time'. The painter Semmel explained that in her work she particularly wanted to make imagery that would respond to female feelings. 'I'm using sex to hang my art on' (Semmel 1974: 55), she states, while another artist, Juanita McNeely, doesn't consider her own art 'erotic', but claims to be dealing with 'woman and her problems, and with sexuality, a human concern' (McNeely 1974: 56). 'Women tend to hide their sexuality, to wear a mask, play a role. But today women are becoming much closer to themselves' (see Mulvey 1974). Other artists who use vagina or womb images in their work include Deborah Remington, Miriam Schapiro, Penelope Slinger, and Rosemary Mayer.

In 1974 in an article entitled 'Vaginal Iconology', Barbara Rose found that artists associated with the feminist movement agreed that there is a 'feminine sensibility' and a subject matter that can be described as 'female'. The question then arose: 'To dignify female "difference", what should feminist art glorify?'

'The answer is obvious, and even if feminist art bears no slogans proclaiming "power to the pubis", that is what it is essentially about. For much of the feminist art that has been labelled "erotic" because it depicts or alludes to genital images is nothing of the sort. It is designed to arouse women, but not sexually.'   (Rose 1974)

What is interesting about those that glorify vaginas 'is the manner in which they worshipfully allude to female genitalia as icons – as strong, clean, well made, and as whole as the masculine totems to which we are accustomed'.

Rose agrees, therefore, that the vagina has been selected by some to represent more than the sexual and generative properties directly associated with it. It has also been taken as a political or social symbol. She writes:

'This category of women's art is profoundly radical in that it attacks the basis of male supremacy from the point of view of depth psychology. At issue is the horror of women's genitals as mysterious, hidden, unknown, and ergo threatening as chronicled by H. R. Haynes in *The Dangerous Sex*.

She continues:

By depicting female genitals, women artists attack one of the most fundamental ideas of male supremacy – that a penis, because it is visible, is superior. At issue in vaginal iconology is an overt assault on the Freudian doctrine of penis envy. . . . The self-examination movement among women that strives at familiarizing women with their own sex organs, and the images in art of non-menacing and obviously complete vaginas, are linked in their efforts to convince women that they are not missing anything. In realizing that "equality" depends on more than equal rights and equal salaries, women are exalting

images of their own bodies. Their erotic art is, in effect, propa-
ganda for sexual equality.'   (Rose 1974: 59)

Perhaps the best-known work of art in which the vagina is the
dominant, and repeated, motif is Judy Chicago's *The Dinner Table*
(see *Figure 4.4*), first shown in March 1979. This took her five
years to construct, with the help of a team of co-workers labour-
ing under her inspiration and guidance. For those who are not
familiar with this complex structure I will note here that it
consists of a triangular table made of three wings each 46 ft 6 ins
long. It stands on a triangular 'Heritage' floor composed itself of
2,300 12-inch triangular porcelain tiles inscribed with names of
famous women. Chicago explained that she 'arrived at the idea of
an open triangular table, equilateral in structure, which would
reflect the goal of feminism – an equalized world.' For Chicago
the triangle was one of the earliest symbols of the feminine and
also the Goddess' sign. She writes of 'the Primordial Goddess,
who symbolizes the original feminine being from whom all life
emerged. She is the Primal Vagina – her centre, dark and molten;
all her energy emanates from her bloody womb and core'
(Chicago 1979: 57). In her view, 'the Primordial Goddess was
originally referred to by primitive markings, triangular shapes
that stood for the vulva, and sacred holes in rocks, the presence of
which on or near animal images was thought to cause animals to
multiply' (1979: 99). We need not try here to assess the basis of
Chicago's assertions, only note them.
   Each of the three sides of the triangular table has thirteen place
settings, a reference to the all-male *Last Supper* paintings. But
here every place setting represents a heroine and consists of a
table runner and a large 14-inch ceramic 'plate'. Each plate has a
different design, often in high relief, based, with varying degrees
of directness, upon the vagina (or more accurately the vulva) but
often capable of carrying other connotations. Thus, just as
Santoro was able to draw parallels between flower shapes and
female genitalia, the plates combine various imagery. Indeed, the
ingenuity by which the plates carry a multiplicity of meanings is
remarkable. At an early stage in her work (on Sunday, 2 June,
1974 to be precise) Judy Chicago noted that 'I want to make
butterfly images that are hard, strong, soft, passive, opaque,
transparent – all different states – and I want them all to have

Figure 4.4   'The Dinner Party' by Judy Chicago, 1974–79

vaginas so they'll be female butterflies and at the same time be shells, flowers, flesh, forest – all kinds of things simultaneously' (1979: 22). Chicago saw 'Poor Virginia [Woolf], a flower of delicacy, a genius, a shaking trembling leaf' (1979: 44).

It seems that these place settings are perceived by Chicago to be 'portraits' of her heroines, and Woolf's 'plate' is described by Chicago in the following terms:

> 'Woolf's image breaks away from the basic plate shape and – though still contained within its place setting – is the most liberated form on the table. The "breaking open" of the plate's structure symbolizes the breaking of the historic silence about women's lives, which can only be fully understood if women possess their own forms of expression. The luminous petals spread open to reveal the bursting center, an image of Woolf's fecund genius.'   (1979: 95)

At the risk of over-repetition, I document Chicago on the question of imagery:

> 'the visual symbology . . . must not be seen in a simplistic sense as "vaginal art". Rather . . . women artists have used the central cavity which defines them as women as the framework for an imagery which allows for the complete reversal of the way in which women are seen in the culture. That is: to be a woman is to be an object of contempt and the vagina, stamp of femaleness, is despised. The woman artist, seeing herself as loathed, takes that very mark of her otherness and by asserting it as the hallmark of her iconography, establishes a vehicle by which to state the truth and beauty of her identity.'
>   (Chicago 1982:143–44)

It is not part of my task here to assess the success of such an enterprise. I will, however, quote a sceptical view put forward by Parker and Pollock:

> 'But what is the effect of these attempts to validate female experience, to reappropriate and valourize women's sexuality? Women, feminist or otherwise, may well feel affirmed by such work, recognizing the way it confronts their oppression by exposing hitherto hidden, repressed or censored aspects of their lives. But because meanings in art depend on how they

are seen and from which ideological position they are received, such images have a very limited effectivity. They are easily retrieved and co-opted by a male culture because they do not rupture radically meanings and connotations of woman in art as body, as sexual, as nature, as object for male possession.'
(1981: 132)

The problem of inadvertently contributing to pornography, about which much has been written by feminists in recent years (see for example Dworkin 1981 and Griffin 1981, among others) is naturally raised. Parker and Pollock publish an explicit photograph of a nude from *Penthouse* magazine to provide an example of males expropriating (or reappropriating) the attempts by women to present a (new) female iconography; presumably in the context of *Penthouse* magazine the image carries different significances. For Parker and Pollock the danger is that

'Both in fantasy and language, woman as woman is not present, except as the cipher of male dominance, the scene of male fantasy. Therefore, within the present organisation of sexual difference which underpins patriarchal culture, there is no possibility of simply conjuring up and asserting a positive and alternative set of meanings for women. The work to be done is that of deconstruction. . . . In art practice, women can engage in work to expose these ideological constructions by questioning the traditional institutions of artist and art, by analysing the meanings which representations of woman signify and by alerting the spectator to the ideological *work* of art, the effects of artistic practices and representations.'   (1981: 132–33)

Juliet Mitchell worries that when feminists break the cultural taboos and turn femininity on its head, 'The danger is that tossing a coin a second time one may land up with the same side one started with' (1971: 69), while Lisa Tickner warns that such visual puns and double-edged irony may indulge rather than challenge derided clichés (1978: 242).

IV

In this paper, I have tried briefly to present some selected material from a range I have collected on various ways in which women have attempted to manipulate the dominant discourse and conventions, which require that women, especially, should see their 'underparts' as shameful and unspeakable. The evidence often shows a blurring of the boundaries of the category but the general message here is, I think, that the 'vagina' has sometimes been used as a condensed symbol to cover all the 'secret' areas of women;[8] providing a unitary counterpart or symbolic inversion to be matched against the undifferentiated unit commonly used to represent the male gender: the penis.

Another candidate for a symbolic pairing with the penis might, of course, be the female breast. There is no space here, nor is it my brief, to consider the symbolism of the breast in any depth, but a few glancing remarks might be made.[9] The pair of breast and penis, unlike the vagina and penis combination, are both external and easily visible on the unclothed body. Both produce (different) life-giving flows. To speculate: the breast and penis may in some ways be seen as having parallel attributes rather than as a conjunction of complementary opposites which fit together symbolically (and physically) – as do the vagina and the penis. In an interesting study, Eichinger Ferro-Luzzi describes how, in Indian iconography, the breast and *lingam* may come to be not contrasted so much as identified one with the other. In speaking of 'the series of absurdities culminating in the equation breast = *lingam*' she makes the point that we are not dealing here with 'an elision of opposites' (Eichinger Ferro-Luzzi 1980: 53).[10]

In recent years there have been more studies of the male nude by women artists and photographers, and at least one exhibition of work by women on this subject. One well-known juxtaposition of penis and breast occurred when Professor Linda Nochlin caused a sensation in 1972. At a meeting of the College of Art Association Nochlin

'showed a slide of a popular French (nineteenth century) illustration of a woman, nude except for stockings, boots, and choker, resting her breasts on a tray of apples [echoes here of Gauguin], then she projected a photograph of a bearded young man, nude except for sweat socks and loafers, holding a tray of bananas under his penis. Instead of the invitation *"Achetez des pommes"* (Buy some apples) inscribed under the maiden, the man advertised "Buy some bananas".'   (Rose 1974: 59)

Nochlin's aim, of course, was to demonstrate how erotic art of the nineteenth century was created by men for men.

Jeannette Kupfermann (1979: 149) believes that the 'Women's Lib' movement has been largely anti-ritualistic. This is a surprising stance since it seems quite clear that feminists have precisely used condensed symbols of various kinds. Indeed in this paper I have tried to demonstrate the attempts of women artists to take on the role of priests in the service of their gender, raising its symbolism as an icon. I have brought into my analysis some contemporary ethnography pertaining to women artists precisely because we have some access to their published thoughts; some, like Judy Chicago, have been particularly articulate as they try to explain their motives and their art. It is clear from what some of them have said that the body imagery they have used has sometimes been overlooked and this raises pertinent doubts as to whether we have in general been as alive to the meaning of female symbols as we have been to those pertaining to males.[11]

The use of gestures and metonymic signs in the way described to repudiate the negative evaluations of a dominant group is, I have suggested elsewhere, a resource of 'muted' individuals or groups (whether composed of women or men or both). I refer to those who have not equally generated or do not equally control the dominant modes of discourse, which embody the values being rejected, and who are unable or unwilling to employ direct aggression, or unambiguous hostility, in order to demand a hearing and a re-evaluation. It seems to me that the story of Iambe and the Baubo statuettes, the beliefs and behaviour of the Bakweri women, the mooning of the girls of Iowa (S. Ardener 1974), the protest marches of the Doukhobors (S. Ardener 1983), and the words and works of the feminist artists all offer mutual help in the understanding of each. In bringing together in one place ethnographic data from very disparate groups and sources I run into deep dangers, of course. 'One must not take material out of context', I hear my betters murmuring, just to start with. I hasten to state that no one-to-one matching is intended. Each event will have its own specificity, context, and history. Various aspects have been discussed, yet in none of the cases mentioned are all the elements present. Faced with such complexities, I personally find it helpful to imagine that, while we are not dealing with ubiquitous 'universals', we may nevertheless be meeting a set of elements which provide a constellation, a 'syndrome', a theoretical model, or a 'register' of related 'vocabulary' perhaps, from which some groups select, or make real more or less partially. From such manifestations an abstract model containing all the elements may in theory be constructable.[12]

I have drawn attention here to the way in which an action-utterance can have an ambivalence. Devereux (1961: 369) notes that 'art can function as a social safety valve' precisely because 'The utterance is understood to be repudiable. . . . The utterance is thereby turned from an idiosyncratic into a conventional, from a non-repudiable into a repudiable, from a straightforward into an ambiguous, from a private into a public, and from a personal into an impersonal statement'. He speaks of the means whereby the artist 'seeks to smuggle his utterance past the inner – and also past the social – order' (p. 373). Double-talk of this kind is not claimed by the feminist artists I have been discussing, as far as I know, but I think it is legitimate to ask whether or not their works of art have a sting in their tails. I have even been led to question whether this paper shares the same ambivalence and to wonder whether it is designed to tease as much as to teach!

Goffman (1956: 37) quotes Durkheim's statement that the 'human personality is a sacred thing: one dares not violate it nor infringe its bounds', and in a poetic flight he wonders whether the individual

'is so viable as a god because he can actually understand the ceremonial significance of the way he is treated, and quite on his own can respond dramatically to what is proffered him. In contacts between such deities there is no need for middlemen: each of these gods is able to serve as his own priest.'

(Goffman 1956: 499)

Deities, of course, may be female, and females priestesses.

Acknowledgements

The author and publishers would like to thank the following for permission to reproduce copyright material in this chapter: the Ashmolean Museum, Oxford for *Figure 4.1*, Baubo statuettes from Wiegand and Schrader (1904); Doubleday and Company, Inc. for *Figures 4.2*, *4.3*, and *4.4*, photos from *Through the Flower* by Judy Chicago. Copyright © 1975 by Judy Chicago. Reprinted by permission of Doubleday and Company, Inc.

Notes

1 I have discussed elsewhere the implications of prudery and social distancing in a study of Oxford colleges, noting Mayer's argument that
the breaking of the boundaries between nature and culture may produce unwelcome 'reminders of the "common nature" of mankind
which is logically opposed to many ideas of social stratification justi-
fying privileged access to scarce resources' (Mayer 1975: 260;
cf. Sciama 1981: 111; S. Ardener 1984: 43–5).

2 I repeat here the gist of an argument set out fully in S. Ardener
(1975b) in order to make necessary connections later.

3 My thanks go to Emily Kearns for help with interpreting some Greek
texts.

4 I have other cases of military intervention reported from France, the
Aztecs, and so forth. In fiction Zola's *Germinal* offers a well-known
example of exposure. Graf reports a case of exposure before a king of
Egypt. Richardson (1974: 217) notes cases of vulgar jesting in Japan
and in Greece (at the festival of the Daedela at Plataea). My attention
has been drawn to a German volume (*Baubo* by G. Devereux) which I
have not as yet been able to read.

5 The vagina has been symbolized in gestures and in other ways by
some feminists, e.g. in the peace movements.

6 Some of her 'boxes' look rather like cowrie shells. Among the Bimin-
Kuskusmin cowrie shells (male wealth) are explicitly identified with
the vagina (Poole 1981: 143). For the association of the cowrie shell
with the female in Japan, see Singer (1940).

7 Among the Maasai it seems that women's subordination is directly
associated with possession of a vagina. Llewelyn-Davies reports that:
'Once men and women were equal. There were no (male) "elders" in
the land, but only women, known as *ilpongolo* (women warriors) and
moran (young men warriors). The women were braver than the men.
At that time they had no vaginas, but only tiny holes for urine to pass
through!' The young men, however, found an occasion to push 'the
sharp ends of their bows into the women's bodies and created
vaginas'. After sexual intercourse the men said: 'Ahah! These are
only women after all!' They married them and women lost their
bravery, and 'life/fertility' began (Llewelyn-Davies 1981: 342).

8 Feminist literature frequently refers to the 'interiority' of women in
one way or another, and 'vagina' symbolizes this concept.

9 A fascinating treatment of 'the single revealed breast' in (mainly
male) western art is the chapter 'The Slipped Chiton' by Marina
Warner (1985).

10 This equation is made possible and acceptable in this Indian case
because 'if there is true devotion, the god will forgive the breach of all
rules be they ritual or commonsense' (Eichinger Ferro-Luzzi
1980: 53). Clara Thompson made the comparison in 1943:

'The position of underprivilege might be symbolically expressed in
the term penis envy using the penis as the symbol of the more

privileged sex. Similarly, in a matriarchal culture one can imagine that the symbol for power might be the breast. The type of power would be somewhat different, the breast standing for life-giving capacity rather than force and energy. The essential significance in both cases would be the importance in the cultural setting of the possessor of the symbol.'   (1943: 52–3)

As for the vexed question of so-called 'penis envy' (on which my views are sceptical) another psychologist, Ruth Moulton, records that

'envy goes both ways. Now that nursery-age children are allowed more freedom of expression and are observed with less bias, normal little boys can be seen trying to sit down and urinate like girls, pretending to have babies and breasts, or envying girls their special privileges, such as the right to wear jewellery, to dress in a range of colours, and to be more protected.'   (1973: 242)

11 I have often myself felt that phallic symbolism is too readily attributed, but those who do give such meanings to certain elongated or perpendicular shapes should at least be prepared to make comparable interpretations regarding spherical hollow or heart/vaginal shapes when they are present. Some studies have been undertaken in which various explicit representations of the female pudenda are drawn to our attention, notably by Margaret Murray in 1934 and Devereux in 1981; there has also been work on more abstract representations, such as that on the Indian Tantra cult of ecstasy. Charlotte McGowan's detailed (1982) paper on some extraordinarily life-like rock formations and their place in fertility rituals of Indian groups in San Diego country, USA, must be noted.

12 Thus we can envisage a set in one society of $a + c + e$, another where $b + c + e$ are found, while elsewhere $a + d + c$ can be distinguished (or perhaps more properly $a_1 + c_1 + e_1$, $b_2 + c_2 + e_2$, etc); sets of 's-structures' where $a + b + c + d + e$ may be regarded as a 'p-structure' (to borrow terminology from E. W. Ardener 1975, 1978) *which exists nowhere*, but which may underlie or illuminate the various partial realizations we find 'on the ground'. Something along these lines I have tried to explain elsewhere (S. Ardener 1975a: xix).

References

Ardener, E. W. (1975) Belief and the Problem of Women. In S. Ardener (ed.) *Perceiving Women*. London: Dent; New York: Wiley.
—— (1975) The 'Problem' Revisited. In S. Ardener (ed.) *Perceiving Women*. London: Dent; New York: Wiley.
—— (1978) Some Outstanding Problems in the Analysis of Events. (ASA Conference). Published in E. Schwimmer (ed.) *Yearbook of Symbolic Anthropology*. London: Hurst; and M. Foster and S. Brandeis (eds) (1980) *Symbols as Sense*. New York: Academic Press.

140   The Cultural Construction of Sexuality

Ardener, S. G. (1974) Nudity, Vulgarity and Protest. *New Society* 27 (598): 704–05.
Ardener, S. G. (1975a) Sexual Insult and Female Militancy. In S. Ardener (ed.) *Perceiving Women*. London: Dent; New York: Wiley. (First published in *Man* (1973).)
—— (1975b) Introductory Essay. In S. Ardener (ed.) *Perceiving Women*. London: Dent.
—— (ed.) (1981) *Women and Space: Ground Rules and Social Maps*. London: Croom Helm; New York: Martins.
—— (1983) Arson, Nudity and Bombas among the Canadian Doukhobors: A Question of Identity. In Glynis M. Breakwell (ed.) *Threatened Identities*. Chichester and New York: Wiley.
—— (1984) Incorporation and Exclusion: Oxford Academics' Wives. In H. Callan and S. G. Ardener (eds) *The Incorporated Wife*. London: Croom Helm.
Beauvoir, S. de (1953) *The Second Sex*. London: Cape.
Callan, H. and Ardener, S. G. (eds) (1984) *The Incorporated Wife*. London: Croom Helm.
Chicago, J. (1979) *The Dinner Party*. New York: Anchor Doubleday.
—— (1982) *Through the Flower*. New York: Anchor/Doubleday. (First published 1975.)
Devereux, G. (1961) Art and Mythology. In B. Kaplan (ed.) *Studying Personality Cross-Culturally*. Evanston, Ill.: Harper & Row.
—— (1981) *Baubo: Die Mythische Vulva*. Frankfurt am Main: Syndikat.
Douglas, M. (1966) *Purity and Danger*. London: Routledge & Kegan Paul.
Dove, L. (1977) Self Help Centres in Los Angeles. *Spare Rib* 55: 26–7.
Dworkin, A. (1981) *Pornography: Men Possessing Women*. London: The Women's Press.
Edgerton, R. B. and Conant, F. P. (1964) Killipot: The 'Shaming Party' among the Pokot of East Africa. *Southwestern Journal of Anthropology* 20: 408–18.
Eichinger Ferro-Luzzi, G. (1980) The Female Lingam. *Current Anthropology* 21 (1): 45–68.
Evans-Pritchard, E. E. (1969) Some Collective Obscenity in Africa. In *The Position of Women in Primitive Societies, and Other Essays* (originally published 1929). London: Faber & Faber.
Firestone, S. (1972) *The Dialectic of Sex*, London: Paladin.
Goffman, I. (1956) The Nature of Deference and Demeanor. *American Anthropologist* 58: 473–501.
Graf, F. (1974) *Eleusis und die orphische Dichtung: Athens in vorhellenistischer Zeit*. Berlin and New York.
Greer, G. (1970) *The Female Eunuch*. London: McGibbon & Kee.
Griffin, S. (1981) *Pornography and Silence*. London: The Women's Press.
Kupfermann, J. (1979) *The MsTaken Body*. London: Robson.
Lambert, H. E. (1956) *Kikuyu Social and Political Institutions*. London: Oxford University Press.
Llewellyn-Davies, M. (1981) Women, Warriors and Patriarchs. In S. B.

Ortner and H. Whitehead (eds) *Sexual Meanings*. Cambridge: Cambridge University Press.

McGowan, C. (1982) *Ceremonial Fertility Sites in Southern California*. San Diego Museum Paper No. 4. San Diego, Calif.

McNeely, J. (1974) Interview in *New York Magazine*, February.

Mayer, I. (1975) The Patriarchal Image: Routine Dissociation in Gusii Families. *African Studies* 34 (4).

Mitchell, J. (1971) *Woman's Estate*. Harmondsworth: Penguin.

Moulton, R. (1970) A Survey and Reevaluation of the Concept of Penis Envy. *Contemporary Psychoanalysis* 7: 84–104. (Abridgement reprinted in J. Baker Miller (ed.) (1973) *Psychoanalysis and Women*. Harmondsworth: Penguin.)

Mulvey, L. (1974) The Hole Truth. *Spare Rib* 17.

Murray, M. (1936) Female Fertility Figures. *Journal of the Royal Anthropological Institute* 64: 91–100.

Nkwain, F. (1963) Some reflections on the 'anlu' organised by the Kom women in 1958. Unpublished ms.

Parker, R. (1977) Censored: Feminist Art that the Arts Council Is Trying to Hide. *Spare Rib* 54.

Parker, R. and Pollock, G. (1981) *Old Mistresses: Women, Art and Ideology*. London: Routledge & Kegan Paul.

Petersen, K. and Wilson, J. J. (1979) *Women Artists*. London: The Women's Press.

Polhemus, T. (1973) Fashion, Anti-fashion and the Body Image. *New Society* 11 October: 73–6.

Poole, F. J. P. (1981) Transforming 'Natural' Woman: Female Ritual Leaders and Gender Ideology among the Bimin-Kuskusmin. In S. B. Ortner and H. Whitehead (eds) *Sexual Meanings; the Cultural Construction of Gender and Sexuality*. Cambridge: Cambridge University Press.

Richardson, N. J. (1974) *The Homeric Hymn to Demeter*. Oxford: Clarendon Press.

Rickles, N. K. (1950) *Exhibitionism*. London: Lippincott.

Ritzenthaler, R. (1960) Anlu: a Woman's Uprising in the British Cameroons. *African Studies* 19 (3): 151–56.

Rose, B. (1974) Vaginal Iconology. *New York Magazine* 11 February: 59.

Santoro, S. (1974) *Towards New Expression*. Rome: Rivolte Femminile.

Sciama, L. (1981) The Problem of Privacy in Mediterranean Anthropology. S. Ardener (ed.) *Women and Space: Ground Rules and Social Maps*. London: Croom Helm; New York: Martins.

Seiberling, D. (1974) The Female View of Erotica. *New York Magazine*, 11 February: 54–8.

Semmel, J. (1974) Interview in *New York Magazine*, 11 February: 55.

Singer, K. (1940) Cowrie and Baubo in Early Japan. *Man* 40: 50–3.

Spare Rib (1974) Don't Get Too Near the Big Chakra. *Spare Rib* 20: 8–9.

Thompson, C. (1943) Penis Envy in Women. *Psychiatry* 6: 123–25. (Reprinted in J. Baker Miller (ed.) (1973) *Psychoanalysis and Women*. Harmondsworth: Penguin.)

Thompson, C. (1950) Some Effects of the Derogatory Attitude towards Female Sexuality. *Psychiatry* 13: 349–54. (Reprinted in J. Baker Miller (ed.) *Psychoanalysis and Women*. Harmondsworth: Penguin.)

Tickner, L. (1978) The Body Politic. *Art History* 1 (2): 236–51.

Warner, M. (1985) *Monuments and Maidens*. London: Weidenfeld.

Wiegand, T. von and Schrader, H. (1904) *Prienne; Ergenbnisse der Ausgrabungen und Untersuchugen in den Jahren 1895–1898*. Berlin: Reimer.

Wilkes, H. (1974) Interview in *New York Magazine* February.

Zeitlin, F. (1982) Cultic Models of the Female: Rites of Dionysus and Demeter. American Classical Studies in Honor of J.-P. Vernant. *Arethusa* 15 (1 and 2).

Zola, E. (1885) *Germinal*. (Everyman edition 1967).

5 Social and cognitive aspects of female sexuality in Jamaica

Carol P. MacCormack and Alizon Draper

Introduction

In Jamaica, for reasons we will explore, sexuality is usually conceptually linked with the desire to create children. For both men and women, perceptions of self-identity and social power are contingent upon the expression of sexual potency which is confirmed by the birth of children. Jamaican art, music, and theatre express the vitality of a society in which women, as well as men, achieve social status through their own activity.

This assertive dynamism is analysed first sociologically, then symbolically. Sex and birth are an affirmation by the self, and by the society, that adulthood has been achieved. Once adulthood is achieved, social influence might be extended through sexual relationships, birth of children, and the building of social networks. On the symbolic level, body imagery and meanings attributed to menstruation give us insights into deeper levels of identity. Especially in this latter type of inquiry we have concentrated particularly on women's perceptions.

METHODS[1]

Research is based upon intermittent periods of field-work in Jamaica in 1983, 1984, and 1985. Three types of data were collected. One type was studies already carried out in Jamaica, most notably by the Department of Social and Preventive Medicine, and the Institute of Social and Economic Research, in the University of the West Indies, which give valuable insiders' insights. A second type was collected from 268 conversational interviews guided by an interview schedule. The interview schedule included a sheet with the outline of a rather matronly female body, and women were led through a series of questions which encouraged them to draw their reproductive system and explain how it functioned. The third type of information came from observations and conversations we made as we stayed in various parts of the island.

We selected a sample of areas in which to interview, based upon the history and economy of the island. The areas were urban Kingston, and areas in and around three provincial towns. These were Alexandria, in the rough and often roadless terrain of the Cockpit Country, to make the greatest possible contrast with Kingston, Black River in a sugar plantation area, and St Ann's Bay in an area long characterized by small farming. In each area we interviewed women waiting to be seen in ante-natal clinics. However, since they constituted a self-selected sample and we were also interested in women who did not attend government health services, we interviewed women in the open-air fruit and vegetable markets as well. In Kingston, for example, a wide socioeconomic cross-section of Jamaican women came to shop in Papine Market, and our sample included a range from a physician and other university graduates to illiterate market traders.

Identity: sex, birth, and social power

SLAVERY AND POWERLESSNESS

In the seventeenth, eighteenth, and nineteenth centuries, political power in Jamaica was controlled by the European minority of planters and administrators. Few brought their wives to Jamaica, and many of the planters themselves remained in Britain, leaving the running of the plantation to European attorneys. However, those men who were attorneys, overseers, and skilled artisans were seldom hired if they were encumbered with wife and children. For them marriage was largely proscribed, but sexual relations with black and coloured women were officially encouraged. If a desired black woman was in an already existing common-law relationship with her husband the relationship was not recognized by whites, and predations on black women did degenerate into frank rape sometimes (Patterson 1967: 42). Slave women often acquiesced in sexual relations with their masters in their own self-interest for they might be excused from demanding field labour and indeed enjoy some small degree of influence and power in the domestic life of the plantation. Thus women's sexuality was in demand from both black and white men. Liaison with a white man usually meant less physical labour and more influence, while a relationship with a black man entailed extra domestic work. After her children were born, a woman devised whatever strategies she could to keep them with her into adulthood, increasing the size of the farming 'provision ground' the household could claim and the labour to work it. Surpluses were then sold, often by women, further enhancing their relative wealth and power.

In this social milieu of trans-racial sex and procreation, a black woman had potential advantages while a black man had much to lose. He could not assert his authority as a husband or father because his 'wife' was the property of another man. Indeed, she might willingly collaborate sexually with the oppressing white men. Even in field labour there was little sexual division of labour and male working prowess and expertise were not overtly acknowledged. Although only about 14 per cent of households at the end of the slave period were headed by women, mothers tended to dominate domestic groups and were often addressed with an honorific prefix to their name as a mark of respect (Patterson 1967: 167, 169; Massiah 1982: 63).

CONTEMPORARY CLASS AND GENDER RELATIONS

In 1978 an élite 5 per cent of the population earned 30 per cent of the income. The bottom 20 per cent of the population earned 2.2 per cent of the income (Jamaica National Planning Agency 1979). Most of the latter group were unemployed. According to a 1979 survey 26 per cent of the labour force was unemployed, 42 per cent being young adults (Jamaica National Planning Agency 1981). Almost 20 per cent of male workers were unemployed, and 39 per cent of women were counted as unemployed (Gonzales 1982: 5). Jamaica has one of the highest official female labour-force activity rates among developing countries. According to official statistics, in 1978 women constituted 47 per cent of the total Jamaican workforce (Gonzales 1982: 8).

Of women who were employed in 1979, 70 per cent were in low-paying, low-skilled, or marginal jobs. Thus, 78 per cent of employed women earned less than the minimum wage of 30 Jamaican dollars per week – the cost of a pair of children's shoes (Gonzales 1982: 10). Among women we surveyed who were pregnant and attending an ante-natal clinic, 83 per cent said they were unemployed. Most of those who were employed had low-paying jobs such as petty trader, washerwoman, handicraft maker, waitress, cook, or farm worker. They were surprisingly well educated, most having between six and eleven years of schooling, with a mean of nine years. Their economic situation was unpredictable and often precarious. Nevertheless, in his survey of urban men who came to family planning clinics, Brody found that 84 per cent felt that Jamaican women were better off than men (1981: 117).

For all these historical and socio-economic reasons, Jamaican women should be viewed as social actors who achieve their own social status rather than passively deriving status from their husbands, particularly since only 29 per cent of women are married (Jamaica 1979: 30).

AFFIRMATION OF STATUS

Where there are few rewarding economic roles for men and women, sex, birth, and the rearing of children provide an important alternative way to seek adult status and enhanced self-identity. In his interviews with men in Kingston, Brody was often given the statement that ideally a man should support several sexual partners simultaneously. His accumulating children would be public manifestations of his potency – of his masculine social power (1981: 60). Similarly, according to our interviews, women's social strength is even more closely identified with the bearing and rearing of children. In the town of Black River, for example, a woman explained: 'Having responsibility is being a woman. Until a woman has a child she is half child herself. After she gives birth and takes responsibility she is entirely a woman.' Even more revealing were the drawings women made of their reproductive system. The uterus was virtually always drawn very large, usually taking most of abdominal space, and the vagina was drawn as a small rudimentary line of channel (see *Figures 5.1, 5.2*). This is in marked contrast to comparison drawings made by British and American university students who drew

Figure 5.1   Drawing by 33-year-old trader in Papine Market, Kingston

Figure 5.2   Drawing by 16-year-old woman attending ante-natal clinic in Kingston

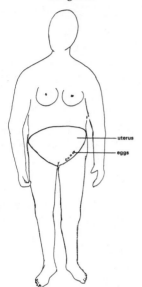

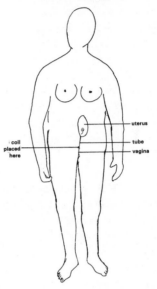

vaginas of large size, often in considerable detail, but had rather rudimentary representations of the uterus and the rest of the reproductive system (*Figures 5.3, 5.4*).

Seeking social power through procreation is not a recent Jamaican social pattern. Nearly thirty years ago Clarke described gatherings of men in a sugar plantation talking of their sexual prowess in terms of the number of children they had fathered (1957: 91). For women, too, sexuality was 'natural', and it was 'unnatural' not to have a child. A childless woman was an object of pity, contempt, or derision (Clarke 1957: 95). Gonzales has suggested that for Jamaica the role of childless adult woman is empty in the sense that it lacks role models and is ill-defined within Caribbean societies (1982: 14).

In an attempt to understand images of adult roles, Hodge looked at Caribbean literature. In novels, white women are usually portrayed as passive and supportive, their lives devoted to serving the interests of their husband (see also Wright 1966). But black women are portrayed as active at home and in the

Figure 5.3   Drawing by 18-year-old anthropology student in the United States

Figure 5.4   Drawing by second-year medical student in Britain

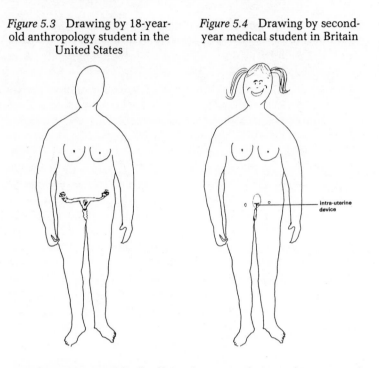

intra-uterine device

extra-domestic world of affairs because their male partner is either absent, a transient figure in their lives, or because even in long-term relationships full maintenance of the woman is not part of the couple's agreed understanding. In this literature a black woman should stand up and fight on all fronts in order to ensure the best possible life for her children. Every effort must be made to educate children and lift them out of the stratum in which they were born, towards a more élite status (Hodge 1982: xi–xii).

But a great deal of frustration, if not social tragedy, is engendered by these conflicting cultural definitions of the black Jamaican female role. Sex and the bearing of children are seen as natural, and a girl of course wants to become a complete woman as soon as possible. But the doctrine of 'naturalness' discourages premeditated contraception and schoolgirl pregnancies abound, in most cases wrecking high hopes for education and social mobility. Women below the age of 20 accounted for 26 per cent of Jamaican births in 1973, 30 per cent in 1974, and 33 per cent in 1975 (Gonzales 1982: 17). A study in 1962 indicated that only

17 per cent of women whose education was interrupted by pregnancy attempted to continue their education later, and 59 per cent were unemployed at the time of survey (Clarke 1965; see also Phillips 1973).

In an attempt to quantify the concept of social passage from the status of girl to the status of woman, we asked women a question with prompted alternatives: 'When does a girl become a woman?' Of the respondents, 48 per cent replied that womanhood came with menarche, 24 per cent said it came with pregnancy, 22 per cent had other answers such as 'at age 21', and only 6 per cent said that having sexual relations marked the beginning of adulthood. Some commented on the contemporary problem of the dropping age of menarche. In a 1978 survey women aged 45 and older had begun to menstruate, on average, at 15.14 years while women aged under 25 had begun, on average, at 14.21 years, suggesting the drop of about a year in a generation (Roberts and Sinclair 1978: 80). When menarchal age was 15 or 16, a girl would already have had years of domestic experience, care of younger siblings, and even possibly years of schooling. Now she is relatively socially inexperienced when her body reaches maturity.

Women in our survey were answering retrospectively. As we shall see, for many women first menstruation and first sexual intercourse came to them unawares, before they had been told the nature or the social meanings of those biological events. Furthermore, women were more comfortable with a conversational reply that explored womanhood as a combination of biological and social achievement.

SELF-AFFIRMATION OF ADULTHOOD

Identity may be analysed from the inside and the outside: from the point of view of self-concept and of social identity. Self-concept connotes a person's consciously or subconsciously held image of himself or herself. Social identity connotes a person's position in society derived from the status they have in the social groups to which they belong. In our Jamaican analysis a young woman's significant social groups are: 1) her own domestic group including her mother; 2) her partner's group including his kin; and 3) peers.

In terms of self-identity, menstruation – a private event – is a powerful sign to a girl from her body telling her that she has become a woman. In this most literal sense we were told, for example, 'A girl becomes a woman when she starts to menstruate. Menstruation shows her that her body is changing.' Some expressed the more sociological aspects of this status transformation by saying, for example, 'When a girl is becoming a woman life is going to change with her, and menstruation is a sign of change.' We had several clues that women were thinking primarily in terms of a mixed process of biology and social experience, as when we were told: 'You become a woman with menstruation, but menstruation and sex with a man give a woman more experience and she becomes more adult.' Giving birth and rearing a child are the final experiences to complete the transformation.

Menstrual blood is viewed as a sign of health and strength in both the physical and the social senses. Regular menstruation is viewed not as weakening a woman but as a sign that she is healthy and ovulating regularly. Her fecundity will alter her relationship with her mother, her kin, her partners, and their kin as she bears children and grows in social strength. But we cannot assume therefore that first menstruation is met with rejoicing by either the woman or her kin. In Brody's study only 7 per cent of women said they reacted positively to their first menstrual period. Rather, they were ashamed, disgusted, or frightened. Few had been told about menstruation by their mothers, a fact we shall explore shortly. In Brody's study 28 per cent had no prior information about menstruation from any source. It was an inexplicable appearance of blood from a place to be ignored, or a 'bad' place (1981: 126). Other studies confirm that girls had been told very little about menstruation and sex before the events overtook them (Clarke 1957: 98; Roberts and Sinclair 1978: 109, 111; Allen 1982: 26; Thompson 1982: 27, 30).

Age of first sexual intercourse tended to be young. In a sample of women attending ante-natal clinic from August Town and Hermitage, Mukerjee found that 29 per cent had their first experience at the age of 15 or younger, and virtually all the rest between the ages of 16 and 19 (1982: 23). In a similar survey Allen found that the youngest was 11 and the mode was 14 years (50 per cent). Allen interviewed the mothers of those young women and found that the time of their first intercourse was later, beginning at the age of 15, with a modal age of 17 (1982: 29). In a comparative study of young women from St Vincent and the Grenadines Murphy found a range of ages for first intercourse from 7 to 18, with a modal age of 15 (1982: 23).

Gooden asked schoolboys and girls in Kingston what they thought about having sex before marriage and 60 per cent of the boys were in favour but only 22 per cent of the girls thought it was a good idea (1966). In Allen's survey, reasons women gave for having their first experience were love (43 per cent), forced (40 per cent), curiosity (13 per cent), and kicks (3 per cent) (1982: 30; see also Clarke 1965). Among the women Brody interviewed, 25 per cent said that they had intercourse for the first time because they liked or loved the man, and 17 per cent said that they were forced. Almost half reported first intercourse as negative, painful, or disgusting (1981: 125–27). Men were even less romantic about first intercourse, and most said it occurred 'by chance' or 'while playing'. Hardly any were in a courtship or dating relationship with their first partner (Brody 1981: 140).

If we view first sexual experience as an event sandwiched in between the important markers of menstruation, which signals fecundity, and childbirth, which ultimately confirms adult status, then it is not surprising to learn that the use of contraception is usually not linked with early sexuality, even though the Jamaican Fertility Survey indicates that between 95 and 99 per cent of Jamaican women knew about contraceptive methods. The lower figure was for women with less than four years of primary education (Jamaica 1979: 71). This high proportion of women knowing about contraception is corroborated by Powell's survey of 2,000 women in 1972 (Powell, Hewitt, and Wooming 1978: 19). Although there was widespread knowledge and availability of contraceptives, only 66 per cent of fecund Jamaican women had ever used contraception, and 45 per cent were using some method at the time of survey (Jamaica 1979: 72, 74). Our study indicates that of those using contraceptives, few use them consistently or effectively. Both young men and women who do use them effectively tend to have alternative means of self-affirmation. They either have strong ambitions for social mobility or have already achieved a level of social status through a good job or other avenue (see Brody 1981: 112ff. for men's use of contraceptives). But many young women were more apprehensive about being infertile and never becoming a complete woman than they were about becoming pregnant at too early an age. Those fears appeared to be heightened in young women who had commenced sexual intercourse before menarche and did not use contraception. Once they began to menstruate they did not know about the period of sub-fertility following menarche, and felt a growing apprehension that they might be sterile. Once they began to ovulate regularly they greeted pregnancy with some relief.

However upon actually becoming mothers many young women appeared to be ambivalent about their status. In Allen's study only 13 per cent of adolescent mothers said they had wanted to have a baby. The mothers of those young mothers reported that 70 per cent of their daughters reacted to pregnancy by crying, 20 per cent were relieved, and 10 per cent showed no particular reaction (1982: 44–5). However, at the same time as realizing the hardships motherhood would cause them, these young women were also realizing that motherhood enhanced their self-image. Of adolescent unmarried women in Clarke's study 59 per cent said people admired them more because they were pregnant and only 5 per cent said people thought less of them (1965).

SOCIAL AFFIRMATION OF ADULTHOOD

If we shift the focus from self-identity to social identity, probably the most important reference group is a young woman's close kindred, and particularly her biological or sociological mother. Mothers expect a great deal of their daughters. They should pass examinations, get good jobs, and augment family resources. But on the other hand mothers view sexuality as both natural and a potential resource, should the young woman make a relationship with a good man who might facilitate the family's social mobility. To reconcile these opposites, mothers seek to guard daughters from sexual liaisons with the wrong type of man (Brodber 1975: 37, 58). Descriptions by Clarke (1957: 97–8) and Brody (1981: 181) also portray daughters, but not sons, as being treated strictly – even repressively – by their mothers. Conflict is therefore inevitable as daughters seek to become socially adult. When sex produces progeny the daughter has become 'big' and her parents have less right to control her. One woman explained to us that a girl becomes a woman with her first baby because she is independent then, no longer under her parents' control. But her biological accomplishment is more than a challenge to parental control. A fecund young woman moves into a position to challenge the very status of her mother. One way for the mother to try to hold on to power is to withhold information about menstruation and sex. But with encouragement from peers, girls work through the frightening events of menarche and sex, acting out what is forbidden. In this way most young women resolve the unacknowledged conflict with their mother who has forbidden the acts which lead to adult status, but who is also the role model for adult status (Brody 1981: 144, 181). However, the inertia and indecision engendered by this conflict are not conducive to seeking contraception.

Turning to the affinal relationship, most women desire a stable relationship with a man. Usually the birth of one or more children to the 'baby father' is a prerequisite for the relationship. But this pattern is often repeated with more than one partner, and a woman's children accumulate. Stable unions tend to occur when the partners are older, with the man in steady employment, after many children are born (Davenport 1961; Powell, Hewitt, and Wooming 1978).

The ideal held by both men and women is that a man should support his children. Among men living in barracks provided by a sugar estate, 71 per cent said the father alone should support the child, 28 per cent said the father and mother, and 1 per cent said the mother alone (Morgan 1974: 30). Of men in seasonal and precarious employment 85 per cent said a man should not become a father until he has a good job (Morgan 1974: 24). But reality falls short of the ideal, and in Allen's survey of pregnant woman aged 11 to 15, 43 per cent were supported by their mother, 37 per cent by their father or stepfather, 10 per cent by a grandparent, 3 per cent by a cousin, and only 7 per cent by their partner (1982: 41).

Many women feel insecure in their union, not knowing when they will be left with all the burdens of child care (Brown 1977: 95). But Roberts and Sinclair present women's more positive views. For some, the independence of a visiting union is seen by them as an advantage. If their partner gives financial assistance the woman can use it all for the upkeep of herself and her children. She is not obliged to use some of it to support her partner as well, as would be the case in residential unions (1978: 249). An even more instrumental view is of men as irresponsible adversaries. They may be useful, but they are not to be counted on as confidants, companions, lovers, or a reliable source of economic support (Brody 1981: 144). In an attempt to measure the quality of relationships we asked women if they discussed sex and pregnancy with their partner; 60 per cent said they did. Of women who said they did not want more children, Powell, Hewitt, and Wooming (1978: 61) found that 40 per cent had never discussed the use of contraception with their partner, and Brody (1981: 43–72) found that many women attending Kingston family planning clinics did so without the knowledge of their partners.

Alas, in spite of all the hopes, a child does not bind a couple into a lasting relationship. In Brody's sample three-quarters of the conjugal pairs had separated and gained new partners by the time the child was aged five (1981: 152). Even though a woman has a child 'for' a man the child is not a very powerful symbol of the relationship. Sexual intercourse and parenthood may be more important for the man and woman as individuals than as members of a partnership.

The irreducible sociological fact is that sex and birth place women at the core of networks with their kindred, affines, and associates. The networks are held together by reciprocities in accommodation, food sharing, child care, and even fostering (Powell, Hewitt, and Wooming 1978: 144–46; Powell 1982; see also Stack 1975).

Identity: body imagery

This section is concerned with cultural analysis, to complement the sociological analysis of the previous section. Everywhere people's understanding of health is informed by folk definitions of the body's form and functions. People give particular attention to the body's margins and its orifices – the breaks in its defences – where the natural and social environment impinge (Douglas 1966). Ideas of cosmological and social equilibrium are also thought by many people to be replicated in the body as a microcosm of the natural universe (see for example Mitchell 1983; Leslie 1976; Manderson 1981). Even in scientific and industrial societies with a long history of universal schooling people still understand their bodies in terms of these folk models, and even highly trained doctors talk to patients in terms of folk definitions (Helman 1978).

MEANINGS OF SEXUALITY

Jamaican men and women look for physical signs to reassure themselves that they are healthy. When they feel strong, energetic, have a good appetite, and are without pain they say they are healthy (Mitchell 1983: 843). The opposite is *maigre*, which means thin, and connotes social as well as physical weakness. Women spoke to us of things that 'draw you down', leaving you thin and tired, rather than full-bodied and fecund. Health has sexual as well as physical connotations.

To have sexual intercourse is to avoid the danger of blocking up natural vitality and therefore it promotes health. Some of the men Brody interviewed felt that sexuality was essential for good mental health (1981: 59). But there is gender asymmetry in that for men sexual intercourse is a good thing, but for women it is sexual intercourse linked to childbearing that is a good thing. A woman who does not release natural vitality by having children may suffer from nervousness or headache, or even become insane (see also Clarke 1957: 95; Kerr 1963: 25; Gonzales 1982: 13).

But the 'natural' release of vitality also alters the natural balance within a person. Losing semen takes something from a man, making him temporarily weak. He must 'put back' his potency by drinking malt, stout, or some other drink following intercourse (Brody 1981: 59). For women menstrual blood signifies sexual and creative strength, but its loss is defined more ambivalently. Menstrual loss puts women in a 'cold' and vulnerable situation, but it also cleanses them, therefore having a health-promoting and strengthening effect.

We were told that having sexual relations is good because it promotes regular menstruation. Roberts and Sinclair report that some Jamaican doctors tell their patients that menstrual cramps are a sign that they need more sex (1978: 116), thus reminding us that at the clinical level there are no pure and separate domains of folk and medical explanatory models.

We asked a sub-sample of 44 urban women if they were more likely to conceive if they enjoyed having sex with their partner, and 27 per cent said yes. A few volunteered opinions such as 'You are not likely to become pregnant if intercourse is rapid', or 'When you enjoy it you are relaxed so pregnancy is more likely'. Two volunteered the view that simultaneous orgasm was more likely to result in pregnancy. However, 73 per cent said pleasure had nothing to do with conception, and many commented 'You can get pregnant even if you are raped'. We asked how many times they thought they should have sex to become pregnant and 85 per cent said one time was enough if it was the right time. Others volunteered the opinion that it was necessary to have sex every day (1 respondent), 3 times a week (2), 8 times a month (1), or 3 times a month (2).

MEANINGS OF MENSTRUATION

In all societies the biological process of menstruation has been brought within the domain of culture: an example of how culture can influence and order the categories through which bodily processes are experienced and explained (MacCormack and Strathern 1980; Snowden and Christian 1983). With reference to Jamaican women's concepts of health and vitality, menstruation is a natural and necessary event which should occur regularly and without hindrance. It rids the body of bad blood and waste matter which has accumulated during the month and must be expelled. When we asked 'Why do women bleed every month?', we were told, 'Waste matter in the body builds up and the irritation causes bleeding to start. Waste matter then flows out with the blood'. Others said, 'Menstruation is necessary to prevent us getting sick', and 'The passing of blood shows you are in good health'. A common expression for menstruation was that it was literally to 'see your health'. The same principle applies to the passage of other bodily substances such as urine and faeces. They should pass freely and unhindered to ensure inner cleanliness and thus health.

   Health may be impaired if the waste matter is not expelled and many women take douches and 'wash outs' (purgatives) when their period is over to ensure that everything has come out. Some think that if this waste does not come out it will accumulate somewhere, or perhaps force an exit some other way. As one woman said: 'It is not natural to go without a period. If the blood doesn't come out the stomach gets higher [swells], with more

sweating, especially under arms, with staining and strong smell.'
A woman expressed uncertainty about how men manage to get
rid of this waste matter since they obviously do not menstruate.
Another was not sure how men avoided high blood pressure since
they were not able to let the excess blood drain away, as women
do.

Despite agreement about the necessity of menstruation there
was no consensus about where the waste blood originated. Many
women thought the source of menstrual blood was eggs which
had burst because they were unfertilized, otherwise the matter
would have gone to form the baby. Others said it came from the
ovaries, the womb, the 'tubes', various organs, a vein, and a few
said it came from the placenta. Most women attributed the
reason for this waste blood to the function of reproductive physiology. Only a minority did not have an opinion about where it
came from or called it general body waste.

Because menstruation, sexual intercourse, and childbirth are
so tightly linked together in Jamaican cognitive structure, we
were not surprised to find abundant evidence that menstruation
is a metaphor for birth (see MacCormack (1982a) for other birth
metaphors). Post-partum bleeding is also a cleansing of waste and
'bad blood' accumulated through pregnancy. As with menstruation, women often gave themselves a laxative to augment the
'clear out'. It is especially important after birth, one woman
explained, because 'the baby does not cleanse itself'. Women
sometimes sat over steaming water to help cleansing, and also to
warm the womb. During both menstruation and post partum the
body is in a 'cold' state. Women did not, for example, drink iced
water which 'makes the blood clot'.

The study by Powell, Hewitt, and Wooming found that only 10
per cent of Jamaican women who stopped using contraception
did so because they wanted to have a child (1978: 36). Our study
indicated that women worry very much about contraceptives
that alter their natural pattern of menstruation. One woman who
had used Depo Provera explained that 'you don't see your
periods so you don't have internal cleansing. Because there is not
regular menstrual cleansing it causes infections in the tube,
which then causes pain all over the body.' (The 'tube' she drew
and referred to in this conversation connected the vagina and the
uterus; see *Figure 5.4*). Another woman explained how she took

the pill and ceased to have periods. She said the pill blocked up her tube and menstrual blood did not come out. She was afraid not only of illness but permanent sterility.

If women did not remember to take the pill regularly their periods would probably be irregular, and many women interpreted this irregularity as a sign that the pill had made them sick. Similarly, Depo Provera which altered the pattern of periods could cause or exacerbate weakness, loss of energy, 'making you drawn down'. This was a sign that the pill or the injection 'does not agree' with the woman, another aspect of the concept of 'naturalness'. It might also cause indigestion and vomiting, suggesting that the drug is regarded as analogous to undigested food.

Many women described the pill as working mechanically, accumulating in the cervix to block it so that sperm could not enter. But fearing a permanent blockage, some would stop taking the pill for a while to let the load reduce itself, or take a laxative to 'have a good clear out'. The woman who described the pill as stopping her periods and 'blocking her tube' drew the tube as the vagina (Figure 5.5). She indicated that this was the tube tied off in tubal ligations, and the prospect worried her not only because it meant she could no longer have a place for sexual intercourse, but also because she was theoretically too young for menopause. How would the blood come out, should she menstruate? Like virtually all women who knew about the intra-uterine device, this woman drew it in the vagina. Even women who had not had an IUD fitted visualized it as being in the vagina to block sperm from rising to the uterus, but also as a foreign body which would poke their partner and perhaps cause pain and infection to them. The condom was widely viewed as a similarly invasive object that could cause sickness, sterility, or even death by slipping off and blocking up the 'tubes'.

Thus we return to the semantics of the 'natural'. Contraceptives tend to be in the Jamaican conceptual category of the nonnatural. They come from a clinic or pharmacy and may elude control by the user (see Brody 1981: 59). The unnatural is: 1) that which the woman perceives as not being under her own control; 2) that which changes normal body rhythms and feelings of health; and 3) invasive foreign objects that may become lost in the body. 'Natural' connotes the innate integrity of the woman's body, and indeed of herself (see Jordanova 1980).

Figure 5.5   Drawing by 17-year-old woman attending ante-natal clinic in Newmarket, Jamaica

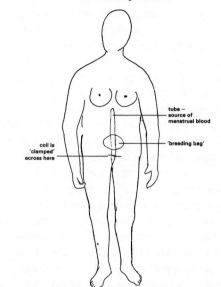

In a comparative framework, these Jamaican women's concepts of regular healthy menstruation are similar to Scott's findings in a study of women from the Bahamas, Cuba, Haiti, and Puerto Rico, and black Americans, all living in Miami (1975: 107). Similarly, Snowden and Christian (1983: 64) concluded from a study in Egypt, India, Indonesia, Jamaica, Mexico, Pakistan, the Philippines, Korea, the United Kingdom, and Yugoslavia that in all those countries women did not want to see a change in what they consider their natural pattern of bleeding.

IMAGES OF THE HIDDEN INTERIOR

In Jamaican thought the interior space from the neck to the bottom of the rib cage is the 'stomach', and the large soft cavity below that is the 'belly'. The belly is further differentiated, as the lower part is perceived as the 'belly bottom'. Belly bottom pain can originate from menstrual cramps, from inflammatory disease which is sexually transmitted or caused by contraceptives – particularly the IUD – or from constipation.

The uterus is the main feature of the belly and women drew it with far more interest and detail than they drew the digestive system (which we requested in a complementary investigation of children's diarrhoea). Also in the belly are 'tubes' which women enjoyed talking about at great length. We encouraged them to draw the tubes as they discussed their form and functions. Some tubes are known empirically, as with one's own vagina, and imagined or 'read' syntagmatically as a more extensive system in the interior. However, because of strict rearing girls are not encouraged to explore tubes on the exterior of the body and many believed that the vagina and urethra are one. Tubes in the hidden interior are also 'known' through metaphorical or paradigmatic association, imagined as various systems of fallopian tubes, alimentary canal and bowels, urethra and urinary system, and blood circulation. The body is composed of these various systems of tubes which should not be obstructed lest illness result. Most women said that infertility was caused by 'blocked tubes' but could not explain – or draw – in much detail what the blocked tubes were. They worried when 'belly bottom pain' signalled that a sexually transmitted disease or a contraceptive gone awry might make them permanently sterile. But 'belly bottom pain' can also be a way to talk about constipation. They often asked doctors for X-rays or medical procedures to blow their fallopian tubes open. But most often they drank bush teas or took laxatives to clear them out.

After many careful conversations, and attempts to clarify conceptual domains by asking women a series of questions with binary choices, we concluded that there is no cultural consensus on whether or not the digestive and reproductive system are a single joined system. In Papine Market two elderly women debated this subject, one sure they were separated and the other sure they were unitary. The latter won the argument by blinding her opponent with science. She had been to hospital and when no one was looking she peeked at her X-ray, 'seeing' them as a single system. Clearly they are in a metaphorical relationship to each other, and taking a laxative in one will help cleansing in another. Also, even if the tubal systems women know by their apertures – vagina, urethra, anus, mouth, and ears – are not conceived as literally joined, the apertures have the shared quality of being breaks in the natural perimeter of the body and therefore points of vulnerability.

DANGER AT THE MARGINS AND ORIFICES OF THE BODY

Because menstruation, but to a much greater extent the post partum, are periods of dangerous 'coldness', women guard parts of the body that come most closely into contact with environmental cold. They do not walk barefoot, wash their hair, or bathe, especially not in cold water. It is dangerous to sit in water and expose the 'open' womb. Most of the women wore a menstrual pad for one to three months after giving birth – some as long as two years – to 'keep the vagina warm so you don't get a baby cold', or 'to keep the cold from going up'. One woman described the way in which she kept her ears plugged against 'cold'. A 'baby cold' can cause illness and pains that might remain for years, or even cripple and kill a woman. Childbirth, especially of a woman's first baby, is a time when she is between the status of girl and complete woman, therefore in a 'dangerous' period of liminality (MacCormack 1982a: 5–6; Turner 1967: 93ff.). Virtually all women told us they did not go outside following childbirth, and commonly waited more than three months before risking the danger of going out at night. They observed postpartum abstinence from sexual intercourse for varying lengths of time, from a month to more than a year, with 48 per cent waiting more than three months. Women spoke of this period as one of danger and vulnerability, a period 'to let the body mend' or 'to give the womb a chance to heal up'. Most women relied on signals from their body: 'A woman can feel when the body comes back'. Then she would resume sexual relations and go about freely in the environment, resuming the routine of mundane life, ending the period of dangerous liminality, and enjoying the unequivocal status of full womanhood.

The social and symbolic, joined by a navel string

In talking of reproductive physiology, we asked women if the hospital gave them the baby's 'navel string' (umbilical cord) to take home and 'plant' under a young fruit tree. They all said it had been thrown away by the hospital. We asked if they would like to have it and virtually all the women said wistfully that they would have liked to take it home and plant it. We sometimes asked the women if they knew where their own navel string was planted. Faces that were old and careworn, or defiant with youthful assertion, softened as the memory turned inward. All could name the tree and the place: 'It is under a coconut tree in St Thomas.' Even though maternity services, run by European textbook methods, do not give the mother her baby's umbilical cord, many mothers still plant the tiny stump of the cord which remains attached to the infant when it comes home. We suggest that the navel string is important because it 'roots' people in a sense of social continuity, a sense of place, and a sense of self.

Slavery strikes at the root of social systems because it makes enslaved people into abject individuals, detached from the political power of kin, and from the ancestral sanctioning power of lineage. Continuity through membership in corporate groups is denied to slaves. Even the minimal unit of kinship, the nuclear family, could not function very well in Jamaica where owners had pre-emptive rights to the labour and sexual services of a spouse. But the irreducible minimum of kinship, the mother–child dyad, just manages a kind of continuity – the continuity of the navel string – in Jamaica. Probably for centuries mothers have buried their child's umbilical cord (and placenta), then planted a fruiting tree which became the property of the child: property which could be passed on to descendants (Cassidy 1961: 254).

People forcibly resettled always mourn for their lost sense of place. The idea of slipping under the ancestral waters, 'going home to Guinea', still has some ritual expression in Jamaica, now more commonly merged with the Rastafarian idea of 'going home to Ethiopia'. But the everyday reality for Jamaican slaves was that there would never again be ancestral shrines, and it was the economic (fruit-bearing) trees of the provision ground that rooted a person in a sense of place.

The type of fruit tree most often named in Jamaica was the coconut. On the coast of West Africa the placenta and umbilical cord are commonly planted with a young fruit tree. In Sande initiation rituals in Sierra Leone, men who will become husbands of girls being ritually conferred with the status of woman come to dance in honour of the girls-becoming-women (wives). They also dance in honour of Sande, the sodality that makes girls into women. As the men dance they carry a bouquet of white coconut flowers (see *Figure 5.6*). Thus they reinforce the emerging young

Figure 5.6 Men dancing with coconut blossoms during Sande initiation ritual, Moyamba District, Sierra Leone, 1970

(Photograph by C. MacCormack)

woman's sense of adult self, a sense of vitality that will be demonstrated in fecundity (MacCormack 1979: 27ff.). In Jamaica, as the young tree planted over the navel string grows and fruits, so will the girl. And in this process there will be conflict with her mother, but it will be resolved for the sake of the navel string that joins them.

Note

1 This paper is an aspect of a larger study generously funded by the Overseas Development Administration at the request of the Jamaican Ministry of Health.

References

Allen, S. M. (1982) *Adolescent Pregnancy among 11–15 Year Old Girls in the Parish of Manchester*. Dissertation for Diploma in Community Health. Kingston: University of the West Indies.

Brodber, E. (1975) *A Study of Yards in the City of Kingston. Working Paper No. 9*. Kingston: University of the West Indies, Institute of Social and Economic Research.

—— (1982) *Perceptions of Caribbean Women: Towards a Documentation of Stereotypes*. Kingston: University of the West Indies, Institute of Social and Economic Research.

Brody, E. (1981) *Sex, Contraception and Motherhood in Jamaica*. Cambridge: Harvard University Press.

Brown, E. (1977) *An Examination of Clients of Family Planning Clinics with Special Emphasis on Inactive Acceptors in the Parish of St. Ann*. Dissertation for Diploma in Community Health. Kingston: University of the West Indies.

Cassidy, F. G. (1961) *Jamaica Talk: Three Hundred Years of the English Language in Jamaica*. London: Macmillan.

Clarke, E. (1957) *My Mother Who Fathered Me*. London: George Allen & Unwin.

Clarke, S. C. (1965) *Some Adolescent Unmarried Mothers*. Dissertation for Diploma in Education. Kingston: University of the West Indies.

Davenport, W. (1961) The Family System of Jamaica. *Social and Economic Studies* 10: 420–54.

Douglas, M. (1966) *Purity and Danger*. Harmondsworth: Penguin.

Gonzales, V. Durant (1982) The Realm of Female Familial Responsibility. In J. Massiah (ed.) *Women and the Family*. Kingston: University of the West Indies, Institute of Social and Economic Research.

Gooden, S. S. (1966) *Adolescent Attitudes to Sex and Related Matters*. Dissertation for Diploma in Education. Kingston: University of the West Indies.

Helman, C. (1978) Feed a Cold and Starve a Fever – Folk Models in an English Suburban Community and their Relation to Medical Treatment. *Culture, Medicine and Psychiatry* 2: 107–37.

Hodge, M. (1982) Introduction. In E. Brodber (ed.) *Perceptions of Caribbean Women*. Kingston: University of the West Indies, Institute of Social and Economic Research.

Jamaica (1979) *Jamaica Fertility Survey 1975/76*. Kingston: Department of Statistics.

Jamaica National Planning Agency (1979) *Five Year Development Plan 1978–82*. Kingston: Government Printer.

—— (1981) *Economic and Social Survey – Jamaica (January–June 1981)*. Kingston: Government Printer.

Jordanova, L. (1980) Natural Facts: a Historical Perspective on Science and Sexuality. In C. MacCormack and M. Strathern (eds) *Nature, Culture and Gender*. Cambridge: Cambridge University Press.

Kerr. M. (1963) *Personality and Conflict in Jamaica*. London: Collins.

Leslie, C. (ed.) (1976) *Asian Medical Systems: A Comparative Study*. Berkeley, CA: University of California Press.

MacCormack, C. P. (1979) Sande: The Public Face of a Secret Society. In B. Jules-Rosette (ed.) *The New Religions of Africa*. Norwood, NJ: Ablex.

—— (1982a) Biological, Cultural and Social Adaptation in Human Fertility and Birth: A Synthesis. In C. P. MacCormack (ed.) *Ethnography of Fertility and Birth*. London: Academic Press.

—— (1982b) Health, Fertility and Birth in Moyamba District, Sierra Leone. In C. P. MacCormack (ed.) *Ethnography of Fertility and Birth*. London: Academic Press.

MacCormack, C. P. and Strathern, M. (eds) (1980) *Nature, Culture and Gender*. Cambridge: Cambridge University Press.

Manderson, L. (1981) Traditional Food Classification in Humoral Medical Theory in Peninsular Malaysia, *Ecology of Food and Nutrition* 11: 81–93.

Massiah, J. (1982) Women Who Head Households. In J. Massiah (ed.) *Women and the Family*. Kingston: University of the West Indies, Institute of Social and Economic Research.

Mitchell, M. F. (1983) Popular Medical Concepts in Jamaica and their Impact on Drug Use. *Western Journal of Medicine* 139: 841–47.

Morgan, K. B. (1974) *Attitudes Toward Family Life Education among 15 to 21 Year Olds in Golden Grove, St. Thomas*. Dissertation for Diploma in Community Health. Kingston: University of the West Indies.

Mukerjee, D. (1982) *A Study of the Characteristics and Community Leadership Role of Family Planning Acceptors Attending the Community Health Centre, Department of Social and Preventive Medicine, U.W.I.* Dissertation for Diploma in Public Health. Kingston: University of West Indies.

Murphy, V. J. (1982) *Factors Associated with Adolescent Pregnancy in St. Vincent and the Grenadines*. Dissertation for Diploma in Community Health. Kingston: University of the West Indies.

Patterson, O. (1967) *The Sociology of Slavery: An Analysis of the Origins, Development and Structure of Negro Slave Society in Jamaica*. London: MacGibbon & Kee.

Phillips, A. S. (1973) *Adolescence in Jamaica*. Kingston: Jamaica Publishing House.

Powell, D. (1982) Network Analysis: A Suggested Model for the Study of Women and the Family in the Caribbean. In J. Massiah (ed.) *Women and the Family*. Kingston: University of the West Indies, Institute of Social and Economic Research.

Powell, D., Hewitt, L., and Wooming, P. (1978) *Contraceptive Use in Jamaica: Social, Economic and Cultural Context*. Working Paper No. 19. Kingston: University of the West Indies, Institute of Social and Economic Research.

Roberts, G. W. and Sinclair, S. A. (1978) *Women in Jamaica: Patterns of Reproduction and Family*. Millwood, NY: K.T.O. Press.

Scott, C. S. (1975) The Relationship between Beliefs about the Menstrual Cycle and Choice of Fertility Regulating Methods within Five Ethnic Groups. *International Journal of Gynaecology and Obstetrics* 13: 105–9.

Snowden, R. and Christian, B. (eds) (1983) *Patterns and Perceptions of Menstruation*. London: Croom Helm.

Stack, C. B. (1975) *All Our Kin: Strategies for Survival in a Black Community*. New York: Harper.

Thompson, T. (1982) *Views of 13–15 Year Olds in High and Secondary School in Hanover Concerning their Parents/Guardians as Sex Educators*. Dissertation for Diploma in Community Health. Kingston: University of the West Indies.

Turner, V. (1967) *The Forest of Symbols*. Ithaca: Cornell University Press.

Wright, P. (ed.) (1966) *Lady Nugent's Journal of her Residence in Jamaica from 1801 to 1805*. Kingston: Institute of Jamaica.

6 Honour and shame: the control of women's sexuality and group identity in Naples

Victoria Goddard

Much has been said on the preoccupation with honour in the Mediterranean area, and in fact this preoccupation, coupled with control over women's sexuality, is frequently used to characterize 'traditional' Mediterranean society. My interest in the literature on 'honour and shame' was prompted by a problem relating to the employment patterns of women. Since the late 1960s there has been a growing body of literature in Italy on women's participation in the labour market and the distribution of women in different branches of production. These analyses have mainly stressed the functional aspects of women's subordination and of the sexual division of labour for capital accumulation; that is, women are conceptualized as a reserve army of labour-power and as a source of cheap labour-power. Women's subordination and the sexual division of labour in the family are taken as given historical products and only their effects from the point of view of production and accumulation are studied.

In this literature there is little that could illuminate a question that emerged from my field-work experience among working-class women in Naples: why were women discouraged from taking wage employment, especially in factories, and furthermore, why was this discouragement phrased in terms of dangers to a woman's chastity in mind and/or body? Why was their employment in small sweatshops or in their own homes, with far lower rates of pay and bad working conditions, considered to be preferable to their employment in a factory that offered higher wages and often benefits, holidays, and fewer health hazards?

At least at first glance, it would appear that the above problem might find an adequate explanation in the literature on

Mediterranean honour and its counterpart, shame. In this paper I will briefly review this literature with the aim of moving away from the economic focus of labour market analyses and of providing a more general framework for the discussion of these questions. Aspects of gender relations and sexuality in Naples (such as courtship and virginity and chastity) are discussed to establish the links between gender relations and the predominant forms through which women are incorporated into the economic sphere. The paper then goes on to suggest that the generalized reluctance for women to enter typical wage–labour relations is to do with the perception of women as the principal agents in important reciprocal relations and as central symbols of group identity.

Honour and shame as a concept

According to Pitt-Rivers, 'Honour is the value of a person in *his* own eyes, but also in the eyes of *his* society' (my emphasis) (1965: 21). It is a quality of groups, not only of individuals – rather a single person symbolizes the group whose collective honour is upheld by its different individual members.

The honourable behaviour of men and women differs. A man must defend his own and his family's honour (which implies control over other members of the family), whereas women must preserve their purity. Men's relationship to honour is therefore seen to involve an active role, whereas the role of women in the theatre of honour is a passive one. This passivitў becomes a burden for men, for 'once the responsibility [of women] in this matter has been delegated, the woman remains with her own responsibility alleviated' (Pitt-Rivers 1965: 45).

Peristiany (1965) suggests that honour and shame are crucial elements in small-scale societies where face-to-face relations are dominant. In such social contexts the total social personality of the individual is relevant for social interaction. Davis (1973) argues that there is a connection between domestic behaviour and reputation and honour in the wider society. This is important in situations where political and economic activities are based on trust: a man's reputation is therefore a central resource, and how a man behaves within his family, and his ability to protect and defend it, will provide a guide to his reliability and effectiveness in the public spheres of economic and political activity.

Most of the work on the 'honour–shame' complex has concentrated on the functions of this code within small communities, from the viewpoint of men competing in the public arena for scarce resources. The honour of women is seen in terms of how it reflects on the menfolk and what effects it has on the capacity of individual men to compete. Women's honour is an element, a resource, which is controlled and manipulated by men. It remains unclear to what extent honour may be an exclusively male code or what perception women may have of this code and of their own honour. John Davis (1973) does actually present women's honour as being somewhat less passive and derivative: a woman's reputation is determined not only by her chastity but also by her capacity to look after her husband and defend his interests.

These approaches are little more than a description of the contents of the code and of its functions and operation, yet this is taken as a valid explanation for its existence. Frequently 'honour' and 'shame' are taken as given, pre-existing elements which are then manipulated in various competitive struggles between men. However, there have been attempts to explain the origins of the codes. Competition is an important element in these approaches as well, for example the code being seen as a response to potential and actual attacks on the group's resources. The control of women's sexuality (and the code of honour as one derivative of this) has been seen as a means of controlling marriage and thus controlling access to property. A high value placed on virginity is likely to be associated with societies with devolving inheritance, that is societies where women inherit property as well as men (Goody and Tambiah 1973). Although the protection of property is likely to be an important factor in determining the need to control women and their marriages, this does not provide a general explanation for the concern with honour. Pitt-Rivers, for example, points out that in Andalusia the local aristocracy, the propertied class *par excellence*, was relatively free from the honour constraints on sexuality that prevailed for the lower classes – for them honour was a birthright, and thus its permanent existence was guaranteed.

In addition to the code being seen in terms of defence of patrimony and economic interest, it has also been seen as a means of creating and defending boundaries. In *The Republic of Cousins* (1983), Tillion argues that an emphasis on endogamy, on 'keeping all the girls of the family for all the boys of the family', which is established through control over women, is a protective measure taken by a lineage society to ensure its survival. However, these boundaries do seem to be reducible to a concern with patrimony for she argues that where Koranic laws of inheritance for women are respected we can expect to find the presence of the veil and the seclusion of women. Female inheritance pulverizes tribal societies. They must therefore defend themselves by keeping their boundaries closed, by maintaining women, and their patrimony, within the group.

This bears a certain resemblance to the argument put forward for Sicily by Jane and Peter Schneider (1976). In their view, the Catholic Church as well as Islam aimed at breaking the solidarity of corporate kinship groups and also their control over their property. The attempt was carried out through the imposition of rules prohibiting marriage between several degrees of kin, and by championing women's rights of inheritance (which in the Catholic Church were associated with the cult of 'motherhood'). Similarly, political empires trying to extend their boundaries and increase their control also attempted to break the capacity of individuals and groups to accumulate wealth and power. The state imposed partible inheritance of property and favoured inheritance to women via the dowry. Kinship groups retaliated in self-defence and challenged the power of Church and state, attempting to maintain their identity through the belief in and implementation of the concept of honour and the control over women and their sexuality. The question of the seclusion of women is also explained by the Schneiders in terms of Sicily's allocated role as provider of labour-power through slave raids in the area (women were preferred captives), as well as through the rights of barons in the seventeenth and eighteenth centuries to take women from peasant households as servants and for their sexual services. The abuse of peasant women by their overlords, exemplified in the *jus primae noctis* was also characteristic of areas of mainland Italy and Spain.[1]

This is somewhat contradicted by Maria Rosa Cutrufelli (1975). She approaches the question of honour from the perspective of providing an understanding of women's economic role in contemporary Sicily. She argues that the importance of honour in the island is not a survival from the past (in fact she points out that in the past Sicilian women, or at least those from the upper echelons of Sicilian society, seemed to have enjoyed much greater freedom than the women of mainland Italy or other parts of Europe) but rather that 'honour' is an integral aspect of social organization that 'fulfils very precise functions of ideological control for capitalism'. What she is arguing is that the ideology of honour and of virginity is involved in controlling the production of labour-power by controlling women's bodies. Through men's operation of the honour code, a regulated flow of labour-power is guaranteed. The code of honour and of the control and segregation of women emerges, according to Cutrufelli, at a precise historical conjuncture: the conquest of Sicily and of southern Italy by the Piedmontese kingdom and the subsequent process of the underdevelopment of the south which became a supplier of cheap labour for the industrial centres of the north of the country, and of Germany and Switzerland. The Sicily of the eighteenth and early nineteenth centuries was not, according to Cutrufelli, dominated by the concept of honour; it was the process of the internal colonization of the area which, by allocating to the south the role of supplier of labour-power, resulted in an imbalanced sex ratio due to the emigration of the men. Within this process of role allocation between north and south, the women of the south emerged as primarily producers of labour power. The control of their sexuality and thus of reproduction became a question of social significance. Cutrufelli and the Schneiders agree in locating the explanation for the control of women's sexuality in a regional division of labour whereby Sicily (and southern Italy as a whole) takes on the function of providing cheap labour-power. But whereas the Schneiders see this as being a phenomenon originating in antiquity, Cutrufelli places the origin of the ideology of honour and the control of women in recent history, that is, in the incorporation of Sicily and the south into a northern-dominated state.

Doubtless, the concept of honour has undergone changes over time and its significance is likely to have varied historically. Yet other authors (mainly for Spain, see Caro Baroja 1974) have traced elements of this code back to the Middle Ages, stressing, however, that the content and significance of honour in Spain, for example, have varied and have undergone crises. Cutrufelli's approach does make the important point that honour is not simply a characteristic of historical backwardness, an ancient value responding to ancient social relations or problems which have not yet been superseded by modernity and rationality (as implied by Peristiany's reference to the 'continuity and persistence of Mediterranean modes of thought' (1965: 9). But there is a problem in accepting the emergence of an honour code as a simple requirement of capital accumulation and the regional division of labour. Without wishing to deny the importance of such cultural values for capital accumulation, it would be an over-simplification to reduce these values and patterns of behaviour to their mere economic effects. A more comprehensive approach to the problem is therefore necessary.

An underlying thread in most of the approaches mentioned is the understanding of the code of honour and the related importance of female virginity in terms of the protection of and competition for resources. The code is represented as an agency of self-defence against encroachment from the outside or as a result of conquest. The operation of the code is thought to be relevant in small-scale social groups characterized by face-to-face relations but it is also characteristic of social units which are part of, or are themselves, a wider unit, within which inequality prevails. It is important to stress that the small-scale village societies studied by Mediterranean anthropologists are, and for centuries have been, incorporated into a nation state. Nor can these communities be said to be socially homogeneous. These two points have too often been ignored or inadequately analysed in the Mediterranean literature on 'honour'. And yet exploitation, usurpation, and class difference would seem to be of key importance here. Perhaps absolute inequality would not require such a code, at least not in relation to the sexual honour of the women of the group – this concern, this preoccupation appears to be relevant where there is at least theoretically the possibility of social mobility and, therefore, competition. Such structural conditions may be found in many cultural and geographical areas and it is interesting to note that manifestations of an ideology of group honour largely based on women's chastity are widespread. The concepts of 'honour' and 'shame' have, however, been turned into a system, a cultural 'complex' intended to characterize a particular type of society, that is to say the non-defined, unexplained, and untheorized 'Mediterranean area'.

With this in mind it is useful to consider Verena Martinez-Alier's work on elopement in nineteenth-century Cuba (1972). She links the preoccupation with female chastity, seen as a symbol of family honour, with the social hierarchy: the code serves to maintain that hierarchy and is thus a structural rather than a cultural element of the social system. For Cuba, she relates the control of virginity in women to class and colour endogamy, and a concern with 'lineage purity' since control over female sexuality represented a control over group membership. Purity and boundaries were a matter for concern not only in relation to individual families but to the total social system. She quotes an offended white parent as declaring:

> 'This is a country where, because of its exceptional circum-stances (i.e. slavery) it is necessary that the dividing line between the white and the African races be very marked, for any tolerance that might be praiseworthy in some cases will bring dishonour to the white families, upheaval and disorder to the country, if not extermination to its inhabitants; (he, a white parent) will never approve of a marriage of their daughter to a mulatto, for this would be covering one stain (the dishonour of the daughter) with another much greater and indelible one.'
>
> (Martinez-Alier 1972: 110)

As Martinez-Alier points out, Cuba hardly fits Peristiany's con-ception of honour as typical of small, face-to-face communities. Rather, Cuba was a large-scale hierarchical society in which family origin was a predominant criterion for status. In order at least to maintain a position in the hierarchy, women's sexuality was controlled so as to ensure isogamic marriage.

From the Cuban study it appears that control over women's sexuality through the honour code is not simply or directly a mechanism for maintaining control over material resources, but corresponds to a more complex interplay of elements and criteria of stratification. The main point seems to be that women are the agents for delimitation and they are ('presumably partly for bio-logical reasons' (Martinez-Alier 1972: 118)) the agents through which family attributes are transmitted across the generations.

Turning back to the original question of the association of wage labour with a lack of honour for women, the literature on honour and shame hardly provides an explanatory framework. This is, at least in part, a result of its concentration on honour as a male code of behaviour relevant in competitive struggles between individual men and families. However, some interesting elements do emerge. Firstly, it can be seen that women are bearers, or perhaps *the* bearers, of group identity, and they thus have a very important part to play in the process of demarcation of group boundaries whether in the exogamous or the endogamous situation.[2]

In the case of group endogamy, control over women's sexuality is likely to be important and perhaps more so when the boundary of the group allows for some degree of invasion. Nur Yalman (1967), with reference to a Sri Lankan village, argues that castes are a solution to the problem of ensuring and perpetuating rank divisions in the society: endogamy provides the means of establishing clear-cut status groups in the context of bilateral descent, as a result of which control over women becomes important. This importance of women for group definition and for the definition of the status of individual families and men results in the subordination of women into a passive role (as Martinez-Alier (1972: 107) points out, a woman's role was 'necessarily largely passive for she was the pawn that was played in the competition for honour'), whereas men are projected into an active role, the role of defender, controller, and aggressor.

This passivity of women is not, however, without its contradictions, which operate at two levels. Although the literature ignores an analysis of honour from a female perspective, women themselves also have a system, if not of honour, then of self-appraisal and self-esteem which is related to their judgement of others. Furthermore, from the point of view of men, women may be seen as passive but they are also seen as a source of danger. This danger may be phrased in terms of the 'dangers' arising from an association of women within a factory-work context or in terms of their sexuality. These points will be explored in relation to the case of Neapolitan working-class women.

Courtship, marriage, and work in Naples

As already mentioned, one of the central questions that emerged during field-work in Naples[3] was the discouragement and sometimes active opposition that many working-class women faced in relation to wage employment outside the home, even where economic circumstances made their monetary contributions necessary.

In many cases women are forced by their domestic responsibilities to leave the factory or find alternative forms of generating an income. But a large number of women opt against factory employment even before the full weight of domestic responsibility falls on them. When pressed, most women explain this decision in terms of the wishes of their fiancés or husbands, and sometimes fathers. The men are very vague on the subject and explain that factories are dangerous places, although the precise nature of the dangers is never confronted. The implication seems to be that the danger manifested itself in the form of a threat to the chastity of the women concerned, although this was not necessarily understood in an obvious, physical sense. It was women themselves who confirmed this apparent link between wage-labour and loss of reputation when they[4] asserted that women who worked in factories were 'whores' (puttane) actually or at least potentially. In the suburban areas where agriculture is still important, women field-hands also knew that they were considered to be sexually corrupt, but as they put it: 'If we were whores we wouldn't have to break our backs for a pittance as we do.'

It is at the point of becoming seriously involved with a man that a woman is faced with strong pressures either to give up factory work, or to seek other forms of employment. This would indicate that it is useful to consider courtship procedures in working-class Naples, in that there appears to be a strong connection between engagement and marriage on the one hand, and restrictions on women's activities on the other. In contrast to what is indicated in most of the literature on southern Italy, which tends to concern itself with rural areas, young women in Naples may enjoy considerable freedom of movement. This movement, however, is usually confined to a certain area: near the home, the distance from home to school or work, to a kinswoman's house or to a local shop or market. For social outings this area may be broadened considerably but the girls will always be accompanied by a group of other women or by a brother or kinsman. Since girls are expected to do a great deal of work in the home from an early age, and often assist in production after school hours, there is not much time left for socializing. Sunday afternoons are usually the time for walks and visits. On such occasions boys and girls meet and establish friendships which may lead to a casual form of courtship known as *fidanzamento fuori casa* or engagement outside the home. These relationships are not considered to be important and a girl may go through a series of them without damaging her reputation. Such relationships tend to be sexually innocent and in fact many girls consider themselves to be 'engaged' in this way with very little prompting beyond an exchange of glances and a slight flirtation.

Serious courtship, or *fidanzamento in casa*, engagement within the home, involves considerably more formalities and signifies a radical change in the girl's life. Her fiancé will visit her parents and if all goes well the potential in-laws will also exchange visits. With this accomplished, the young man is accepted by the girl's household and he is thereafter likely to become a more or less permanent presence and a fairly regular commensal. The girl is in turn expected to visit her mother-in-law and the closeness of the relationship which she is ideally expected to develop with her is indicated by her use of the term *mammà* (mum), to address her.

From now on she will no longer be able to go out with a group of friends or in fact to go out at all except with her fiancé or to visit her mother-in-law or kin. At this point her relationships with women friends will deteriorate. She is likely to give up work or become an apprentice at home or in the workshop of a trusted friend or kinsman/woman. The girl's father officially takes on the role of controller of his daughter's behaviour and reputation – he 'takes care of her' for the man to whom he has promised her. The sexual content of relationships seems to follow a development parallel to these circumstances: there is very little if any physical contact in the engagement 'outside the home', whereas once a couple become engaged 'within the home' they may well become involved in sexual experimentation which can result in full sexual intercourse.

This does not mean that virginity is not important. On the contrary, it is a crucial element in the relationships of men and women. In a city like Naples people are subjected to many influences (including that of the feminist movement). Therefore there can be little pretence to homogeneity of values or behaviour, such as that suggested by the 'honour and shame' literature.[5] But even male comrades of the left-wing parties, activists at the level of party or trade union, want or even expect, to marry a virgin. Yet nobody is likely to be surprised if they discover that a bride dressed in white (and the vast majority of women dream of a white wedding) is not a virgin or is even pregnant. This is not considered a great dishonour although the news will hardly be broadcast. Nonetheless, a woman is expected to marry her first lover. Although this is not its explicit function, the *fidanzamento in casa* can provide a framework which allows women to engage in full sexual activity should they wish, without forsaking the ideal of the white wedding. Sex in this case is an anticipation of the right which the couple expect to obtain through the marriage ceremony. A woman who goes through several such engagements may well lose her reputation and seriously weaken her chances of finding a husband. The explanation for this is that people will murmur that 'there must be something wrong with her' if she has been unable to carry through any of her engagements. But it is possible that another, hidden, cause of loss of reputation is that she is considered to have been 'sullied'.

Marriages are not arranged by the couple's parents and in fact young women are likely to meet their future companions in a variety of ways, through friends, at parties, or even in the street. A large number of older women I interviewed had also met their husbands in the street, at fairs, or on the beach. Thus at this stage parents have relatively little control over their daughters except through the girls' siblings, cousins, or neighbours. But through their necessary approval and acceptance of the young man into their home with the *fidanzamento in casa*, parents do exert some influence. Once the young man becomes 'of the house', much stricter control is exercised over the young woman to prevent contact with other men. On the other hand, in the case of pregnancy, parental pressure and control will also be exercised on the young man to resolve the problem. Marriage *di riparamento* (of repair) is very common.

Ultimately, and excluding of course those cases where violent means are used, it is the women themselves who control their sexuality and decide whether or not to dispose of their virginity; the forms of courtship described are ways of attempting to control women but also to provide some protection from error.

Women in fact can make the wrong move. A woman can decide to engage in full sexual intercourse knowing that it may result in pregnancy and that this should have the often desired effect of shortening what is usually a long period of courtship (five to six years). Alternatively, she may resist attempts by her fiancé to persuade her to give him a 'proof of true love' knowing that she may lose him because of this refusal. Or a woman can engage in some form of sexual activity as a sort of 'promissory note' to try to establish a relationship with a man of her liking and will then judge how far she may or must go according to his reactions and behaviour. So every woman must face these decisions carefully, for a miscalculation can have dramatic consequences.

A woman who has engaged in sexual activity outside the protective framework of the *fidanzamento* system is in a very vulnerable position and she may be rejected by her family and of course her lover as well. On the other hand, even though a *fidanzamento* may be broken off, if it is known to the parents that the fiancé has been their daughter's 'first man', they are very likely to exercise pressure to have the relationship re-established. Thus the withholding or the disclosure of such information allows the young woman some degree of manipulation. Going to bed with a man can be an insurance in terms of marriage – unless he outwits her. Should this happen it is generally said that the only options left open are the streets or a relatively inexpensive and simple operation to re-establish virginity, since generally in a large city like Naples the only proof of transgression is pregnancy or lack of hymen; otherwise suspicions can only remain such.

The problem of the 'allocation' of women's sexuality is not of course resolved with marriage: marital infidelity is also considered to be a grave problem if the woman is the culprit. The infidelity of women is considered to be a grave insult to men and a serious threat to family stability. Many men felt that they would react violently in such a situation, although all those questioned were 99 per cent certain that their wives had never been unfaithful to them and they were most emphatic about this. On the other hand, it is expected of a 'normal', 'healthy' man that he will take every opportunity for sex that presents itself and his self-image will be thereby enhanced. A woman who was to engage in the same kind of behaviour would be realizing her potential corruption and forsaking her chances of being seen as a woman in the positive sense. Although this double standard is generally accepted by men and women in a fairly fatalistic way, many women (and some men) question the fairness of this. When a young woman asked why men should be allowed to engage in extra-marital relations when women are not, her husband (jokingly) replied: *'Perche l'uomo é cacciature e la femmina é zuoccola'* ('because man is a hunter and woman is a whore' – the term *zuoccola* also means 'rat'). This comment suggests that the position of women is a contradictory one. Man is the predator but woman is not simply the victim that may be preyed upon. Her vulnerability in fact gives her a negative value. It renders her corruptible and therefore to a certain extent corrupt. In another sense 'woman' is seen as being predatory herself: the rat is to be hunted down but it is also a renowned aggressor; the prostitute is to be approached, her services bought, but at the same time she must take some initiative to earn her living through selling her sexual services.

By focusing on the normative aspects of the 'honour' code from the point of view of the interests of the men of the society, the 'classical' literature on this subject does not provide insights on the operation and implications of the code for women. Nor does it provide many clues to the contradictions that might emerge in the operation of the code. A comparison of the Neapolitan case with the anthropological literature presents certain difficulties. It is to be expected that Naples, being a large and important port, and having been the political and courtly centre of a kingdom[6] would show marked differences from the small hinterland villages usually studied by anthropologists. Yet certain continuities are evident with regard to the concern with controlling women's sexuality and the importance of female chastity for male social reputation.

The Neapolitan material indicates that although the 'rules' restrict women's capacity for autonomy and very much determine the direction of their self-realization, these rules can also be played by women to try to gain recognition, self-respect, and fulfilment within socially established terms. There is no reason to assume that these contradictions and possibilities of manipulation are absent in the rural situation.[7] The *fuìta* (elopement) in Sicily, like the *scappata* in Naples, constitutes an attempt to force parental consent in the case of partnerships considered to be unsuitable. One night, or even several hours, which the couple spend on their own is usually sufficient to persuade parents to save their daughter's reputation by agreeing to the marriage. Although in Sicily and possibly elsewhere there are cases of bride kidnappings, in most cases it seems feasible to assume that women are consenting and active participants in this manipulation of 'honour'.

As we have seen, the literature emphasizes the importance of the code of 'honour' for the operation of local-level politics in small communities governed by face-to-face relations. Although in working-class Naples much social, political, and economic activity does take place within a sphere of neighbourhood and kinship networks, it is inadmissible to reduce Neapolitan social structure to a small-scale community level. In this respect Verena Martinez-Alier's comments are helpful. Although contemporary Naples cannot be likened to nineteenth-century Cuba, it is evident that both are class societies based on relations of inequality and exploitation, although of course there are many ways in which this class structure may be interpreted and understood.[8] I would therefore suggest that the idea of male competition for scarce resources based on personal honour will not take us very far in our search for an 'explanation'. Instead it may prove more helpful to explore the question from a broader perspective that attempts to envisage the social structure with its historically given complexities and contradictions.

To return to our original question: the conditions of life in both rural and urban areas oblige many women to work. Yet there seems to be a continuity between rural and urban situations in respect of an association between women's work, and especially wage-labour outside the family enterprise, and a loss of reputation which is generally expressed in sexual terms. This problem, which is not addressed by the honour and shame literature, remains open. By moving away from a framework of individual competition and by locating the problem within a broader perspective and seeing women as agents who are integral to the social structure, we may provide a clearer understanding of this question and of the contradictions inherent in women's image and role. Taking a cue from the work of the Schneiders, Tillion, and Martinez-Alier, it is useful to approach this problem by conceptualizing women as carriers of group identity and as social boundary markers.

Women as carriers of identity

Mary Douglas (1966) argues that the human body can be used as a model for the 'collaboration and distinctiveness of social units'. Many instances of sexual pollution of one sex – usually but not always males – being endangered by contact with the other sex, are analogies of social relations, of social symmetry or hierarchy. Thus the limits of the body can represent the limits of the social unit. Rituals expressing anxieties about the body's orifices reflect a preoccupation with defending the political and cultural unity of a group.

Both the male and female physiologies can serve as models to express this concern for group integrity, yet in the Hindu caste system the onus of responsibility for caste purity falls on women. Douglas points out that there is frequently a double standard in sexual offences which relate to the maintenance of social boundaries: in patrilineal societies the wife holds a place analogous to that of the sister in the Hindu caste system for she represents the 'door of entry' to the group and the wife's adultery introduces impure blood into the lineage.

It is this social responsibility of women in maintaining group boundaries which I wish to explore as an alternative to the existing honour and shame literature. If women are seen as the boundary markers and the carriers of group identity, it follows that their 'integrity' should be safeguarded. The concept of the group can operate at different levels of inclusion: the family, the kinship group, the village, region, class, or caste. The integrity of the women of a group cannot be understood solely in terms of ensuring appropriate marriage arrangements, which would, however, explain many aspects of behaviour resulting in the isolation and 'protection' of women. The role of women as carriers of identity has further repercussions of a less obvious nature, which, I would argue, are related to women's role and power as reproducers. Women may also be seen as the guardians of the 'secrets' of the group. By the very process of their control by men and their relegation to and identification with the domestic sphere, women are in a unique position to provoke a crisis within the group.

That women's vulnerability is thought to be greater and more important than that of men is suggested by Nur Yalman (1967) in relation to Sri Lanka, where 'a woman's lineage (or fecundity) must be protected'. Women are prohibited from having sexual relations with the wrong man, that is with a man of lower caste. Women are internally polluted through sleeping with men of lower caste and furthermore, unlike a man in similar circumstances, they cannot be ritually cleansed from such a pollution. This seems to be very much related to women's capacity to bear children. When a woman has sexual intercourse with a man of lower caste she may bear a child. This child will be 'a perpetual witness to her deep pollution and the mother will be forever associated with another caste' (Yalman 1967). The polluted woman and her polluted child bring pollution on to the group (the family and the caste); consequently the ritual purity of each group must be protected through its women.

Mary Douglas (1966) makes a similar point. Sexuality is of crucial importance especially to the higher castes, since an individual's place in the hierarchy of purity (of the Hindu caste system) is biologically transmitted. Children assume their mother's caste membership even though she may marry into a higher caste. Women are therefore the 'gates of entry' to the caste. Because of this, women's purity is carefully guarded and a woman who is found to have had sexual intercourse with a man of lower caste is severely punished.

Women may also be seen to represent, and perhaps most forcefully through their sexuality, the privacy and intimacy of the group. In an agrotown near Naples, a woman fruit picker caused a scandal which had repercussions as far away as Milan. She managed to do this by explaining in her local dialect how while working in a field she had had a miscarriage.[9] Her story was told simply and was accompanied by a brief gesture intended to illustrate the size of the lost foetus. All this was filmed and recorded, and later shown on a national television network. As a result she was criticized and ostracized by her town, and the most active agents of the attack were her husband and the other women. It was said that the husband locked her up for shame but ended up by locking himself away as well because he could no longer confront the condemnation of the town. Her daughter telephoned from Milan to tell her that she thought her home town had gone mad and that 'certain things are best kept to ourselves'. A group of women from the town admitted that abortions in the field were a frequent occurrence. Most of them had had experiences of miscarriages as a result of overwork, or of deliberately provoked abortions. It was not considered incorrect to tell the world how hard they worked and how difficult their life was. Their objections revolved around other things the woman had unwittingly revealed. They felt that the incident had exposed something very private about themselves as a group and that this exposure would present them to the world as being backward and ignorant. Had she explained the same experience in standard Italian, it would not have had the same impact, for it would have seemed more impersonal and 'scientific'. But it was as though the gesture and the use of their own language had opened a window not only into their most sacred and intimate experiences as women, but also as women belonging to a particular group and a particular town.[10]

This incident reveals the association of group identity with those intimate experiences of women as they are predominantly defined, that is experiences related to reproduction. These experiences should not be disclosed to the outside world for in doing so one renders oneself, and one's group, vulnerable. In this case the identity of the group is seen in defensive terms. It raises the question as to who the 'other' is against whom the group is defining itself. The 'other' would, like the group, operate at different levels of inclusion: family versus family, village versus village, region versus region, and the most inclusive valid levels of identity in this case for most people most of the time would be Naples and the south.

Most Neapolitans are aware of their reputation and image abroad, and agree with many elements of this image. Most see the people who surround them as ignorant, sometimes dirty, crude, and lazy, and to some extent everybody attempts to distinguish themselves from the 'masses', partly through the often pained use of Italian rather than dialect and partly by recognizing that their neighbours are 'a bit ignorant' or 'more backward than us'. But Neapolitans also have a great sense of pride, not so much in their fellow Neapolitans as in the city itself, its climate, the natural beauty that surrounds it, and, very importantly, its food. Food has a very positive symbolic value. There are certain dishes and culinary traditions which, for Neapolitan sentiment, are on a par with those traditional songs which extol the beauty of Naples and its inhabitants' capacity for love. Food is not only considered to be an important source of pleasure but it also represents the essence of 'Neapolitanness', of the family and home life, and especially of that most positive of figures, the mother.

Neapolitans are by no means hostile to visitors, and tourism is an important economic resource. Yet high crime levels in the city mean that many people retain unpleasant memories of their visit. Neapolitans are of course aware of the incidence of crime in their city but on the other hand explain that they are a warm people and that in spite of their 'backwardness', 'no one here will just walk past someone who is lying in the street'. Mistrust towards outsiders is focused on various representatives of the state, regardless of origin. There is always the fear that a 'foreigner' walking about may be an agent of the state: a tax collector or inspector. The police are also viewed with hostility and it is said that they will not follow a suspect into some areas of the old city, for fear that they may not emerge in one piece.

Relations with the nation state are, then, generally perceived as being negative, an attitude which reflects the historical reality of the incorporation of the south into the Italian state and the subsequent policies of the latter. Most feel the state is uncaring and exploitative and that they, as poor people and as southerners, are excluded from the benefits it may offer. There is also the feeling that the state is far removed from them both socially and physically, and they find it hard to deal with the various ramifications of state power; for this reason, many people expressed a preference for having a single person, a 'strong man', in power. It has been suggested that the Neapolitan popular classes' defiance of legitimate (state) authority pushes them into a readiness for violence and often a romantic mystification of violent figures such as the 'guappo', the mafia-like gangster figure so frequently encountered in Neapolitan popular theatre and newspaper chronicles, whose use of violence responds both to the defence of economic or political interests and also to a rather strict application of the code of honour. Here we see an identity which has both a class dimension and a regional, local, one. The ambiguities of Neapolitan identity must be understood within the context of the history of Naples and of the south as a whole, which is a history of conquest and foreign rule. We must also understand it in terms of how southerners have been, and largely are, perceived by northern Italians. During the nineteenth and into the twentieth centuries there were contradictory visions of the south: on the one hand it was seen as a kind of 'primitive paradise', and on the other as backward and miserable. In the late nineteenth century there were theories which attempted to explain the poverty of the south as a consequence of the inferiority of the southern 'race'.[11] Thus Neapolitan identity, and southern identity, is an identity *contra* the north and *contra* the state.

To what extent does this group identity versus the state involve women? It is interesting that Hegel (1980) develops this point and does so by drawing on Greek tragedy. Antigone sought to bury her dishonoured brother in the religiously correct manner, against the wishes of the ruler. Because of this she was condemned, for she had gone against the law of the state. Antigone's sense of duty towards her family and her family's honour prevailed over her sense of duty towards state authority. Inspired by this account, Hegel suggests that women are the carriers of family law and of the private sphere, but in this drama it is the public sphere, which for Hegel is the sphere of men, which wins. The state wins and subordinates the kinship group. For Hegel, family piety as expounded in Sophocles' *Antigone* is one of the most sublime presentations of virtue; it is principally presented as being the law of woman, a law which is opposed to public law, the 'law of the land'. So women are primarily identified with the family and become the representatives of family law which is inevitably in contradiction with the law of the state. This suggests that, like Antigone, women are perceived as being the defenders, actively or passively, of a certain set of rules, values, and loyalties against outside forces. Given the defeat of the private sphere, women hold on to its vestiges whereas men have been separated from it.

It is possible that women, as carriers of group identity and of an ideology based in kinship, are themselves seen to be in contradiction with the 'outsider', be this the state or all those who represent state ideology or ideologies contrary to that of kinship. Furthermore this can be said to hold in many societies beyond the frontiers of the 'Mediterranean area' where the maintenance or establishment of hierarchy is achieved through marriage, and therefore cannot be taken as the product of Mediterranean culture and its prime characteristics. But taking our cue from the Antigone story, we can suggest that women are not only the agents of boundary marking in hierarchical social structures, but are also the bearers of a deeper identity and its associated values, the carriers of the problematic of 'us versus them'.

It is in these terms and not in terms of a static and arbitrary concept of 'Mediterranean values' that we can explore the question of the objection to women's wage employment. On Africa, Esther Boserup comments:

> 'It is obvious that in countries of female trading, the absence of women from white collar jobs cannot be due to resistance against their working outside the home, as it is in the Arab countries. But in Africa we find another objection to female employment for a wage: African men loathe the idea of their wives or daughters working under the authority of a *foreign man.*'   (1970; my italics)

Similarly in Naples the objection to the employment of wife, fiancée, or daughter in impersonal wage-labour conditions, whether in factory or field, is an objection to them working for a boss who is outside their own social sphere and is therefore unlikely to share their system of values, in other words, a 'foreigner'. Given economic needs, there is a preference for their employment in petty commodity production, where they are recruited through personal networks, and where the dominant relations are not the impersonal relations of wage-labour but the very personal relations of kinship and friendship. This form of employment can be highly exploitative but it is felt to be appropriate for women especially once they are completely incorporated into the social relations of kinship and marriage through the *fidanzamento in casa.*

Women are the ones who are principally responsible for maintaining networks of neighbourhood and kinship and this they do through reciprocal exchanges of favours and goods. Women 'of the group' are valued most as mothers, carers, and guardians. Motherhood in turn is seen as being the clearest embodiment of the 'pure gift', the best example and inspiration to all being the Virgin Mary, mother of Christ and therefore mother of all. I would suggest that women are the bearers of values based on generalized reciprocity, generosity, self-sacrifice, and devotion, and are the focus and carriers of the group's identity as seen in these terms. It is therefore thought to be important to separate them from the impersonal, profit-orientated relations of capitalist production. In this way the group defends through women its sanctity against the apparently balanced relations of wage employment which its members accurately perceive as being imbalanced and exploitative, even though such work may, of course, be more materially beneficial than work in a small workshop. Could this be an aspect of the 'law of the family' still fighting the public sphere – the state and capitalism? Is this another re-enactment of Antigone's tragedy – of woman being attached to the ethics of the family but not being strong enough to combat the state and therefore becoming its victim?

To a large extent women themselves would share the above view: motherhood is crucial for a woman to achieve full status. There is a sense in which being a woman is different from being a person and hence regardless of her achievements a woman is not fulfilled, is not a proper woman, until she bears a child. A woman's identity is therefore very closely bound up with her caring, nurturing role as mother. There is an association between a woman's performance as a caring figure and her being good, and therefore also chaste. Cleanliness of the home is associated with cleanliness of the body and chaste sexual behaviour. A woman who has a dirty home is not only frowned on for not fulfilling her caring role properly; she is also likely to be considered sexually loose. There is a conflation of the various facets of woman's identity so that failure in one aspect is likely to bring about the collapse of her total identity. The only case I encountered of a mature woman leaving her husband (one of the very few who left her husband at all) was a woman living on a council estate whose husband had the eccentric indulgence of dirtying his clothes and going around looking like a tramp. Although it was acknowledged on the estate that the man was a bit funny, the woman exhausted herself by washing, mending, and generally struggling to make him look clean and tidy. Her failure to manage this meant that she suffered daily humiliation every time he left the house and finally she and her daughter walked out on him. Although she came back to cook and clean for him on a regular basis, she was now free from full responsibility for his appearance. She enjoyed the total support and sympathy of her women neighbours.

It was mentioned earlier that food, and more specifically Neapolitan food, was a central concern. Neapolitans are extremely

conventional in their food tastes and are on the whole very suspicious of 'exotic' dishes (for example dishes from the centre and
north of the country). Sunday dinner follows a set procedure and
deviations from this procedure are not tolerated. Men hanker for
their favourite dishes, 'as mother used to make them'. Young
women learn the secrets of the art from an early age, unless they
enter a factory or workshop, in which case, given the division of
labour within the household, the mother or a sister will concentrate on the domestic chores. The major manifestation of hospitality is the offering of cooked food, an offering that will be made
with a great deal of pride by the woman of a household. Within
the rather strict terms of what constitutes an appropriate dish and
how this must be prepared, a woman will perfect the art of its
preparation with the feeling that her identity and reputation, and
those of her household, are bound up with this. Food is therefore
a channel for the expression of a woman's worth and in turn
becomes a symbol of the nurturing role of motherhood, of the
family, and the private sphere with the values and sentiments
that they involve. I would suggest that Neapolitan identity is felt
to be emotionally and practically linked to certain culinary tastes
and that this symbolically important food is in turn identified
with the most positive female figure and the personification of
the positive values of generosity and sharing which are associated
with the family.

A woman who is involved in a wage-labour relationship is, on
the other hand, seen to be involved in an activity and an ethic
which are diametrically opposed to what she must personify:
giving without expectation of immediate return. This therefore
challenges her capacity to perform adequately as a woman, that
is as a mother. As mentioned, women who enter productive
activity at an early age are likely to miss out on the learning
process of such activities as cooking which are important for
female positive identity.[12] Their involvement in such impersonal
relationships and their consequent weakness *vis-à-vis* nurturing
chores are contradictory to their 'being a good woman'. In
addition it must be said that the burden of housework in Naples is
great and demanding, not only in terms of time and energy, but
also because it is perceived as a task that requires total dedi-
cation; regular wage employment outside the home is then, *ipso
facto*, considered to be a betrayal of this principle. In short, if a

woman is not totally dedicated she is not a proper mother, therefore she is not good and must be a whore.

If women are passive to the extent that they serve as agents for social boundary definition and as 'pawns' in the hands of others, this is reflected in men's view of women as either dangerously vulnerable or eminently available and seducible, which dichotomy broadly corresponds with the dichotomy 'us/them'. But there is a further contradiction within the category of 'woman' which stems from the awareness that in spite of all attempts to control and contain women, they are the ones who ultimately decide how and when to 'allocate' their sexuality. Most men claimed that they were sure their wives were not unfaithful, yet men have many anxieties about women, their sexual needs, and their own capacity to satisfy them. Brandes (1980) points out how popular sayings and songs in an Andalusian village reflect men's view of women's sexual voracity; this can be conveniently used by men but it also represents a grave danger to them. He finds a strong male preoccupation with the idea that too much sex wastes them away and that their wives may in fact even be plotting their death by an overdose of sex. This paranoia is also reflected in the very popular Italian film *Matrimonio alla Siciliana* (*Marriage Sicilian-style*) in which a young woman, widowed by a Mafia bullet, takes revenge on behalf of her dead husband by marrying the Mafia boss and proceeding to kill him by seducing him continuously and forcing him to have more sexual intercourse than his body can cope with, until he dies. She dutifully returns to her husband's grave to announce that he is avenged.

It is tempting to suggest that these anxieties not only reflect men's awareness that they cannot totally control women, but also represent a recognition of women's oppression at the hands of men, an oppression which they are likely to want to overthrow. A quote from the Spanish Father Haro would suggest this: 'It is through their sex that women acquire power over men and women have naturally the ambition to attain command and liberty, and they wish to invert the order of nature, attempting (even though it may involve the greatest cruelties) to dominate men!' (Pitt-Rivers 1965: 68). Just as slave owners based their right of ownership of people in the 'laws of nature' yet lived in fear of slave revolt and reprisal, it may be suggested that men base their privileges on 'natural' differences yet remain aware of the strains of this imposition.

The allocation to women of the role of bearers of the intimate identity of a group imposes restrictions on their sexuality and more extensively on their activities, and this results in the dichotomy of good versus bad woman, pure versus corrupt, positive versus negative. The social role and importance of women idealize them on the one hand in the form of the mother and oppress them into conforming with this ideal. Yet because of their importance to the identity of the group, women may also bring disgrace to it, either through their vulnerability or by wilfully going against the rules, often in an attempt to secure their own well-being. It is because of an awareness of the danger of the capacity of women to break the rules that it is thought that they must be not only protected but controlled.

No doubt both men and women serve this function and, as Mary Douglas argues, the human body, male or female, its orifices and excretions can be used to map out concern for group boundaries. Two questions emerge: why are *sexuality* and sexual behaviour so important in social delimitation and why is it especially *women's* sexuality and sexual behaviour that are subject to control?

In many instances sexuality can be argued to be important because group membership is inherited. Where inheritance is determined more or less independently of actual sexual behaviour there is relatively little concern about sexual transgressions (Douglas 1966). But where inheritance is thought of as closely linked or determined by sexual activity, then there is much greater concern for correct sexual behaviour, particularly so in the case of women for they are the bearers of future generations of group members. There is generally much greater tolerance of loose sexual behaviour in men, although many cultures consider restraint to be a positive value in men, or at any rate there is a felt contradiction between the image of male predatory sexuality and anxieties about wasting away (Brandes 1980).

However, the problem probably does not end with biological transmission of group membership. In the Hindu caste system a woman is internally polluted as a result of improper sexual intercourse. Douglas points out that food is an important focus for pollution anxieties, both because of the social division of labour which produces food and because ingestion results in internal pollution which is far more difficult to rectify. Food crosses the boundaries of the body and penetrates it just as the penis crosses the boundaries of the female body and invades it. I would suggest that although these anxieties are not codified in the way they are in the Hindu case, nevertheless they may find expression in non-caste societies in many conscious and unconscious reactions to women's sexuality. Furthermore, women who are the repro-ducers of the group are at the same time, in a patrilineal society, outsiders. So women are themselves potentially dangerous for they *are* the margins of the group, being within and yet not of the group, being outsiders to the group and yet crucial for its sur-vival.

Conclusion

What I am suggesting is that the control of women and their sexu-ality, resulting in their exclusion from various activities and spheres, could be explained in terms of women's role as boundary markers and carriers of group identity. The concepts of 'honour' and 'pollution' are cultural attempts to express this. This role of women becomes particularly important in historical situations of actual or threatened destruction of socio-cultural groups in the face of religion, the state, and/or capitalism. The necessity for controlling women's sexuality in these circumstances meets a crucial obstacle: the fact that ultimately it is women themselves who can control their sexuality. Women have the capacity to provoke crises in the system precisely through their sexuality. The contradiction between the power over women established to control them and the power of women to subvert the relations through which they are controlled is expressed, in the case of southern Italy and Andalusia at least, in the ambivalent per-ceptions of women as passive victims and predatory nympho-maniacs.

Notes

1 This refers to the right of the noble lord to enjoy a peasant bride on her wedding night, i.e. to be the one to end her state of virginity.
2 According to Levi-Strauss (1969) the repercussions of these two systems (endogamy and exogamy) are likely to be different for women, although subordination would be implied in either case.

3 Field-work was carried out in working-class and lumpen-proletariat areas of the city, in the old city, and the new 'dormitory' suburbs. Work was focused on women outworkers, but artisans, factory workers, housewives, and agricultural labourers were also interviewed.

4 Housewives, i.e. women not engaged in productive wage work, were the most likely to express strong views on the subject.

5 But Pitt-Rivers does point out that the contents of 'honour' vary according to status and class:

> 'A system of values is never a homogeneous code of abstract principles obeyed by all the participants in a given culture . . . but a collection of concepts which are related to one another and applied differentially by the different status-groups defined by age, sex, class, occupation, etc. in the different social (not merely linguistic) contexts in which they find their meanings.'   (Pitt-Rivers 1965: 39)

6 Naples was the capital of the Bourbon kingdom of Naples until 1861 when it was incorporated by Piedmont into the state of Italy.

7 Anthropologists have tended to emphasize consensus in relation to cultural values and their internal logic and consistency rather than exploring the potential contradictions they may hold, although many have been aware of the complexities involved, especially in a stratified society (see Pitt-Rivers in Note 5).

8 There are many people who think of the social hierarchy as God-given and therefore eternal and universal. Others approve of a class system and in fact advocate a stronger government and a more disciplinarian and punitive regime. This is especially the case where the poor are seen to be so as a result of their laziness or incapacity.

9 Work-induced miscarriages, fairly frequent in Italy, are called 'white abortions'.

10 In fact the women of a nearby agrotown did accuse them of being 'more backward than us' but this was because of the reaction of the town and in particular of the husband who was referred to as *chillo struonzo di Qualiano* or 'that shit from Qualiano'.

11 For a reflection of some of these ideas in the early anthropology of the area, see Banfield (1958).

12 Middle-class and professional women seem to be less likely to miss out on the acquisition of these skills than working-class women who become involved in wage-labour from an early age.

References

Banfield, E. C. (1958) *The Moral Basis of a Backward Society*. New York: Free Press.

Boserup, E. (1970) *Women's Role in Economic Development*. New York: St Martin's Press.

Brandes, P. (1980) *Metaphors of Masculinity: Sex and Status in Andalusian Folklore*. University of Pennsylvania Press.

Caro Baroja, P. (1974) Honour and Shame. In J. G. Peristiany (ed.) *Honour and Shame, The Values of Mediterranean Society*. Chicago/London: University of Chicago Press.

Cutrufelli, M. R. (1975) *Disoccupata con Onore*. Milan: Gabriele Mazzotta ed.

Davis, J. (1973) *Land and Family in Pisticci*. London: Athlone Press.

Douglas, M. (1966) *Purity and Danger*. London: Routledge & Kegan Paul.

Goody, J. and Tambiah, S. J. (1973) *Bridewealth and Dowry*. Cambridge: Cambridge University Press.

Hastrup, K. (1978) The Semantics of Biology: Virginity. In S. Ardener (ed.) *Defining Females*. London: Croom Helm.

Hegel, G. W. F. (1980) *The Philosophy of Right*. Trans. T. M. Knox, repr. from O.U.P. by Encyclopedia Britannica.

Levi-Strauss, C. (1969) *The Elementary Structures of Kinship*. London: Eyre & Spottiswoode.

Martinez-Alier, V. (1972) Elopement and Seduction in 19th century Cuba. *Past & Present* 55.

Peristiany, J. G. (ed.) (1974) *Honour and Shame, The Values of Mediterranean Society*. Chicago/London: University of Chicago Press.

Pitt-Rivers, J. (1965) Honour and Social Status. In J. G. Peristiany (ed.) *Honour and Shame: The Values of Mediterranean Society*. Chicago/London: University of Chicago Press.

Schneider, J. (1971) Of Vigilance and Virgins: Honor, Shame and Access to Resources in Mediterranean Societies. *Ethnology* 10 (1).

Schneider, J. and P. (1976) *Culture and Political Economy in Western Sicily*. New York: Academic Press.

Silverman, S. (1975) *Three Bells of Civilization: the Life of an Italian Hill Town*. New York: Columbia University Press.

Taussig, M. (1980) *The Devil and Commodity Fetishism in South America*. Chapel Hill: University of North Carolina Press.

Tillion, F. (1983) *The Republic of Cousins*. London: Zed Press.

Yalman, N. (1967) *Under the Bo Tree: Studies in Caste, Kinship and Marriage in the Interior of Ceylon*. Berkeley, Los Angeles: University of California Press.

7 Beyond the Samoan controversy in anthropology: a history of sexuality in the eastern interior of Fiji[1]

Allen Abramson

'Hence I do not envisage a "history of mentalities" that would take account of bodies only through the manner in which they have been perceived and given meaning and value; but a "history of bodies" and the manner in which what is most material and vital in them has been invested.'   (Foucault 1976)

Introduction

In *Coming of Age in Samoa* (1928), Margaret Mead declared the possibility of a human childhood liberated from the western traumas of puberty. Under suitable cultural conditions, she wrote, the emotionally painful experience of adolescence could be entirely mitigated. In Samoa she claimed to have found these conditions, whilst the islands themselves have long been cele-brated by western thought for what Mead wrote of their culture's handling of sexuality.

In *Margaret Mead and Samoa: The Making and Unmaking of an Anthropological Myth* (1983a), D. Freeman dismisses the crux of Mead's ethnography and rejects its theoretical underpinnings. Freeman insists, instead, that young girls in rural Samoa are subject to a powerful cult of pre-marital virginity which they transgress only at their peril. Indeed, Freeman thinks that human culture everywhere develops only through the very repression of animal sex (and violence). According to this theory, the society which results cannot then undo itself by cultivating the erotic play of autonomous currents of sexuality.

This essay is also compelled to doubt Margaret Mead's liber-tarian optimism. However, I put forward a viewpoint which is more sceptical of the representations of ruling élites than that of Freeman, by concentrating my analysis upon forbidden and muted forms of sexuality that, while subterranean, are none the less powerful in fomenting systemic change. It is in this realm of subcultural structure and movement that a *historical* analysis of sexuality abandons Freeman's ideology of ethology to meet up with Mead on her own informants' ground. It is there that Margaret Mead's findings can be genuinely appraised.

My own analysis[2] explores a 'cult' of virginity in neighbouring Fiji identical in its ritual and organizational context to that with which Freeman seeks to undermine the *The Coming of Age in Samoa*. The argument he puts forward affirms the repressiveness of the 'cult' and, moreover, the claims for its hegemony made by the gerontocratic establishment. However, a historically orientated theory reveals how the 'cult' is doomed to failure against the grain of a powerful sexual counterculture which arises internally as a logical inversion. The premise of this counterculture conceives the body as 'naturally free' and predisposed to the pleasures of carnal adventure.

It is, therefore, impossible to make of these data – as both Mead and Freeman wanted – an ethnography which testifies to either the innate repressiveness of culture in relation to human sexual nature, or to the former's liberatory potential. South-west Oceanic 'cultures' are as promiscuous as they are repressive and this contradiction has to be unravelled.

Some theoretical remarks

This being the case, it becomes apparent that 'the Samoan controversy' in anthropology must recede to leave behind it a puzzle of quite different proportions. A question sums up the puzzle. How can the same people, once promiscuous youths, deny as elders the fact of promiscuity, and impose upon their own children the metaphysics and the 'cult' of bridal virginity? How is *this* contradiction to be unravelled when its unearthing reveals not merely the sham of a hypocritical class – a frequent phenomenon as we know – but a deep and dire crisis in the whole cosmogonic system of 'human' reproduction?

It is this second paradox which becomes the real – because historical – puzzle. This will be my manifestly Foucaultian conclusion.

Three theoretical obstacles bar the way to even a preliminary understanding of how sexuality has been historicized in this – and any other – cultural environment. I refer to these obstacles as those of naturalism, functionalism, and the essentialization of genders.

NATURALISM

Naturalism characterizes 'human', 'male', and 'female' sexualities as vectors with given physiological and/or psychological needs, effects, and desires that enter the social structure as the rough and ready sex of unsocialized human nature. Naturalism's study of sexuality develops into detailed or comparative analyses of the ways in which different cultural forms and institutions indigenously represent and co-organize these natural ensembles of needs, effects, and desires.

Both Mead's and Freeman's studies of the Samoan sexual milieu are naturalistic theories. Their descriptions scrutinize 'Samoan' customs for the way in which they impinge upon raw sexuality. For Freeman's 'ethological science', the Samoan social order has evolved by repressing this sexuality. In Mead's cultural approach, it has evolved to express it fully. At no point can naturalism ask questions about the imaginative constructions of indigenous sexuality or, more importantly, about the part played by these constructs in particularizing both the 'cult' of virginity and the resistance which it occasions. Naturalism can only presume that these constructions are in fact mythic or ideological *representations* of what is given, real, and 'natural'.

FUNCTIONALISM

The second obstacle in the way of a history of sex can be represented as functionalist. Functionalist theories split up 'human nature' into a plurality of distinct components, each component being not only a need but also the impulse towards a practice that has to express and socially satisfy its originating human drive.

The effect of such functionalist concepts upon the study of sexuality is to reify the latter as an autonomous impulse. Sex, in parallel with the other compartments of human nature, directs for itself the erection of a special domain in social space: the realm of sexual relations. Moreover, male and female sexualities will strive to externalize themselves in separate sexual realms, which can be read off against their separate sexual physiologies.

This approach predicts the crystallization of women's representations of sex in a women's field of action, and male representations in a male field. If there is a radical enunciation of this
position, male representations and structures are shown as
having invaded and dominated the expressive space of women.
Such spaces may well exist. What is problematic, however, is the
'oversexualization' of these domains, their reduction to sites of
satisfaction and/or repression where sexuality functions as an
end in and for itself through its social forms.

   Such functionalist concepts are unable to come to grips with the
ways in which psychobiological sexualities always first present
themselves for symbolic signification. Such signification fixes
specific sexual practices as means in the performance of much
broader 'human' projects. Consequently, when human, male and
female, sexualities achieve collective significance, it is as a result
of a partial and selective reconstruction of sex in imagery. From
the infinity of imaginable possibilities defining the reservoir of
the erogenous, imagery formalizes an essential sexual identity.
This essential sexuality has first to achieve a presence in a general
discourse to become at all potent. It is thus already socially integrated when functionalists come to define it as 'human' and (just)
sexual. It is already written up as a complex language, already a
marriage of instinct and ramifying image.

   This being true, it is not really feasible to speak of a distinct
domain of the sexual. If the broader schemes and scenarios
described in this paper are to be understood in their own terms,
sexuality as a primary category has to be liquidated. Such
schemes and scenarios lay down the structure in which sex is
precipitated as a biocultural quality.

THE ESSENTIALIZATION OF MALE AND FEMALE GENDER

In social space the male and the female connote more than a differentiation of the body's sexuality. The essence of sexual difference is always indigenously conceived in Fiji as spreading out
from its genital loci to dichotomize the immediate milieu and the
cosmos beyond. As a result, objects and roles tend to become
imaginatively annexed to either the male or the female in a way
that, conjuncturally, may appear to be 'natural' and eternal. The
sexing of the world through the differential objectification of

sexuality ramifies male and female, so transforming them into genders.

Many social studies of gender compile a list of dualities which sum up, simultaneously, the genderization of the relevant world and, within it, the basic experience of maleness and femaleness. For relativistic studies this ethnographic compilation stands as analysis: comparative knowledge subverts the 'naturalistic' claim made by any society in relation to the substance of its genders. The aim of such studies is to say that maleness and femaleness are differentially externalized and experienced in different ethnic contexts and that, therefore, a universal maleness or femaleness does not in fact exist. These studies stand in familiar opposition to other analyses of the same materials which assert universal images of male and femaleness, and superimpose them upon the empirical. Measured against these ideals of 'authentic' gender, societies, classes, and genders can be ideologically criticized for their oppressively inauthentic constructions and impositions.

Such analyses are theoretically disposed towards the reduction of gender to a unitary experience. Although cross-culturally gender varies, in any one 'society' it remains the same and can be unproblematically characterized on the strength of its unity. Even where inconsistencies obtrude, the unity of gender and its experience are rescued by reformulations which typify, say, femaleness as ambiguous. Sometimes femaleness means one thing, it is said, sometimes another.

A historical investigation of the social present, however, sees structures of gender undergoing critical change. History in the very same place subverts the eternalization of gender associations, creating in the process sexual identities that slide between alternate and contradictory chains of gendered objects and practices. Applied in this paper, this point of view abandons the idea of a Samoan or Fijian experience of maleness and femaleness. It discovers, instead, a dispersion of gender and a fluidity of sexualities structured across a complex social totality.

This complex totality posits for young women positions of oppression. However, as it is unravelled, every axis of oppression also offers a form of freedom. The structure is, consequently, as much one of sexual possibilities as it is a commanding edifice of sexual actuality. However, when young women resist the cult of virginity – as the essay describes them doing – they cannot be seen as replying in the name of universal womanhood and for the right to be sexually autonomous. This complex Oceanic structure defines, in its historico-cultural specificity, particular modes and experiences of oppression, particular modes and experiences of freedom.

The political culture of young female virginity

The large village-chiefdom of Serea lies about 50 miles north-west of Suva city on the largest island in Fiji. Approximately 300 people live either inside the chiefdom or immediately outside it in the forest on land held by Serean patriclans. Since the climate of the eastern interior is wet and fairly hot, and since soils in the river valley are basically good and plentiful, garden agriculture is productive and trouble-free. People fish as well as plant crops, hunt, and gather a little in the forest, and supplement their subsistence with a few commodities.

BESTIAL ATTRIBUTIONS

Roughness, coarseness, and an insatiable sexual appetite are traits which are said to define young men's nature. Lust, in the form of 'heat', is said to well up out of the male body as a spontaneous impulse. It is recognized, though, that somehow this impulse must be channelled out of Serea and exported abroad. Serean men are given to understand that their bodies are promiscuous but must be 'exopromiscuous'. Young women of Serea must be virgin brides.

Thus, before the practice became illegal, a bride's vagina was checked on her wedding day when the village would enquire after the state of her hymen. If she was pure and intact her blood was smeared on a barkcloth and held up for all to witness. This practice was common throughout the whole south-western Pacific. Today in eastern Fiji, if a bride disgraces herself at her nuptials, she is sent back to her agnates in shame. To prevent hostilities, they must reply with an appropriate substitute consisting of an earth-baked pig, lacerated about its head and with a banana thrust into its anus.

This substitution symbolizes the errant woman as a beast of the forest deprived of proper female sexuality. The carnal excesses of womanhood are represented as the bestial incarnation of an erogenous, but infertile orifice: the anus. In this way, the image of the pig, 'sexually' penetrated at its anus by a phallic other, announces for Sereans a union of human beings steeped in feral abomination.

This ceremonial iconography in abomination makes two very important cosmological and moral points about the fall of the deflowered women into the order of the forest.

Death and savage fertility

In the first place, by sexually uniting plantain and slaughtered pig, this symbol hints at that critical process of decay which is the fulcrum of the forest's regenerative cycle. For beyond contributing biomass to organic succession in the forest, decay perennially mutates the population structure of its ecosystem. It succeeds in blurring and then destroying the reproductive distinctness of separate species, dissolving each deceased generation into an undifferentiated realm of potency, called *vanua* or 'nature'.

Serean humans are born into patriclans which are thought of as embodying wild species. Truly exogamous marriage 'humanizes' the existence of patriclans by individuating and personally naming the separate bodies of their membership, and in this way, by constituting domestic organization as the reproductive framework of a nucleated 'humanity'. The death of these separate bodies is not considered to be an organic death: as detritus they remain a part of the forest's continuous growth. Death, very definitely and very sadly, however, dissolves these boundaries. It terminates the social relations which make these bodies specifically 'human' in Serea. Dead bodies are placed, anonymously, in pits belonging to the patriclans, in which, since time immemorial, all of their members' bodies have been ceremoniously interred. Here decomposition collectivizes the erstwhile separateness of their bodies, fusing them into the regenerative whole of the common territory (Leenhardt 1979).

The symbol of a young woman's promiscuity reflects abomination because it interpolates this sense of death into the flow of social life. It does this by short-circuiting the ritual currents of kinship which marry a savage man to a cultured and celestial woman, and which promote the new couple as a detached and unique identity.

Errant female sex thus reincarnates the sexual involutions of savagery and its killing off of an individualized, true 'humanity'.

The omnipotence of the savage phallus

In the second place, this image of abomination reflects back to its audience the fundamental gender asymmetry of Serean thought. The forest is represented as the abode of origin-beings, or *vu*, all of whom were (and still are) the first ancestors of the chiefdom's patriclans. These origin-beings are held to be consubstantial with particular wild species that reproduce themselves in the savage mode: which is to say, through the active nature of the male organ.

The savage potency of the *vu* is incarnated in both the male and female genitals of all clan descendants. Penis *and* vagina are jokingly identified in public under the name of the clan origin-being or under the name of its embodied species. However, the *vu* was a male, and not only that, but his potency is transmissible only through the active sexuality of clan sons. Female sexuality in the forest realm – and in the period of pre-social history in which that realm was dominant – is considered absent as a potent force, and only present as an agency of nourishment. Thus, every old clan village in the forest is surrounded by coconut palms. These are said to grow up every time an umbilical cord falls away, and is placed inside a growing nut which is planted in the soil of the ancient village. Forest maternity is nurturative rather than pro-creative, and female sexuality is represented as a passive phenomenon, specifically as a receptacle into which phalluses deposit already formed organisms. Consequently, because the agency of savage reproduction is masculine and because collective descent is rooted in the chiefdom's savage past, Serean clans are patriclans.

The bride resignified as a wild pig is, thus, automatically signified as product and incarnation of a savage masculinity. As such – and unlike the virgin bride, her opposite – she cannot contribute her vagina to active, reproductive effect. She is signified mockingly by way of her anus which, therefore, appears as a sign of her sexual subsumption to the masculine, her vicarious fall into the realm of the forest.

THE SIGNIFICATIONS OF PUNISHMENT

A licentious woman in Serea is punished as well as resignified. If found to be pregnant outside marriage, she is beaten heavily and publicly by her parents. She is harangued and insultingly equated with a pig, a cow, and a dog, all of which creatures are similar in important respects to the Serean human body. What they lack, and what makes them animal rather than human, is a *yalo* or 'soul'.

Serean 'soul' is formed out of *mana*, a transcendental power. It gells with maturity as the repository of *kila*, social knowledge, the power which inducts a child's body into the spheres of kinship which mystically transform it. Pigs, cows, and dogs do not enter these circuits and their bodies, consequently, are not transformed. The 'soul' is located inside the human head. Not surprisingly, therefore, as promiscuity proves the bestiality of the young woman, her 'soul' is known to have fled and her hair is entirely shaved off. She is thus stigmatized by reduction to the state of an anthropomorphic animal – an infant, in effect – for babies are born almost bald. Moreover, babies are also beaten like animals when they cry at night, and so, too, is a young woman beaten when she abandons human society by renouncing her virginity. Promiscuity, thus, destroys her human 'soul'.[3]

Finally, a profligate girl is thought to have returned to the wild and become a soulless beast if she indulges in the rough game of *muria mai* or 'follow me'. This game is probably mythical, but the evidence cited for it is a mark on the male body. Nearly all young Serean men insert hemispherical pebbles or halves of glass marbles into the folds of skin on their limp penises. The operation in question takes place in secret beyond the gaze of any adults or young girls. It is said that a girl with a promiscuous disposition, once penetrated by such an organ will hungrily pursue it for the rest of her sexual life, the reason given being that promiscuous vaginas are cavernous entities not stimulated by the normal penis. A similar image is invoked by the claim that some young women in Serea – particularly those with illegitimate children – will 'go convoy' in the forest. They are said to fornicate gleefully there with a whole host of men simultaneously. The vagina of such a woman, is, of course, counterposed to the virgin vagina which only opens up in marriage as a narrow passage, an opening for just one man. Licentious young women are thus said to lapse into bestiality when their 'soul' abandons their head and when their vagina expands for polyandry – the sexual norm of the beast.

In this way, forms of punishment on the one hand, and forms of (reputed) perversion on the other, elaborate – both publicly and in secret – the antithesis of the 'cult' of virginity. The passion with which the abomination is punished, and yet at the same time made the object of a perverse male diversion, takes place in the context of the same system of ideas and imagery which idealizes the virgin bride. Punishment, perversion, and adoration: these conflicting practices about the body and sexuality of young females announce the fluidity and the ambiguity of womanhood within the Serean cosmos, and, hence, the imperative of ensuring virginity for the nuptials.

THE HISTORIC TASK OF YOUNG FEMALE VIRGINITY IN
THE CHIEFDOM OF SEREA

In indigenous terms, the vagina belongs to the wild as a subordinate object in its reproductive cycle. However, through discipline, segregation, regulation, and the associations imposed upon it by the kinship system, a woman's body – thought of as the expression of her vagina – can be wrenched out of the natural realm and be reconstituted as a transcendental power in marriage.

Virgin vaginas concentrate *mana*, a power which does not generate fertility, but which acts upon savage fecundity to imbue it with cultural substance and so structure it as a social relation. This social relation is the Serean state of 'humanity'.

Mana possesses a young girl's vagina by dissolving its connections to her organic and corporeal body and by turning her into a 'god-soul', a reincarnated divinity. In fact, Serean women, as brides in every generation, ideally reincarnate the goddess Adi Waimaro and repeat her legendary coming to the forests of Serea. In so doing, brides are said to arrive from the realm of *lagi*, located across the ocean and beyond the horizon, in the heavens above the sky. Today Adi Waimaro is said to exist as a whales-tooth – a *tabua* – wrapped up in barkcloth, and locked up in a box in a secret corner of the chiefdom. At her wedding, a virgin bride can pass to a young man only after his father has presented the sacred whalestooth to her father. All whalesteeth sympathetically carry the identity of the divine prototype; thus virginity, under the special conditions of the rites, receives its divinity from the sacred gift. This form of 'exchange' does not function as an interchange of equivalences undertaken with political or economic interest in mind, but as a cycle of cosmic transfigurations wrought on a social stage. Such wife-goddesses are generated by the incest taboo and by the other operations of the Serean kinship system. These work towards the rites of marriage and for the man who will acquire his wife-goddess.

Prior to his marriage, a youth tends to run wild with 'the boys'. In Serea, this group of turbulent adolescents is known as the 'Green Army'. Its members celebrate being wild and unruly; participation in its activities draws young men away from the disciplined, individualizing regime of garden agriculture to an anarchic, hunting gang in the forest. Fathers give sons individual gardens of their own to tend, but sons give up these separate gardens to their Green Army, or else abandon them entirely for collectively chasing, trapping, roasting, and eating the wild pig in the forest, outside the civilized structures of individual domestic life inaugurated by goddess-brides.

The pig is well-known in the chiefdom for eating anything – including its own kind. For this reason, it achieves what promiscuous womanhood is thought to achieve through illicit sex. That is to say, it liquidates the boundaries between species by recreating in its stomach the condition of primal unity, of undifferentiated 'nature'.

Thus, the ideal of the male adolescents in Serea appears to be the subsumption of body and mind to the unthinking spontaneity and unboundedness, to the sheer freedom, of this unity. What is abhorred by adulthood is adored by the Green Army of the chiefdom's youth. They kill the pig not because they hate it, but because it is their adolescent hero, their veritable anti-god. They absorb this anti-god not only through the medium of the hunt but also through 'bestial' promiscuity.

THE OBJECT OF THE 'CULT' OF VIRGINITY

What then do young men acquire when they marry? They acquire the opposite of their anti-god, that is a goddess who is simultaneously the embodiment of control and individuality, of rules (*lawa*) and named souls (*yaca*). Virginity kills off the essence of 'the wild pig' in female bodies, and its appropriation in marriage by a man is also expected to kill off a man's desire for the pig. Henceforth, males will become the husbands and, as such, owners of a regulated male body and a private domestic economy. A man's wife, if she was virgin, splits him off from the primitive corporateness of his patriclan. She *is* his private being in the modern Serean world, the foundation of his home.

This specification of female chastity shows, therefore, that the 'cult' of virginity in the chiefdoms of interior Fiji has little to do with the socio-biological function of repression as decreed by 'the science of ethology'. True enough, a psychic repression of libidinous drives may well be engendered by the institution. However, the origins of the 'cult' are to be found not in the needs and processes of human nature and society, but in the culturally constructed realities of Serean 'nature', 'human nature', and 'history'.

Consequently, the 'cult' of virginity works by repressing a biological phenomenon which is first delineated by cultural process. It is shaped, institutionally, by the culture of the very 'nature' it has to suppress and by the culture of domestic existence it has to create. It is, thus, for all its repressiveness, a doubly creative practice.

Transgression as biocounterculture

DEVIANCE OR COUNTERCULTURE?

Freeman's Samoan analysis insists that young girls are socialized to a rigorously repressive morality, infractions of which may invoke such strong feelings of shame as to lead to suicide. Infractions to the law of pre-marital chastity do occur in Samoan chiefdoms, however, just as they occur in the similar Fijian milieu. Freeman's naturalistic viewpoint can only see these as cases of deviance, social pathologies caused by a feeble internalization of the norms of the 'cult'. In effect, the ethologist's concept of transgression pits anti-social instinct against culture, narcissistic drives of the individual body against the altruistic constitution of society. However, where transgression is theorized as being due to a failure in the machineries of socialization, it is refused the possibility of being and becoming a culturally creative resistance, and is denied the status of praxis.

In fact, young men's and women's resistance to the dominant culture arises precisely out of an indigenous discourse, whose imagery, language, and set of possible objectives are culturally laid down by the dominant structure as its own antithetical object.

SEDUCTION AND TRANSFORMATION

On the western, outer margins of the village site – in the area still called 'forest' and notionally associated with it – there stands a dimly illuminated, windowless hall. This serves just a single function: it houses the regular dance of the Serean unmarrieds. The married sector does not visit this hall and, conversationally, only alludes to it. The intimacies that are hatched there are not monitored by the adult order.

The hall exists in the area formally designated 'outside the chiefdom'. In this space young men are known to 'go wild'. It is a space within which, though rules of kinship and chiefly authority undoubtedly persist in the mind, they do so but weakly. Beyond the pale of House, Liege and Church, as it were, the young male body in particular is understood to throw off the shackles of both imposed restraint and moralized self-control. It is for this reason that though the forest along the road has long been chopped down, the road, the fields, and even the city are still considered spatial extensions of wild reality and as such, movement into this space is seen as threatening to the body's moral fibre.

Thus, invariably, the boys sponsor the dance in a drunken state. The function will not seem right to them until, inebriated, they are unable to contain their lewdness and violence and appear to lose control in a spontaneous explosion of inner energies. The ritual drink *kava* – and even more obviously the alcohol they put away – furnishes the physiological basis by which they can heighten their experience of the wild as they conceive it. This seems to be the entire point of the evening. I was assured once that young men in this state who cannot find a woman to go with will resort to the cows of Serea. After all, aren't their subincised penises prepared for this very contingency?

Sometime after dusk, cued by the strumming of cleverly dissonant strings, small groups of young women converge coyly upon the dance hall. Whilst the boys are typically unkempt, the new arrivals are impeccably turned out. They have, to a woman, oiled and scented themselves, bedecked their hair with flowers, and changed into their brightest, cleanest clothes. The boys reel wildly and madly about the dance floor. The girls, on the other hand, stay standoffishly to the side. The dance, at the outset, is a thorough mismatch of disposition and style.

Initially the girls make few concessions to the unrestrained forwardness of the boys. They communicate their sexual reticence by insisting on dancing à la quicktime, during which time, their partners try to reduce the space between them. After an hour or so, though, the band – which consists only of male instrumentalists – turns down the tempo. The dance is forced into slow step. Bodies are brought together. The women abandon their standoffishness.

As the rhythm becomes still more pacific, partners 'make appointments'. Secret rendezvous are selected, always somewhere beyond the village perimeter. With a deftness finely cultivated during adolescence, lovers slip away in secret.

THE ORGANIZED 'SPONTANEITY' OF PROMISCUITY AND
THE REPRESENTATIONS WITH WHICH IT IS IMBUED

This subversive promiscuity is as much socioculturally endowed as is the 'cult' of virginity which it inverts and evades. Indeed, these adolescents dance as much to the image of mythic promiscuity – to that of Serean 'nature' untrammelled – as they do to the music seductively conveying an imagined spontaneity. The sexual excesses of promiscuity, therefore, never appear and are never experienced as 'just biological', but in stark opposition to the other mythic bases of kinship and marriage.

Drunk as they are or sometimes, perhaps, pretend to be, the boys are apt not to calculate kinship too stringently and while they are unlikely to elope with a 'sister' who is a daughter of a father's biological brother, it is quite probable that the capriciousness of attraction and seduction at this dance will unite male and female from the same patriclan, a union which is otherwise always considered too close.

There is a relative indifference of partners as to whom they go with after the dance. Pairings are made only in the expectation of their being ephemeral and after many dances both young men and women will most likely have been with many partners. The dance serves to break down and reassort sexually consorting couples. It is, thus, in the long term, the institutional means by which sexuality is collectivized and – in Serean terms – the means by which the savage totality of 'prehumanity' is reconstituted beneath the domestic realm and in contradiction to it. The image of this subversive totality forms the determinant presence at the dance.

LIMINALITY AND THE CONFESSION OF AN ILLUSORY SECRET

However, whilst an arena of idealized fornication prevails amongst Serean adolescents, it does so only in the invisibility of a liminal 'underground'. Mead was grossly in error in thinking that her young female informants might openly flaunt sexual codes determined by the order of marriage. They did – on the strength of her own account – boast of their lovers and love affairs. However, Mead had set herself up just outside the village: a 'professional inadequacy', according to Freeman. But just outside the village, Mead had positioned herself right within the domain of the chiefdom's adolescents. Here – but nowhere else – could promiscuity be happily put into words. The spatial co-ordinate of Mead's 'professional inadequacy' meant that she could hear what Freeman, drinking *kava* with Samoan chiefs at the ceremonial heart of the village, could not hope to hear. Not 'having entered the community' meant that, inadvertently, she could listen to the transgressive discourses at its margins.

Somehow, this charade can be pursued: young men who will supposedly be beneficiaries of this chastity know that most of the girls have been deflowered already and know, furthermore, that their own bride will almost certainly not be a virgin. Moreover, they in turn will become parents and will organize the same scenario for their own children.

What role does this conspiracy of silence play? What power does this illusion of secrecy hold?

Its systematic misrepresentation censors the taken-for-granted awareness of the chiefdom's promiscuity; in lieu of a policing of the mischief, it tries to deconstruct it and turn it into its opposite. In a very real sense, it is heretical for a Serean to announce that promiscuity is rife because the more important 'truth' of the ideals of the system must prevail. Only exceptionally is promiscuity announced, and then in a bout of punishment which is quickly ritualized.

It is interesting to find that Malinowski offers strong support for a more general occurrence of this type of deconstruction by means of silence.

> 'The careful avoidance by a man of any knowledge about his sister's amorous prospects is, I am certain, not only an ideal but also a fact. I was over and over again assured that no man has the slightest inkling as to whom his sister is going to marry; although this is the common knowledge of everybody else. I was told that if a man came by chance upon his sister and her sweetheart when they were making love, all three of them would have to commit LA'U (suicide by jumping from a coconut palm). This is obviously an exaggeration which expresses the ideal and not the reality: if such a mishap occurred, the brother would most likely pretend that he had seen nothing, and would discreetly disappear. But I know that considerable care is taken to preclude any such possibility and noone would dream of mentioning the subject in the presence of the brother.'   (Malinowski 1929: 439–40)

This bracketing off of sexual abomination makes room for the unfolding of the countertendency in promiscuous sexual unions.

Contradiction and the politics of Serean sexuality

SUBTEXT: THE CULTURAL SOURCE OF FEMALE PROMISCUITY

To win young women to the sexual regime of the forest, the strategy of the young men must be to break into the circuit of divine feminization. This phenomenon can be accomplished. As the last section observed, many young women do indeed give themselves over to the Serean 'forest of unmarried phalluses' and as they do so, they abandon with their virginities the ritual reality of their celestial station. Doesn't, then, this imaginary displacement prove that a Serean maiden's mythic status is just that: only mythic? Aren't young Serean women seducible, because underlying a notional virgin divinity, their libido is, from the very first, governed by the universal power of Eros?

These questions must be answered in the negative if the 'ethological' view of promiscuity as unconditioned pathology is to be wholly dispatched. In fact, it can easily be shown that illicit desires can only be aroused in Serea in consequence of some very precise cultural conditions. Seduction is effective because its propositions resonate with a muted imagery of 'nature' in women's cosmic self-awareness. This subtext of women's 'nature' fractures the unity of female gender, so that women may be one thing – but they are also something else.

WOMEN'S GENDER IS STRUCTURED SYMBOLICALLY IN CONTRADICTION

In effect, the gender of young women is symbolically structured in contradiction. Their female biology is represented to them as a cosmically nodal point in the conveyance of human souls from the Fijian heavens to the land and men of Serea. Their femaleness is also, however, thought of and experienced as corporeal and animal, as a passive receptacle for the savage phalluses of these same 'wild' men, and, consequently, as the embodiment of a purely masculine principle of regeneration. Thus, when the young men plan and carry out their seductions, they do not mobilize against the Serean myth of femaleness. Rather, their appropriate technologies of seduction resonate with and elicit the forbidden image of young women's 'masculine' sexuality. In the end, female gender – like most phenomena in Serea – has to be seen not as a thing, but as a process on a continuum. One extreme on this continuum is materialized by the wedding ceremony, when a virgin bridge may indeed feel that she is transcendental and divine – just for the instant – and a true champion of what possession of a vagina affords the cause of the chiefdom's 'humanity'. Here, it can be argued that Serean womanhood finds itself an indubitable reality, a sacred and exclusive authenticity safe from the destabilizations and transformations which normally characterize the complexity of female gender. The other extreme is materialized, illicitly, when coitus, staged not by rules but by the inner bodily energies and their textualized masculinity, dislodges the sense of transcendental femaleness. As a result it may well have to be argued that *there exists no true praxis in female freedom in the chiefdom of Serea*. In effect, young Fijian women must 'choose' between being a regal power which is appropriated and unfree and a freedom which is palpable but ultimately unfemale.

Further evidence has to be cited to illustrate this critical contradiction in the materialization of a woman's gender. It is realized, of course, that women do possess a body, but many of its biological functions are zealously hidden from public view and conversation and, thus, denied 'true reality'. These include eating (women eat after men have retired to the public forum of the *kava*), menstruating, childbirth, and death. The very rigour of these concealments, though, confirms the basic suspicion of both men and women that despite a special contact with divinity, women's bodies are as organic as men's.

Moreover, young women say that they embrace the Church in Serea in order to evade the clutches of Satan. The indigenous image of the Christian devil equates this Antichrist with the Serean Tevoro, the He-Creature of the primal forest, who, naked, shaggy-haired, anthropophagous, and incestuous, survives there to terrorize the wayward. Tevoro/Satan attaches civilized bodies to his wild and savage space when he invades and annexes them. His work is represented and felt as a snatching of the flesh which repels the soul, and which impels women – and men – towards uncontrollable 'madness' (*lialia*) or sickness, both of which are properties and weaknesses of uncultivated flesh. Thus, the devil in this hybrid cosmology is the primal flesh that makes up human bodies. He is simply nature in the wrong place, in command of dehumanized bodies which are devoid of souls. He is, in point of fact, the Christian personification of the Serean wild pig, the beast which represents the totality of 'nature' in opposition to all of its separate species, and (in particular) the savage 'nature' of masculinity engulfing the divine reality of femaleness. It is interesting to note that during one Easter celebration in the village, those who hunt the pig refused to attend church to commemorate the death and resurrection of Christ. Instead, they retired rebelliously to drink, making themselves wild with methylated spirits.

It is not at all surprising, therefore, to see that Serean women religiously embrace the Church with an urgency that expresses the continual nature of this cosmic struggle for their bodies. These days, in urban areas, young women submit to exorcisms, a developing technology for ridding the spirituality of 'true' female gender of the invasions of savage maleness.

FLAWED 'HUMANITY': THE UNCOMFORTABLE TRUTH
UNDERLYING TRANSVESTISM

It is also interesting to reflect upon the fact that old and widowed women are expected to return from their husbands' to their fathers' quarter of the village when their husbands die. They are given small, single huts exactly akin to those frequently occupied by 'wild' unmarried boys, and here they practise the art at which they are considered expert: the massage and manipulation of wounded male bodies. Moreover, at weddings, these old women – venerated matriarchs within the patriclan – are called upon to publicly display the masculinity concealed within their own being.

As ceremonial transvestites, they dress up in men's clothes and feign to poke imaginary phalluses into imaginary orifices. Unconstrained laughter erupts and flows at this ridiculous manifestation of biological maleness teased out of female bodies. Why do old women stage a manifestation of Serean maleness? Why does the crowd find this demonstration so ridiculously funny? Why does this theatre take place at a wedding? In effect, when the chiefdom laughs at these female transvestites, it laughs not at what is clever make-believe but at the dramatic starkness of the truth. The starkness in this truth is its contradiction. Serean women have, in fact, two genders, yet the logic of producing viable 'humanity' through the kinship system and its rites decrees that they have just one. Thus, weddings throw doubt upon their own ritual efficacy. Old women's perverse performance poses a question mark over the authenticity of the rites and, more to the point, over the authenticity of Serean 'humanity' as a state of being.

In effect, Serean women are precipitated into the field of a specific politics of sexuality in which they ought to become divine but in which they cannot evade the pull of primordial Serean savagery. This polarization registers the fact that the whole mystic circuit tends to be driven into contradiction and turned back upon itself. This tendency exists for three separate reasons: 1) young men are programmed by and within this system to be promiscuous and dangerously so in the end; they are socialized to transform, should they not be transformed; 2) these same young men are politically underpoliced so that they *can* try to undermine the dominant norms; and by so doing, they actualize the state of 'nature' they are born to stand for; 3) young girls are endowed with a contradictory, unstable gender.

TRANSVESTISM, CONTRADICTION, AND THE EVOLUTION OF A THIRD POLITICS OF SEXUALITY

As a result, the chiefdom of Serea knows, or at least senses, that its primary cultural transformation may never be taking place. Beneath the pronouncements of marriage and the restrictive regulations of domestic nucleation lives the fear that Serean women are unceasingly being exposed to a promiscuous regime. Consequently, as a man grows into the Serean polity, he risks being abandoned and, thus, losing everything that constitutes him as an independent citizen.

In this context, should a wife leave her husband, he simply becomes one of the male herd, and young men and married men together flock to his house, to drink, eat, and sleep alongside him. Such communal companionship, though, can only consign the forlorn husband to the futile comforts that were destined to be Job's lot. For in the very bosom of company comes the dissolution of all that a presumed virgin bride stood for: the recognition of his standing as a wholly autonomous individual installed supremely alone in the upper end of his own house.

The first response to this contradictory situation has been described and analysed already: female promiscuity is wishfully smothered in silence. This conservative tendency, however, is countered by a novel transformation, by way of which chiefs are held to have come to Serea to eclipse the 'cult' of virginity.

In the period before the *pax britannica*, coastal paramount chiefs shattered the autonomy of rival communities by crushing them in battle and bonding their plantations to the imperial body of the god-chief himself (Sahlins 1985). Annual tributes in yams metaphysically fixed this organic absorption of the ruled into the ruler's being. Additionally though, each conquered chiefdom was taxed to the tune of a hereditary princess, once a village chief's daughter and now the concubine of a polygamous god incarnate. Rape, politically engineered and religiously sanctified, formed the cruel apotheosis of this mastery of the cosmos within the structures of empire.

Chiefs welded 'lands' into 'nature' by swallowing the economies of men and by penetrating the sexualities of women. This unification of the savage realm about the absolute spirit of the god-chief replaced the project of 'humanity' and gave a new cosmic function to sex. Male sexuality in particular was completely redefined. The contradiction in women's sexuality was violently resolved.

In Serea today rape *in deed* appears to occur but infrequently. However, the *idea* prevails generally that chiefs ought to take as many women as possible and indeed, that young girls might well want to surrender their bodies to his *mana* voluntarily, to masochistically 'enjoy' within them the divine substance of domination (Sahlins 1985). It is impossible to gauge the extent to which this transformation has gained a foothold in practice. One thing is certain, though: the idea itself has become a powerful force enlarging the awe in which men behold their chiefs and, perhaps, too, the fear with which women walk beside them.

Conclusion

Thus, so long as savage males in these formations were entirely dependent on the acquisition of virgin brides to achieve their 'humanity', young women would ever be fated either to submit to the cult of virginity and its system of punishments, or secretly transgress. For male elders in Serea this is how the situation still stands. However, for the chiefs themselves, and for those who are ideologically predisposed towards their forebears' claims, the 'cult' has been superseded as *the* civilizing organ of savage being. Its new ideal of an integrated body-politic – the chief's second body (Kantarowicz 1957) – no longer requires young women to be adulated and virgin. It requires them, in fact, to project themselves publicly as subjects of their bodily sex. It *requires* them to transgress against the 'cult' and its objectives.

Thus, quite paradoxically, the arrogant chauvinism of this chiefly élite tends to free young women from the extraordinary denials of the body required of a female goddess. It frees them for sexual excess, but under conditions of surrender, and failing that, of submission. This being the case, it can be seen why in this Fijian chiefdom and most likely in other parts of the same region, young women are both sexually repressed *and* sexually expressive (and also, moreover, threatened by sexual violence). It is not the fact that both forces are symbolically structured which gives them an equal presence and determinacy. The reason why both movements are equally contributory to the experience of adolescent sexuality in the region is ultimately extrinsic: it is because of the crisis prompted by transgression and by the space won for the promiscuous cause by the evolution of a third political culture of sex. The 'nature' of the 'cult' of virginity and the culture of the 'nature' of sexual freedom can both only be understood in their simultaneity if their 'overdetermination' by this third term is positively understood.

This being the case, it is apparent that an orthodox anthropology of sexuality must give way to a history of its cultural politics.

Notes

I have to express my gratitude to the Social Science Research Council without whose funding this paper could not have been researched, and to Dr Pat Caplan of Goldsmiths' College, University of London, without whose comments and painstaking efforts on the draft manuscripts, the paper could not have been published.

1 This essay appears in the wake of an already expansive discussion – industry? – of The Samoan Controversy. (Strathern 1983; Shore 1981, 1982, 1983; *Canberra Anthropologist* Special Issue (1983) 6 (2)). Shore offers the most detailed and subtle description of Samoan 'society' to date. His work also affirms the symbolic construction of transgressive as well as dominant sexuality, at the intersubjective level. Hence, the 'mystery' of the Samoan way.
2 Beyond Shore's helpful Samoan parallel, I have incurred three serious debts in the composition of this paper. I am manifestly indebted to

The History of Sexuality (Foucault 1981) for its formulation of a valid
historical object of sex. Secondly, I am indebted to Marshall Sahlins
who, though he may not know it, taught me more in two or three
conversations about anthropology, than I'd learnt in the previous ten
years. Sahlins transmits an awesome, infectious energy which seems
to originate as much from the informant's realm as he sees it, as it does
from its ordering discourse. Finally, I am indebted to my own
informants – to all of them – but particularly, here, to boys of the
Serean 'Green Army'. Understanding that I had always to return to the
kava bowl to sit alongside their chiefs and fathers, they skilfully
conducted me in and out of their realm, but never into the sort of
'trouble' that defined it. This took some doing. Without their patience
and skill, therefore, this paper could never have been conceived. I had
to be an equal occupant of both 'the structure' and its antithesis.
3 In *The Gardens of Adonis*, Marcel Detienne (1977) provides a model
analysis of a dominant polity steeped in ritual, and of a 'spontaneous'
movement back to 'nature' which is none the less culturally constructed.

References

Detienne, M. (1977) *The Garden of Adonis: Spices in Greek Mythology.*
Hassocks: Harvester Press.
Foucault, M. (1976) *La Volonté de savoir.* Paris: Editions Gallimard.
—— (1981) *The History of Sexuality.* Harmondsworth: Penguin.
Freeman, D. (1983a) *Margaret Mead and Samoa. The Making and
Unmaking of an Anthropological Myth.* Cambridge, Mass.: Harvard
University Press.
—— (1983b) Inductivism and the Test of Truth: a Rejoinder to Lowell D.
Holmes. *Canberra Anthropologist* Special Issue 6 (2).
Kantarowicz, E. (1957) *The King has Two Bodies: a Study in Mediaeval
Political Theology.* Princeton: Princeton University Press.
Leenhardt, M. (1979) *Do Kamo. Person and Myth in the Melanesian World.*
Chicago: University of Chicago Press.
Levi-Strauss, C. (1962) *Structural Anthropology. Vol. 1.* London: Allen Lane.
Malinowski, B. (1929) *The Sexual Lives of Savages in North Western
Melanesia* (3rd edn) London: Routledge.
Mead, M. (1928) *Coming of Age in Samoa.* New York: William Morrow.
Sahlins, M. D. (1983) Raw Women, Cooked Men and Other Great Things
of the Fiji Islands. In P. Brown and D. Tuzin (eds) *The Ethnography of
Cannibalism.* Special Publication. Washington, DC: Society For
Psychological Anthropology.
—— (1985) *Islands of History.* Chicago: University of Chicago Press.
Shore, B. (1981) Sexuality and Gender in Samoa: Conceptions and Missed
Conceptions. In S. Ortner and A. Whitehead (eds) *Sexual Meanings: the
Cultural Construction of Gender and Sexuality.* Cambridge: Cambridge
University Press.

Shore, B. (1982) *Sala'ilua: a Samoan Mystery.* New York: Columbia University Press.
—— (1983) Paradise Regained: Freeman's Margaret Mead and Samoa. *Canberra Anthropologist* Special Issue 6 (2).
Strathern, M. (1980) No Nature, No Culture: the Hagen case. In C. MacCormack and M. Strathern (eds) *Nature, Culture and Gender.* Cambridge: Cambridge University Press.
—— (1983) The Punishment of Margaret Mead. *The London Review of Books* 15 (8).

8 'Selling her kiosk': Kikuyu notions of sexuality and sex for sale in Mathare Valley, Kenya[1]

Nici Nelson

Introduction

Views about the nature of sexuality form a significant part of a society's total complex of cultural constructs relating to the nature of men and women and the right and proper relationship between the genders. However, ascertaining these views is a difficult task for an anthropologist since they are among those intimate areas of life which are verbalized with reluctance to strangers and outsiders. It may also be that most anthropologists, for reasons of tact or personal shyness, have either not pursued this area of inquiry or not written much about it. The paucity of data on this subject in the literature is indicative of the reluctance of both anthropologists and their informants to discuss sex and sexuality. When, as was the case in this particular research, the major thrust of inquiry has been in areas only tangential to that of cultural constructs of sexuality, it is obviously difficult to generalize these constructs at a later date. This chapter, there-fore, represents only some tentative thoughts on the nature of Kikuyu views of sexuality. It is an area which would necessitate a thorough, more focused inquiry at a later date. For the moment I am interested in examining one aspect of Kikuyu sexual relations – that of the commercialized sexual relationship – in order to see what the 'sex for sale' syndrome can tell us about the more normative sexual relationships between men and women. It is also of interest to see whether a careful consideration of Kikuyu ideas on the commercialized sexual relationship can tell us some-thing more general about gender relations.

The research on which this paper is based concentrated on the migration of female heads of household in a Nairobi squatter

settlement,[2] on their migration histories, their urban careers, and
their economic and social strategies for survival. For this reason,
my data on the ideology of sexuality are relatively scant and un-
systematic. It is also skewed since my informants were not
'respectable' married women, but members of a small but growing
category of free women living in town and partially exploiting their
sexual relationships with men for overt economic gain. In the
parlance of Kikuyu English, they were women who 'sold from their
kiosks' (a small store, often just a hut). In addition, I have used data
on sexuality gathered from married women who lived in Mathare,
as well as the many men who drank with the beer brewers of
Mathare. I lived in Kenya for nearly four years and many of my
friends were Kikuyu, so I also have impressionistic data from
everyday interaction and living. It must be recognized, however,
that most of my systematic data come from Kikuyu women who
were less 'normative' in terms of the larger society. How much
their views on sexuality differ from those of their 'respectable'
sisters is impossible to gauge without further research.

This paper, then, will concentrate on Kikuyu views of the
sexual nature of men and women and the nature of the sex act,
and how sex relates to other aspects of society, as well as views
about the proper sexual relationship between men and women
(which naturally are part and parcel of the proper total relationship between men and women). It is also an exercise in
speculation into the true role of the commercialized sexual act in
the total picture of a society's concepts of sexuality. Perhaps the
most interesting question, namely the ways in which the
relatively recent introduction of commercialized sex into Kikuyu
culture and society have altered their constructs of sexuality,
cannot be explored because of lack of data. However, I hope to
show that at the present time the commercialized sexual
relationship[3] is both a mirror image and a logical extension of the
contractual marital sexual relationship. In addition the comparison between the marital and the commercialized sexual
relationship tells us something about the Kikuyu view of
sexuality and male–female relationships.

Kikuyu views of sexuality

This section summarizes Kikuyu views of sexuality, concentrating on their ideas about the sexual nature of men and women.

Wherever possible I note differences between male and female views of the same topic, and between the views of married women and of free women in Mathare Valley. It would be wrong to assume that Mathare free women's views on sex and sexuality are entirely typical, since their sociological position in Kikuyu society is not. There would of course be many areas where their views would converge with the more normative Kikuyu views. The problem is to identify the convergences and the divergences.

KIKUYU MALE SEXUALITY

There is agreement by all Kikuyu men and women that the male sex drive is strong. Men *need* a lot of sex and a variety of sexual partners. Faithfulness is not a real issue for men, as it is for women. There is a sense, conveyed more by men than women, that regular sex with a variety of partners is a man's *right* – a logical extension of a commonly held view that men are naturally polygynous (though women should be monogamous by nature). Frequently, when challenged on this fact of men's lack of faithfulness, men would point to the 'African way' of polygynous marriage which they would use to justify men's need, not to say right, to have regular sex with a number of partners. Thus men who migrate to town without their wives take it for granted that they will have sexual liaisons in town. It would seem that their wives resign themselves to that fact as well. Formal polygyny today is decreasing in incidence, but it is the feeling of many that the reasons are economic rather than ideological. Men are re-defining polygyny into a situation of one legal wife (to whom they owe a variety of long-term socio-economic responsibilities) combined with a number of lovers or mistresses (for whom they have only short-term responsibilities) or even shorter-term com-mercialized sexual relationships with women, like those who sell beer in Mathare. Only the most devout Christians make any attempt to adhere to an ethic of faithfulness and strict monogamy.

All Kikuyu men are circumcised. Circumcision marks the transition from boy to man, both sexually and socially. In earlier Kikuyu custom it would have been unheard of for a woman to have sex with an uncircumcised man. Today, Mathare Kikuyu women have as customers men from ethnic groups which do not circumcise their members. These women complain that such men smell (are sexually undesirable?) and hint that their performance leaves much to be desired sexually. Whether this was just a symbolic way of saying that they defined these uncircumcised men as boys or whether women truly perceived them as sexually less potent or active is impossible to determine.

KIKUYU FEMALE SEXUALITY

Just as men are thought to have a strong sexual drive, so are women, and both men and women recognize this fact. Only virgins can do without sex. This is the reason which migrant men give for forbidding their wives in the rural areas to use any form of contraception. They fear that while they are gone their wives will have affairs and will not be found out. Thus, at least in the eyes of men, women's *right* to have regular sex must take second place to the male demands for control of women's fertility, though their *need* for sex is recognized. Men fear that women left alone in rural areas for months on end will be unfaithful, even though they hope and pray that their own wives will resist temptation. Women themselves feel that they have a right to sex, and this is a frequent source of complaint by wives in such separated families, and often a major reason given by women in Mathare for having divorced migrant husbands to come to town.

How faithful, then, are women, and how willing to forgo variety in sexual partners for security? According to Kenyatta, there were mystical sanctions forcing women to be faithful when their husbands were away on long trips, as otherwise they jeopardized the safety of the men (Kenyatta 1962). Thus Kikuyu custom placed a strong supernatural importance on women's faithfulness. Women, both married and unmarried, claimed that women can be faithful and even are so by nature, as long as they are well treated by their husbands and receive sufficient economic support, tenderness, and sex. Men, however, are less certain. As long as a woman had had only one sexual partner, it was said that she would probably remain faithful. However, once she had had more than one man she would be 'spoiled for faithfulness'. As one man explained to me, 'Once women have tasted the variety of many men, they can never again be satisfied with having sex with only one man.' It is interesting to contrast this attitude with the one displayed by the Hausa men in Cohen's book. In the Hausa quarter of Ibadan, women who had been prostitutes were valued as having sowed their wild oats and thus being more inclined to be faithful to their husbands (Cohen 1969).

The link between female circumcision[4] and female sexuality is more explicit than it is in the case of male circumcision. Circumcision for females had all the social and religious significance that it had for men, marking a cut-off point between child and woman. It signified the transition from the state of ignorance, inactivity, impotence, and asexuality into one of activity, knowledge, sexuality, and reproduction (Mbiti 1969: 123). But sexuality for women has more to do with procreation than with pleasure, and more specifically procreation for the patrilineage; it also implies a concern with controlling women's sexual drive.

Medical doctors and Kikuyu women to whom I talked agreed that circumcision, even the moderate form practised in Kenya, would limit women's sexual pleasure since the most sensitive tissues of the female genital organs, the clitoris and the labia minora, are excised (WIN News 1984). Old women interviewed during a return visit in 1984 (I collected almost no data on circumcision in my first period of field research in 1971–74) confirmed this. They said that girls were circumcised to limit their sex drive and to keep them under control. In my original survey, most older (and therefore in all probability circumcised) women said that sex was for procreation only rather than for pleasure.

THE SEX ACT AND SEXUAL BEHAVIOUR

The Kikuyu would seem to have a very pragmatic view of sex. Coitus is viewed as necessary for health and sanity, and any person who does not have regular sex will suffer various illnesses, both nervous and physical.

Furthermore, it is thought that celibacy, as a voluntary state of abstention from sex, is a physical and psychological impossibility. Indeed there is no Kikuyu word for celibacy. Most uneducated Kikuyu maintain stoutly that nuns and priests secretly have sex and only tell people that they are celibate in order to underline the precepts of their religion. There is no concept of a man or woman who is uninterested in sex. Impotence is confused with barrenness, and the same word (*thaata*) is used for both, although some informants will, when pushed, say that a man who is impotent can be called *kuhahurwo*, the name for castration of animals. Neither is there any word for frigidity in women, since granting a husband sexual services is an essential part of a wife's duties.

Sex is the cornerstone of marriage. It is necessary for the union of men and women. Impotence or refusal to have sex is, and always was, grounds for divorce. Lack of sex was named as the worst aspect of living alone for women when their husbands migrated to work. I got the impression that Mathare women assumed that they considered it proper for husbands and wives to have sex nightly.

This attitude to the expected sexual behaviour between men and women, however, does not seem to indicate that sex is necessary for reasons of pleasure. Out of sixty-three Mathare women interviewed, only 36 per cent named pleasure or love as a reason for a sexual relationship; 52 per cent of women stated that sex was for procreation, 20 per cent said it was needed to keep healthy, 10 per cent said it provided money or shelter for women, both married and unmarried; in other words, it was seen as a form of payment made by women for the resources they receive from men.

This instrumental attitude to sex in Kikuyu society would seem to be echoed by the generally unromantic view of sex held by Mathare women, although it is difficult to say how prevalent this is among Kikuyu women generally. Is it a widespread cynical assessment of the sexual relationship, or rather a cynicism born of the particular circumstances in which Mathare free women find themselves?

Sex definitely does not seem to be highly elaborated. Nothing in Kikuyu myth emphasizes its pleasurable aspects. There is no instruction in how to please a man in the initiation of women, as there is in the customary practices of other societies (Richards 1982; Caplan 1976). On the contrary, in the past there seems to have been a complex of beliefs and practices which, in the opinion of modern manuals on sexual techniques, could not have contributed to the sexual pleasure of the partners. According to Leakey, wives were forbidden to touch their husbands' genitals, or husbands to touch their wives' nipples with mouth or hand.

The man had to lie on top of the woman and her legs had to enclose the husband's. Any failure to adhere to these strict rules could lead to death unless the parties involved purified themselves (Leakey 1977: 787–88). This basic and unelaborated approach to the sex act seems to have survived to the present day. Many Mathare women confirmed that most Kikuyu do not regard sex as something that one learns how to do. It is for begetting children and physical release. There is, to the best of my knowledge, no word in Kikuyu for orgasm, either male or female. Some informants claimed that many Kikuyu men were uninterested in their partners' pleasure or lack of it.

It is important, however, that this point should not be over-emphasized. Mathare women often said that they enjoyed sex for its own sake and were frequently willing to bend a rule in order to let a penurious customer stay the night if he was good in bed; similarly they would get rid of a customer whose performance was less than satisfactory. As one woman remarked to me, 'I don't like overripe bananas!' But it was clear that as a rule Kikuyu men did not expend much effort to please their partners. Sophisticated women who had had sexual intercourse with Europeans often commented wistfully that Europeans took more time and touched and caressed them more, enabling them to experience pleasure even if they were circumcised. One witty young woman, with an excellent command of English vernacular, caustically described the average Kikuyu man's performance in bed as 'pump and shoot, roll over and go to sleep'.

Kikuyu preliminaries to the sex act are revealing and tell us something about expected male/female attitudes to sex. To quote one informant (not a Mathare free woman, but a married man):

'In the old days if a man wanted to have sex with a woman he approached her and said in Kikuyu "I want". If the girl was interested she replied "What do you want?" So it goes with the girl making complications to the man to make him work harder. So it goes on like that until the man realizes that she is interested only she will not admit it. Now the man turns it into a rape. The woman doesn't fight back, she only pretends to until the man penetrates her. And so it goes till it is finished.'

The coy and reluctant girl, the act of penetration compared to a rape, convey a sense of male power and physical strength rather than tenderness and gentle wooing. Other remarks by Mathare women confirm this. 'Sex is exhausting work. One doesn't have time to talk', said one woman. Another woman, commenting on the fact that a man had had sex with her and had not paid, said 'He crushed my chest for nothing', an image which calls up a vivid picture of violent physical activity. One would not expect men to woo women whom they were paying for sex in the same way that they would wives and girlfriends. But even married women or women with lovers made similar disparaging remarks which create a picture of sexual intercourse as athletic rather than sensual.

LOW-INCOME MATHARE WOMEN AND 'SEX FOR SALE'

Before going on to talk about the connections between Kikuyu views of sexuality and commercialized sex, it is necessary to say something about the history of commercialized sex in Kenya, its organization in Mathare Valley, and the way it is viewed.

In the precolonial era, the Kikuyu were a widely scattered horticultural people who were patrilineal and patrilocal. Girls married soon after puberty, divorce was almost unknown, and widows of child-bearing age remarried at the death of the husband. It was a subsistence horticultural economy where most production was for use, though there was barter in local surpluses of vegetable produce, salt, iron, and cattle. It is highly unlikely that there existed any institutionalized form of commercial sex. However, it was not long after the arrival of the Europeans and the beginning of the building of the railway in Kenya that many Kikuyu women began to take the opportunities offered for freedom from marriage by selling sex to the workers on the railway or the migrants to the city (Bujra 1982; Whyte 1980). The number of women practising commercialized sex has increased over the years in most urban areas. It is an unsubstantiated perception by many observers that a preponderance of these come from the Kikuyu–Meru–Embu–Kamba groups. Even in Luo areas and on the coast, a large number of women working in bars for this purpose would seem to be Kikuyu or Kikuyu-related.

In Mathare the commercialized sexual relationships are casual and generally carried on in connection with each woman's private business of retailing the local maize-millet beer. Women sell this beer in their own rooms, and similarly any sexual relationships they have are started by their choice and carried out on their home ground. There is no pimp or madam, familiar figures in the context of commercial sex in so many countries.

Mathare women have a variety of sexual relationships with men that vary in duration and in the directness with which payment exchanges hands; they form a continuum from something called 'Quick Service' (a twenty-minute stint) to a form of 'Town Marriage' that could last for years. Except for Quick Service, most of the short-term relationships include some form of domestic service, such as allowing the man to wash and preparing drink or food for him. Luis Whyte, in her historical analysis of commercialized sex in Nairobi, has shown how in the early days of Nairobi, when housing was in very short supply, spending the night with a *malaya*[4] was one way that very poorly housed urban migrants obtained domestic service as well as sex. For many it was the only way to spend a night in a real bed (Whyte 1980).

Attitudes to this type of sex and the women who make it available are difficult to determine. Men, and Kikuyu society at large, certainly view these women as bad, corrupt, dangerous, and beguiling creatures who would suck migrants dry of money, life substance, and desire to go home. Letters to the newspapers and images in locally produced novels portray urban women as either the good mother or the urban whore (Wachtel 1979). Clergymen and politicians consistently rant against the evil and corrupting influences of such women. Though there is no law against prostitution in Nairobi, the police carry out sweeps in low-income areas where they pick up women with no visible means of support (that is, a husband or a job). The courts co-operate by sending them back to their place of origin in the rural areas (a futile action, since the women merely climb on the first bus back to town). These sweeps, ostensibly to clear the streets of vagrants, are in part directed at 'prostitutes' in order to rid the city of Nairobi of their immoral activities.

The ironic thing is, of course, that many men would seem to have very ambivalent attitudes to women who are free with their sexual favours. The very men who write the letters to the newspapers, complain to their MPs, and condone police raids which limit the freedom of movement of women who practise commercialized sex, are often those who come to Mathare to seek female companionship and sex. Men employed in Nairobi but whose wives stay behind in the rural areas visit Mathare Valley and enjoy short-term commercial relationships and longer-term friendships or conjugal relationships with women there. The very police who arrest them are often their customers, friends, or lovers. Such men obviously care and express admiration for the women they know, and sometimes even for the whole category of Mathare free women, making such comments as 'they work hard to educate their children' or 'they have many troubles'. In the general climate of condemnation of women who are not married and who profit from temporary sexual liaisons with men, some men would seem to have a more understanding and non-judgemental attitude to the matter.

It is impossible to know how the majority of Kikuyu married women perceive and define the sexually free women of Mathare and their commercialized sexual relationships. It would be entirely understandable if many, especially those left alone in the rural areas by migrant husbands, were resentful and morally indignant. After all, it is their husbands who are spending their money on such women in towns, money which would otherwise be expected to come to their family. This would explain the commonly expressed image of such women as rapacious blood-suckers who squeeze men dry of all they have before they cast them aside. Men, in this stereotype, are seen as helpless victims of these women's charms who are almost bewitched into forgetting their homes and families. How widespread this image is and how many married women really agree with it cannot be known. Certainly the married women in Mathare whom I knew expressed great sympathy for women who sold sex. They said that it was one of the things women were frequently forced to do in order to survive. Perhaps living in close proximity with free women, married women had come to understand and empathize with their situation. Perhaps it is a function of shared poverty. Certainly I found middle-class and élite urban women more likely to moralize and be judgemental about *malaya* than those living in squatter settlements.

Mathare unmarried women themselves quite naturally had an instrumental and pragmatic definition of commercialized sex. Although not every woman brewing and selling beer in Mathare also sold sex, very few free women condemned it and most put a positive construction on it. Of a survey population of Mathare beer sellers, only 11 per cent saw anything wrong with commercialized sex or the women who sold sex (*malaya*), and these thought that such casual sexual relations spread disease or were against the teachings of the Christian Churches. The other 89 per cent of the women in the survey felt either that commercialized sex was neutral (e.g. a business, like any other, or a short-term form of conjugal relationship in which women exchanged sex for money instead of for food and rent as married women did) or else gave it positive characteristics (e.g. it gave women the money to care for their children or aged parents, or it prevented urban men from suffering sexual frustration which would inevitably lead to their running wild and raping innocent women). The 16 per cent who considered commercialized sex as just another form of male–female dependency were interesting, since they reflect a more instrumental view of marriage and the role of sex within a marriage (i.e. that sex is a service a wife gives to the husband in exchange for his supporting her and the children of the union). At this point, without more widely based research, it is impossible to say how common is this point of view on sex and marriage. Mathare women, coming as they do from broken marriages or being barred from marriage through having borne a child out of wedlock, might be expected to have a more than normally jaundiced attitude to such things as sex and marriage.

It is a frequently expressed opinion in western countries that women who are involved in commercialized sex are frigid. This was not the case in Mathare. Women frequently discussed their previous night's clients from the point of view of their sexual prowess or techniques. As I have said before, they would be willing to let a promising customer stay longer than he had paid for, or get rid of a sexually inept one before his time was up. Some claimed to prefer western men, not just because they paid better, but because they took more care about their partners' feelings and enjoyment.

Sex for sale and Kikuyu concepts of sexuality

What does an examination of the 'sex for sale' syndrome tell us about the larger area of Kikuyu beliefs about sexuality?

A search through the literature yields almost nothing about concepts of sexuality in relation to commercialized sexual relationships. Katherine Arnold (1977, 1978) has examined commercialized sex in a Peruvian brothel to gain a greater understanding of images of masculinity and femininity. The situation is not exactly parallel to that in Mathare, since in Peru the commercialized sex act is not privatized and individualized as it is in the Kenyan situation described above. In Peru, women operate out of organized brothels, which men, even those with relatively low incomes, attend, selecting their partners in rooms loud with music. The women dress in smart, provocative dresses and dance with the customers in an uninhibited fashion designed to stimulate their passions. Much drink is consumed by men and women. Men frequent brothels for both sexual release and also to experience a wider range of sexual techniques, since these women are paid to adopt 'poses' (positions during the sex act) which respectable married women would not assume.

The search for sexual partners in Mathare seems very basic in comparison. Women do not dress in any special way, in fact quite the opposite. Most of them look like women who have had a long day of hard work brewing beer, doing housework, and caring for children, followed by a busy night serving customers. Cotton dresses and rubber sandals are the usual wear. Their behaviour is more bold and jolly than provocative in any obvious way. In fact those women who made a practice of unbuttoning their dresses or sitting on men's laps in an overt bid for seduction were frowned upon by other free women as silly or wanton. Music is rarely played and dancing non-existent. Some women drink as the evening progresses, but the majority feel the need to keep their wits about them and will only become drunk on evenings when they are not serving beer.

There are bars frequented by women who offer sex for sale all over Kenya where the women (still operating independently, as a rule) dress prettily and dance provocatively. However, these are a more recent phenomenon and cater to the wealthier men of the African or European élite. It is my impression that the majority of Kikuyu men who seek women to purchase sexual services do so in circumstances close to those described in Mathare Valley.

Kikuyu men do not seem to ask for anything elaborate or special in the form of sexual services when they pay for sex.

Kikuyu women who offer sex for sale are not offering the exotic or the unusual: they are providing an outlet for sexual release. It is conceivable that they are also offering men sexual variety in a simple, easily obtainable fashion. Such women do, however, take more initiative in beginning the relationship than so-called 'respectable' women would, but their initiatives would seem restrained compared to those of the Peruvian prostitutes. Mathare women indulge in sly innuendo and sexual joking as well as touching men in ways which make their intention obvious.

Arnold sees the image of women in Peru as split between the respectable married woman and the woman who sells sex; this dichotomy she characterizes as that of the virgin and the whore (see *Table 8.1*).

Table 8.1   *The Peruvian image of women*

virgin/asexual	*whore/sexual*
domestic	extra-domestic
familiar	exotic
safe	dangerous
manso	*macho*
feminine	masculine
asexual	sexual

Women who sell sex in Peru are seen in opposition to married women because they take the sexual initiative, are sexually active, are economically independent and 'masculine' in the eyes of the society. They are not under the control of male relatives or husbands, so that sex with such a woman diminishes no man's honour and increases no man's machismo.

This dichotomy, according to Arnold, serves in some way to mediate the tension caused by concepts of masculinity and femininity which are simplistic and distort reality: 'Where there exist models of male and female that attempt to ignore or transcend reality (in this case the true complexity of men and women, masculinity and femininity) there is inevitably, a great deal of tension' (1977: 190).

If one attempts to compare stereotypes of wives and free women expressed in the Kikuyu material, a much less clear opposition emerges. It is even more problematic if one tries to create

Table 8.2   *Kikuyu males' views of married women and* malaya

wives	malaya
faithful/potentially unfaithful	unfaithful
provide children for patrilineage	children conceived stay with mother
safe	dangerous
provide sexual outlet	provide sexual outlet and variety
provide domestic services	sometimes provide domestic services
need long-term support	need short-term payment in cash
basic sex	basic sex
good	bad(?)
sexual	sexual
feminine	feminine
do not take sexual initiative	take sexual initiative

this opposition from the point of view of men and women (or at least Mathare free women). From the data available, the Kikuyu male conception of married women and *malaya* might look as shown in *Table 8.2*.

The conceptions are polarized in some respects, but by no means to the extent shown in Arnold's model. The lack of polarization is even more evident when the same dichotomy is constructed from the views of Mathare women (see *Table 8.3*).

In comparing the two dichotomies, it can quickly be seen that Kikuyu men do not split the image of women so clearly between sexually pure and impure as do the Peruvians. The differences which are singled out are structural (only one category produces children for the patrilineage), economic (mode of payment), and moral (one is good and safe, the other bad and dangerous) rather than sexual. In this male view the one significant difference in sexuality between wives and free women is in the area of taking the sexual initiative.

Mathare women deny even this difference. This would seem to contradict the observable facts of male–female interaction in Mathare, but the rationalization is very interesting. Mathare free women view men as the sexual aggressors. They 'corrupt women with money'. Because they come to Mathare and offer money to poor women for sex (poor women who cannot by implication refuse it) *they* are the *malaya*, not the women. Presenting a poor person with an 'offer they cannot refuse' is a form of blackmail,

Table 8.3 *Mathare free women's views of married women and* malaya

wives	malaya
provide sexual services to one man	provide sexual services to many men
sexual	sexual
need sex	need sex
enjoy sex	enjoy sex sometimes
provide domestic services	sometimes provide domestic services
raise children (majority of responsibility)	raise children alone
produce children for husbands' patrilineage	produce children for themselves
faithful to one man as long as he fulfils responsibilities to the family	not faithful because men do not fulfil responsibility to the family
married	not married
good, kind, generous	good, kind, generous
do not take sexual initiative	do not take sexual initiative
like sexual variety but do not express it	like sexual variety and get it
do not control own sexuality	control own sexuality

so Mathare free women view themselves as technically forced into selling sex for money and claim they cannot really have taken the sexual initiative. True they flirt with their customers and may in the last analysis initiate the sexual liaison (they also claim that in comparison with wives, they have more control over their own sexuality), so in one sense they can be seen to be sexually aggressive. But it is men, by the act of coming to Mathare and acting in a manner which is described locally as 'hunting' (the equivalent to the English phrase 'on the prowl'), who take the sexual initiative in the first place. In this way free women of Mathare perhaps try to absolve themselves of the guilt of stealing other women's men.

One important aspect of sexuality which Mathare women see as different between wives and free women is the control of sexuality. Quite correctly, free women perceive and even value the greater control they have over their bodies. This is of course helped by the circumstances in which they practise commercialized sex. They own their own rooms, entertain their customers there, owe allegiance to no pimp, and can call on the assistance of the community to deal with unpleasant or difficult customers. When men refuse to go, threaten physical violence, or refuse to pay, women can call upon their neighbours for immediate help.

A question which remains unanswerable at the present time is the extent to which married Kikuyu women's characterization of wives and *malaya* would agree with that of Kikuyu men or of Mathare free women. It is my tentative assumption that it would share elements of both. A possible model of married women's views is shown in *Table 8.4*.

The three dichotomies constructed in *Tables 8.2, 8.3,* and *8.4* (though the last one is largely hypothetical) show that the separation between wife and *malaya* does not occur as strongly as in the Peruvian material. The sources of the Peruvian association of strong sexuality with bad women are undoubtedly complex but one of the most important influences would be 400 years of Catholicism. The Judaeo-Christian tradition has always distinguished between those women meant for domestic and procreative purposes and those intended for pleasure. This would appear to some observers to have its origins in the conflict between male sexuality and male patriarchy. Men are thus seen to be torn between their desire for control of women's sexuality (couched in terms of morality) and their desire for pleasure. Dividing pure wives from bad prostitutes resolves this dilemma between men's patriarchal need for female monogamy, and the

Table 8.4   *Married women's views of married women and* malaya

wives	malaya
faithful	unfaithful
sexual	sexual
need sex	need sex
basic sex	basic sex
feminine	feminine
do not take sexual initiative	take sexual initiative
provide domestic services	provide some domestic services
raise children for husbands' patrilineage	raise children for themselves
take major responsibility for raising children	take sole responsibility for raising children
bridewealth has been paid	no bridewealth paid
home creators	home wreckers
good	bad

'latent polygyny in which men take pride' (Sullerot 1971: 38). One way to solve men's need for a variety of sexual partners would be to permit all adults sexual freedom, but this would challenge the patriarchal tradition. In other words, the Christian Churches find it easier to recognize the institution of commercialized sex for some women than sexual freedom for all women. 'Prostitutes' are a pool of women common to all men. As individuals they are not restricted to one man, but are available to every man. The existence of this category of sexually available and socially uncontrolled women allows men to indulge the demands of their sexuality without losing control of the sexuality of their wives, daughters, and sisters.

Kikuyu, in common with many non-European peoples, could be seen to have devised another solution to the conflicting demands of male sexual 'needs' and patriarchy. Polygyny means that many (though not all) men can have a variety of sexual partners and a regular supply of sex even though individual wives may be away from home, pregnant, or sexually unavailable because of post-partum taboos. Yet simultaneously polygyny enshrines the firm principle of female monogamy. While in Kenya polygyny amongst Kikuyu would seem to be on the decline, other groups are still marrying polygynously. Parkin (1978) has described how polygynously married Luo men keep one wife in the rural area to manage the farm and one in town to maintain their domestic and sexual comfort. It is still a useful institution in the urban, industrialized sector.

Henriques (1962) recognizes the possible connection between polygyny and the absence of institutionalized commercialized sex in his world history of prostitution. Writing on the relative absence of prostitution in so-called 'primitive' societies, he rejects ideas of early sexologists such as the innate chastity of primitive peoples, or their deficient sex drive. He hypothesizes that prostitution does not exist in societies where polygyny existed. Yet the most cursory overview of the African ethnographic record will show that no simple equation exists between polygyny and absence of prostitution. Prostitution existed in a number of preindustrial African states which also had polygyny: Ashanti, Nupe, Hausa, Bunyoro, Haya. To my knowledge, there was no form of commercialized sex in the acephelous societies of Africa. Obviously free commercial sex is associated with social stratification, personal mobility, the weakening of the minimal lineage (a localized subunit of a lineage), and heterogeneous, densely populated settlements. Under these circumstances there are unattached men (soldiers, travellers, traders) who desire access to unattached women. Increased social stratification and personal mobility may mean that there are categories of women free to provide those services, more open to exploitation by others, or anxious to sell services they can provide in the market-place.

However, this African form of commercialized sex existing in preindustrial states does not seem to be associated with the nega-tive stereotypes common in Europe. Where good ethnographic data exist, it is noticeable that the perceived division between wife and free woman is very weak indeed. Indeed, among the Nupe it is wives who engage in commercialized sex while on long-distance trading journeys (Nadel 1942). Among the Hausa, Cohen describes a situation where women alternate between the roles of wife and free woman, trading off a life of security and seclusion for one of independence and relative insecurity (1969). Women from Haya (a small intralacustrine Bantu kingdom in Tanzania) travelled far afield in early colonial times to urban areas selling sex with the permission of their husbands, sending money and any children they might bear home to their families, throughout their working career (Swantz 1985).

What accounts for this relative lack of distinction between married women and free women? In polygynous, patrilineal societies (either preindustrial states, or acephelous societies gradually being absorbed into modern states) women who pro-vide sexual services are regarded as a logical extension of the wife. They are in most ways exactly like women who are wives, except for the obvious dyadic roles they play with the men who are their partners (who are customers and not husbands). Perhaps it would not be too far-fetched to hypothesize that African men view such women as temporary wives existing on the fringes of marriage. It has frequently been observed that in Africa the relationship between husband and wife is a fairly instrumental contract with the close involvement of the two families. It displays few of the mystical, romantic, 'soul mates till death do them part' elements which European monogamous marriage has developed over the last few hundred years. The only way in which wives and free women differ significantly is that one produces children for her partner's patrilineage and the other produces children for herself. This then may be the critical element which accounts for the moral opprobrium which is levelled at women who engage in sex for sale; it is not the fact that they are sexual creatures.

Christian philosophy has always made a separation between body and spirit: things of the body (sexuality?) are valued less than things of the spirit. As Figes (1970) has made clear, the sexuality of women has been loathed and feared since the inception of the Judaic tradition. This fear of women's unbridled sexuality has continued through the Christian era and permeated the work of philosophers and psychologists until the twentieth century. While it is true that women's sexuality is feared because it threatens men's total dominance of women, I would maintain that it is also feared because for women it is more difficult to ignore the reality of the flesh. Men can copulate, then forget this yielding to the demands of the flesh. Women menstruate, they become pregnant, they give birth and lactate. So to perpetuate, as far as possible, the conception of the body which associates it with sin, women must be discouraged from being sexual. Good women are passive, asexual, and do not enjoy sex. Bad women are aggressive and sexual. These few 'bad' women are a necessary evil which allows men to satisfy the cravings of the flesh, while maintaining the purity of their wives. Christian men have always salved their consciences after their sexual indulgences with prayers and invective against 'bad women'.

In Africa, this division of the flesh and the spirit into immoral and moral does not seem to exist. In pre-Christian philosophy: 'Man's power is both physical and mental, and the coordination of the two makes him a full man' (Parrinder 1969: 28). According to Parrinder, African philosophy sees a unity and continuity of spirituality from the lowest form of life to the highest. This would imply that African world views would recognize a holistic, integrated human being, made up of body and soul, neither of which is more holy or moral than the other. A healthy human being gives full recognition to both aspects of the self. Allied to this is a concept of ethics which 'receive sanction from a consideration of whether actions help or harm human power' (Parrinder 1969: 29). Humans are members of a community and ethics are defined in social terms. Even the human relationship to the supernatural seems to be that of a series of ongoing obligations (sacrifices for example) performed to the gods or the ancestors in exchange for help or services rendered in time of trouble.

Thus it is possible to view the judgement of immorality levelled against free women in a different way from that in a Judaeo-Christian culture. Free women are not immoral because they have a strong sex drive, or enjoy sex, or like a variety of sexual partners. They are immoral because they have separated sex from procreation for the patrilineage. Uncontrolled sexuality is not a sin because of its venality or its essentially nasty character, but because it denies the lineage its future generations. Virginity before and chastity during marriage are emphasized (but not over-emphasized as is the case in many societies where women's chastity is instrumental in creating male honour) not for some abstract principle of right and wrong, but for the entirely practical principle that women should direct their sexuality in to their most important social role, that of reproduction.[5]

In Kenya of the 1980s Kikuyu are nominally Christian (though some are Muslim) and many are devout adherents of strict evangelical sects. Inevitably indigenous concepts of morality and sexuality must have been affected by contact with outside ideas as well as recent, internal socio-economic changes. The effects of more than sixty years of Church activity must be recognized in any analysis of Kikuyu views in this area. However, it is clearly impossible at this juncture to differentiate neatly between those elements of current thinking which derive from local ideas and those which have their origin in Christian teachings.

Pre-Christian Kikuyu views of sex and sexuality were largely consistent with the constructs developed above. To a great degree, present-day Kikuyu views still are, despite more than sixty years of Euro-Christian teaching. A strong sex drive and a need for sex were, and still are, recognized as part of every healthy person from an early age. Young Kikuyu boys and girls used to be allowed a certain freedom (well supervised) to experiment sexually, short of full penetration (thus avoiding possible pregnancy). Today, it is wryly recognized that boys and girls will inevitably continue to experiment 'in the bushes' on the way to and from school but the fact that the experimentation is now totally un-supervised is regretted. In earlier times, a pre-marital pregnancy (as long as the girl was circumcised) resulted in a fine for the boy responsible and pressure on the couple to marry (hardly very severe punishment by cross-cultural standards). Today the same thing happens, but if the boy does not marry the girl, she is likely to suffer from stigma through having a child out of wedlock (perhaps a result of Christian teachings?). Within marriage a woman's status and importance were and still are created by her bearing sons and daughters for the patrilineage so that, if she is childless, the marriage will probably not last. Women are recognized as full sexual beings but their rights to indulge their sexual natures must take second place to the control of the patrilineage, even perhaps to the extent of their having their clitorises excised in order to limit their sexual enjoyment. Men, on the other hand, have both the need for and the right to a number of sexual partners. In the preindustrial situation, they obtained these via polygynous marriage. Today, a man may do this by a series of temporary liaisons with free women in town. Sometimes, men seek the company of these women and in many cases live with them for years. None the less, such women do pose a threat to the normative Kikuyu marriage where women reproduce the lineage, and so they must be labelled as 'bad'. This may have more to do with the fact that they control their own sexuality and children (through their independent economic status) than that they are active sexual beings.

In conclusion, it can be seen that examining local perceptions of the roles of Kikuyu wives and *malaya* in urban Nairobi has given us insights into the way the Kikuyu world view defines sexuality and sex. Questions have been raised on the relationship between polygyny and the perception of commercialized sex, and the role and purpose of sexuality in a patrilineal system, as well as on the perceptions of sex and sexuality in African religious philosophies. Firm conclusions must await further data.

Notes

1 'Selling one's kiosk' is a local expression (translated roughly from Swahili) used by women to denote selling sexual services. A kiosk is a small place of business – usually a small shop. It is interesting because it indicates the way in which Mathare women viewed these transactions as purely business.

2 The data on which this chapter is based were collected between 1971 and 1974 in Nairobi. Research was conducted in Mathare Valley, a large squatter community in the north-west sector of the city. There I conducted general participant observation on community life and the operation of petty commodity production, but specific interviews were carried out on female heads of household who brewed beer and sold their sexual services to provide entertainment for the many men living in Nairobi without their families. Life histories and intensive interviews on a variety of subjects were collected from nearly 120 women and a village-wide survey was held at the end of the research period. In the course of these two periods of research I was greatly assisted by Veronica Njoroge and David Irungu, without whose help the results would have been infinitely poorer.

3 In this paper I will not use the common English word for women who practise commercialized sex, 'prostitute'. While I realize that the circumlocutions I will use (e.g. 'offering sex for sale' or 'practising commercialized sex') are unwieldly, I prefer them to 'prostitute', which I feel is a culturally specific word with connotations which I wish to avoid.

4 The Kikuyu practise the form of female circumcision called clitoridectomy. It was an extremely important rallying point for early Kikuyu opposition to European domination and was the cause of the so-called independent schools of the pre-war years (see Kenyatta 1962). Clitoridectomy became a very emotion-laden issue because it was felt (and still is felt by many) that it established a female's status as an adult woman ready for sex and marriage. Establishing independent schools for girls was one way of ensuring that Kikuyu girls could be circumcised. They were forbidden to be circumcised in the Christian-run schools. Whether a Kikuyu woman is circumcised or not is a function of her age, her education, class, religion, and birthplace. Older women will probably all be circumcised. Women from lower socio-economic categories without much education are more likely to be circumcised than women from families of higher education and economic status. Women from certain Christian sects are not circumcised because of religious prohibitions. Rural women are more likely to be circumcised than urban. It is difficult to obtain good data on this subject, but some sources suggest that nowadays only one-third of Kikuyu girls are circumcised (WIN News 1984).

4 This is the Swahili word for a woman who has sex for sale. There was, to my knowledge, no word in Kikuyu for a woman who practises this activity. I do not like to use the nearest English equivalent, 'prostitute', because of its inappropriate, culturally specific connotations.

5 For this thesis to be consistent, it would have to be the case that in matrilineal systems there was less concern for a woman's engaging in commercialized sex. In such a system she would be producing children for the matrilineage. In any case, the control of the husband over his wife is limited by the authority of the matrilineage (Schneider and Gough 1974: 17). A careful search of the ethnographic literature would

be necessary to determine this. The above-mentioned symposium does not touch upon the subject. Another test for consistency would be if men had no misgivings about barren women selling sex free of the bonds of marriage. In the case of a barren woman, who can produce children for no one, her operating outside marriage does not threaten the reproduction of the patrilineage. However, she still poses a threat to the current structure of marriage by providing a model of an independent, unattached woman controlling her own economic and sexual life. My data cannot provide confirmation of this point.

References

Arnold, K. (1977) Introduction of Poses to a Peruvian Brothel. In J. Blacking (ed.) *The Anthropology of the Body*. London: Academic Press.
—— (1978) The Whore in Peru. In S. Lipshitz (ed.) *Tearing the Veil*. London: Routledge & Kegan Paul.
Bujra, J. (1982) Women Entrepreneurs of Early Nairobi. In C. Sumner (ed.) *Crime, Justice and Underdevelopment*. London: Heinemann.
Caplan, P. (1976) Boys' Circumcision and Girls' Puberty Rites on Mafia Island. *Africa* 46: 215.
Cohen, A. (1969) *Custom and Politics in Urban Africa*. London: Routledge & Kegan Paul.
Figes, E. (1970) *Patriarchal Attitudes: Women in Society*. London: Faber & Faber.
Henriques, F. (1962) *Prostitution and Society*. New York: MacGibbon & Kee.
Kenyatta, J. (1962) *Facing Mount Kenya*. New York: Vintage Books.
Leakey, L. (1977) *Southern Kikuyu Before 1903. Vol. II*. London: Academic Press.
Mbiti, J. (1969) *Concepts of God in Africa*. London: SPCK.
Nadel, S. F. (1942) *Black Byzantium*. London: Oxford University Press.
Obbo, C. (1980) *African Women: Their Struggle for Economic Independence*. London: Zed Press.
Parkin, D. (1978) *The Cultural Definition of Political Response*. London: Academic Press.
Parrinder, G. (1969) *Religion in Africa*. London: Pall Mall Press.
Richards, A. (1982) *Chisungu*. London: Tavistock Press.
Schneider, D. and Gough, K. (1974) *Matrilineal Kinship*. Berkeley, Calif.: University of California Press.
Sullerot, E. (1971) *Women, Society and Change*. London: Weidenfeld & Nicolson.
Swantz, M.-L. (1985) *Women in Development: A Creative Role Denied*. London: Hurst.
Wachtel, E. (1979) The Mother and the Whore. Institute of Development Studies, Nairobi, Working Paper 45.
Whyte, L. (1980) Women's Domestic Labour in Colonial Kenya: Prostitution in Kenya, 1905–1950. African Studies Centre, Boston University, Paper 30.
Women's International Network News (1984) Genital and Sexual Mutilation of Females 10–14 February.

9   Rank, gender, and homosexuality: Mombasa as a key to understanding sexual options

Gill Shepherd

Introduction

In presenting the material which follows on male and female homosexuality among the Swahili Muslims of Mombasa, I have two aims.[1] Firstly, the interplay between heterosexual gender roles and homosexuality, in a society with marked sexual segregation in most contexts, illuminates the local meaning of sexuality and gender. Most of the paper is concerned with this. However, the conclusions reached are instructive, I hope, for a sharper theoretical understanding of male and female homosexuality in other societies.

There has been too much of 'the biological and the psychological' (Ashworth and Walker 1972: 147) in discussions of male and female homosexuality.[2] Explanation has tended to focus on the individual and on precipitating factors within the family, to the exclusion of asking why particular societies allow homosexuality to occur without strong negative sanction, or indeed why it is that homosexuality is totally unknown in some cultures, and common in others. It seems that sociologists have, by and large, been the prisoners of their own societies' attitudes to homosexuality instead of making these very attitudes the objects of investigation. What I hope to show is that homosexuality may be a rational decision, bringing fuller participation in and better benefits from the society of which the homosexual is a member.

Mombasa: the social context

There are roughly 50,000 Swahili – mixed blood Arab-Africans – in Mombasa, of whom I estimate perhaps 5,000 are homosexual. It is important to remember that, because of the way in which men and women shift over a lifetime between homosexuality and heterosexuality, a still higher percentage has lived or will live homosexually at some time. Boys may first have homosexual experiences at puberty or thereabouts; girls must have been married before any adult activities, including choice of sexual partner, are allowed them and so lesbians are all married, divorced, or widowed women. It is thus rare to find very young lesbians, in the way very young homosexuals exist.

Lesbians and homosexuals are open about their behaviour. There are well-established rules for fitting them into everyday life and nobody would dream of suggesting that their sexual choices had any effect on their work capabilities, reliability, or religious piety. However, close kin are saddened by a boy's homosexuality, since it reduces his later marriage chances, and some men are highly reluctant to visit lesbian kin or affines, so it would over-simplify the picture to pretend that such choices are entirely unproblematic.

The contribution of Islam to the institutionalization of homosexuality in Mombasa is examined later. It certainly *is* a factor, for non-Muslim Africans living nearby are scarcely involved; yet explanation cannot rest there, for a glance through the literature on the Middle East reveals that attitudes to homosexuality vary from acceptance to horror.

Mombasa, for most of its history, was a port existing for the trading of African raw materials (ivory, gum copal, and for a while grain) against imports of cloth, beads, wire, and so on. Omani Arabs competed with the Portuguese for the town, and at the beginning of the twentieth century it became a part of the possessions of the Omani sultan of Zanzibar, under British indirect rule. The British found a cosmopolitan society with an élite of leisured Arab landowners and Arab and Indian entrepreneurs, a large middle and lower-middle class of Swahili and substantial numbers of slaves drawn from all over East Africa, who worked at a wide range of urban and rural tasks.

The British brought great changes to Mombasa. Slavery was abolished in 1907 and the Arab and Swahili population, the majority group in the town until 1897 (Topan 1972: 36–7), gradually came to be dominated numerically by immigrants from surrounding coast tribes and from further inland. Before the abolition of slavery and Mombasa's economic expansion, the town was almost 100 per cent Muslim. Pagan slaves and wives invariably converted and the heterogeneous origins of the town's inhabitants were smoothed, through incorporation into Islam, into a single hierarchy where social position was plotted on the basis of a combination of three factors: strength of claim to Swahili-Arab ancestry, wealth, and Muslim piety. After the establishment of colonial rule, however, new immigrants were far less dependent on acceptability to Muslims and were no longer obliged to take much notice of Islam and its norms. By the 1960s, non-Muslims were in the majority.

Nevertheless, Mombasa old town and the adjacent older suburbs are still almost entirely Muslim today. Most of the mosques are here and, whatever goes on in the outer suburbs, it is here that Arab standards are still admired and an Islamic lifestyle still aimed at. Men frequent the streets with their mosques, coffee-sellers, and stone benches for open-air discussions. Women stay indoors or, if they must go out, put on their black *buibui* veils and slip through back alleyways to their destinations.

MALE AND FEMALE GENDER ROLES

Islam stresses several virtues important for both sexes which the Swahili endorse: assiduity in religious devotion, generosity to the poor, hospitality. Good men and women should both show these virtues.

The Muslim attitude to sexual intercourse is also important for what follows here. While sex is obviously concerned with pro-creation – 'women are your tillage', says the Koran (Surah II: 223) – Islam also seems to accept that sexual intercourse is a pleasure and should be enjoyed as such (Tanner 1962: 73). It is explicitly present in the Muslim paradise and the Christian dichotomy between earthly bodily pleasures and heavenly spiritual ones is not repeated in Islam. Thus sexual skilfulness is taught to Muslim girls, through the medium of dances, as a preparation for marriage quite as important as domestic skills.

Sex and romantic love in Mombasa have something of the troubadour tradition about them. Men's and women's songs commemorate the bliss and agony of love, especially illicit love, yet hold up divinely happy permanent unions as the ideal. In real life there is frequently much dissatisfaction with marriage partners and one in two marriages end in divorce (Strobel 1975: 87–8); nevertheless, the quest for the perfect partner continues through one marriage after another (Tanner 1962: 70). A respectable adult is a married adult and most men and women continue to contract marriages until well into middle age if they can.

The attributes of women

Sexually, Swahili women are assumed by men to fit the classic Islamic picture: they are thought to be sexually enthusiastic and sexually irresponsible, given the opportunity. Men fear the power of women to pollute, particularly through their menstrual blood. They are kept out of all mosques except those with a women's section because menstrual blood pollutes[3] and men have no certain way of avoiding this pollution otherwise. A man who has made his ritual ablutions and is on the way to prayer may not even shake hands with a woman below the age of the menopause, unless she is his mother or actual sister (and clearly ruled out, therefore, as a sexual partner) without losing *udhu*, purity.

Women are regarded as the dependants of men, whatever the actual situation. True womanliness involves accepting gracefully the Koranic statement of the matter: 'Men are in charge of women, because God has made the one of them to excel the other, and because men spend of their property (for women's support)' (Surah IV: 34). Obedience is honourable, freedoms come by permission, not by right. Modesty, gentleness, and quietness should spring from these perceptions, say men. Women, like their sexuality, must be confined and ordered by men for if this ordering is lost, ungodliness and corruption must follow.

The attributes of men

Complementarily, it is almost impossible to talk about the meaning of maleness, in Islam in general and in Mombasa in particular, without talking of women. An admirable man is a person who supports and therefore controls women and children. This control is at its strictest and most effective when exercised over the virginity of unmarried daughters, and is less effective at dealing with the faithfulness of wives.

In Mombasa, where the ambiguous Arab and African origins of the Swahili are ever-present in people's minds, the rule which insists on the marriage of a woman to her equal or superior tends to mean that men are seen as more 'Arab' and hence more Muslim than women. Their knowledge of Islam is likely to be better than that of women and these days the degree of western education (also higher among men) combines with it to produce an image of men as knowledgeable and equipped to cope with the world beyond Mombasa.

Women expect support as a right and are unsympathetic to weak providers. 'Women go to men for money like men go to banks', they say, glossing over the work men may have done to get the money. Men who can afford it are eager for dependants, for both earthly prestige and heavenly reward (*thawabu*) accrue to providers. In the past slaves were part of the retinue. Today elderly kin, stepchildren, fostered or adopted children, unmarried teenagers, and servants, swell the households of the wealthy.

Finally, men are the creators of women's status, at certain key moments. A Swahili father is dutybound to arrange for his daughter the best match he can for her first marriage. Her status at that moment, with all its implications for the future marriages of her siblings and children, is a crystallization of his: ascribed to her, but achieved by him. Secondly, whatever the status of the girl's first husband, the marriage and its consummation are the only pathway to female adulthood.

Rights and duties of women

Women have the right of support for themselves and their children from husbands, or men of their natal family. In conforming to rules for the segregation of the sexes, women have the right to co-opt men's help for shopping, the running of errands, and as occasional escorts.

Married women may attend weddings and funerals in their entirety, go out visiting or to the cinema with other married women, and may smoke. But they must accept that the higher their status is, the less frequently should they exercise the right to go out: they should stay at home and let others come to visit them.

The list of a woman's duties is rather longer. She must permanently accept greater restriction than the Christian and pagan African women living in Mombasa do. She must run the household and know how to cook a wide range of different dishes. She must rear small children patiently and indulgently and ensure that bigger girls have learnt the complete range of wifely skills by the age of 15 or so, including receiving instruction in menstrual and sexual matters from another woman. She should set girls an example in her own regular prayers. She should behave cheerfully to her husband. A wife has no duty to contribute to the household's income, by sewing, weaving mats, or cooking food for sale, but if she does so she expects a more prominent role in household decision-making, and usually gets it.

As a woman gets older she may, through her personality, become significant as a mediator, a trusty neighbour, a rearer of children for others, or a helper of the poor or elderly. Husbands vary in their attitudes to these activities. Some appear to prefer a passive and childlike wife to the last; others approve their wives' qualities.

When men complain of their wives, it is of their laziness in household tasks and their extravagance with money. More quietly, because it shames them, they complain that they are sexually unreliable, and that women connive with women to hide extramarital adventures from their husbands.

Rights and duties of men

Men have a right to their wives' exclusive sexual services, their obedience, and their domestic labour. In return they have a duty to support wives and children – defined at its minimum as providing for their day-to-day needs (this very often includes a servant's wages) and new clothes annually at the end of Ramadan. They should sleep with their wives regularly and treat them fairly by local standards.

Women who complain of their husbands, complain of being left alone too much and of their suspicions that there is a secret second wife, or one in the offing. Sexual escapades as such are not a threat if they do not lead to a new marriage. They will manage cheerfully on very little money from a semi-employed husband, but make strenuous complaints if they suspect that money is being diverted elsewhere. A woman is much angered by a husband who, in a family quarrel, takes the side of his natal family against her.

Appearance and reality

There is a broader background to the unsatisfactoriness of the relationship between man and wife so often expressed, and it is this. Swahili Muslims, the men especially, are trying to work with an Arab-Islamic, patriarchal, patrilineal model of society which does not at all fit with the bilateral, matrifocal realities. In the area of gender roles the discrepancy is potentially conflict-ridden.

Women are veiled,[4] have limited legal autonomy, ought to inherit only half as much property as their brothers. Yet in fact, the high divorce rate and the rarely broken custom of leaving children with their mother when divorce or death removes the father, mean that in reality women are much more significant nodal points here than in the Middle East. In fact, Sharia law is modified in the woman's favour by Swahili customary law (Shepherd 1982).

Thus it does not fairly represent reality when men say, as they do in describing the part played by the woman in conception and pregnancy, 'She is the oven I cook my child in'. Indeed a woman to whom I quoted this laughed and replied, 'No, the woman is the machine that makes the baby: the man just pushes the button to start the machine'. Men and women can recite their patriline back for several generations but there is a far more ample knowledge of matrilateral kin collaterally.[5] For all this, most women *think* it is right to follow Islamic norms (even to their own detriment) because of the status that correct behaviour brings among the Swahili themselves, and because Islam and its symbols act as features distinguishing the Swahili from mere Africans. At the same time marriage is *actually* marked by the inability of men and the refusal of women to conform to the Middle Eastern pattern when it comes to rights and duties. A glance at economic realities for men and women shows why.

Swahili men have a picture of a golden age, which existed in reality a couple of generations ago for some, in which a gracious leisured life could be led on the basis of the ownership of slaves and land. If work must be done, it ought ideally to be clean, sedentary, and unhurried. Unfortunately, real life is different. Coast Muslims have been in steady economic decline since the abolition of slavery, mortgaging the land they had to Asians and often losing it. Most have been unable to take up work requiring a secular English education because of tardy provision of English-medium schools on the coast during the colonial period.

The families that did not lose all their land have experienced a great rise in the value of what they had left, as Mombasa's suburbs have grown. Many carved their land up into plots, built cheap housing, and now live partially or wholly from rents. Women as well as men have benefited from such practices, since they have been allowed more than their rights in Islamic law. Indeed, where a sibling group has had at its disposal houses in the Old Town *and* suburban land, there has been a tendency for sisters to be given the houses. This is because brothers assume that divorced sisters will need somewhere to live sooner or later. Women with houses try to pass them on to daughters not sons, successful prostitutes buy them (Bujra 1968: 82), lone women are occasionally given a room in a house free, in return for collecting the rent from the other tenants and keeping the house clean and in good order. As a result, I estimate that at least 50 per cent of Swahili women – older ones on the whole – live in their own houses, or are at least housed independently of provision by a husband. These women are divorced or their husbands are living uxorilocally, or with another wife. The pattern may have been even more common in the past. Bishop Steere noted in 1870 that on the Swahili coast, 'the bride's father or family should find her a house, so that the husband should go to live with her, and not she with him' (Strobel 1975: 92 n. 159).

Some men own houses and collect rents from them; some have had an education fitting them for work as clerks, teachers, or civil servants; some make a living as Koranic teachers and *kadhi* (Sharia judges) and some have blue-collar work in Kilindini docks. But very many Swahili are underemployed – doing a little trading, tailoring, or shopkeeping but scarcely making ends meet. Since Kenya's independence in 1964, Mombasa has gradually filled with educated, English-speaking, up-country Africans. The tourist industry employs only a minute fraction of the coastal dwellers themselves, and shop leases which become available when Asians leave the country very rarely go to locals. Unemployment among the young, in particular, is very high. Those who can leave Kenya for Saudi Arabia and the Gulf states do so by hook or by crook.[6]

In face of the difficulty men may have in supporting women, women themselves seem able to earn small sums of money in a great variety of ways, filling small gaps and catering to modest needs. Some sell cooked food from their kitchens or make cakes, coffee, or ice-lollies for their children to sell in the street. Some plait mats or embroider men's caps. Those with sewing machines can make a steady income which rises dramatically just before each big Muslim festival. Much more trading from the privacy of the home is done than the casual observer would realize. Cloth is bought by the bale and retailed in dress lengths; women's *leso* (the cloths worn by East African women over dresses) were smuggled from Zanzibar, Tanzania, and the Comoro Islands when they ran short locally in 1974 and were sold by women; goods stolen by men can at times be entirely disposed of in a morning by women, messengers running from back door to back door with the news that 'such-and-such is available at so-and-so's'. Small sums can be made teaching children the Koran, giving nubile girls menstrual and sexual instruction, as officials in spirit cults, or by membership of dance societies performing at weddings (Strobel 1975: 12ff; Topan 1972: passim).

While a Swahili woman with status to maintain would prefer to live from rents or home-based trading, poor women will turn their hand to almost anything. In this way a household may at times depend more on a wife's earnings than a husband's, if it is a poor one, for when men become unemployed they rarely turn to the small-scale money-making ventures of their wives, but wait for another job. Very few Swahili women are entirely self-supporting, but many can mitigate the hardships which inadequate support from men can bring, through their earnings and through the ownership of houses.

Finally, there are both male and female prostitutes in Mombasa among the Swahili. Those who are careful with the money they earn are likely to be able to build or buy a house and eventually rent out rooms in it. Prostitutes find some customers among wealthy locals, but Mombasa is also full of tourists, and sailors from ships berthed in Kilindini docks.

Only the very wealthiest men can order their households in imitation of well-to-do Arabs, refuse to allow their wives any economic activity beyond domestic labour, and confine them on the whole to the house. These wives, even if they are wealthy in their own right as many are, must allow their husbands to administer their affairs for them if they are to accept the role that goes with their status. But the lower the status of the partners to a marriage, the greater the incongruence between the notional ideal and the accepted reality of gender roles. No doubt this has been accentuated by the events of the last half-century, but it must always have been like that: Swahili bilateral kinship patterns indicate an adaptation both for the absorption of male Arab immigrants through marriage and for alternatives if such alliances fail. One result is that women are generally in a much superior position to that of Arab women in the Middle East, in real economic terms.

Friendship

This examination of heterosexual gender roles is not complete without some mention of non-sexual relationships between members of the same sex. Men and women dwell within very different subcultures which are rich and engrossing for their members and overlap so little that there is a tendency for relationships *between* the sexes to be one-dimensional. The most enduring dyad in Swahili society is the mother–daughter relationship. Much else hangs on it and the two may manage to spend a surprisingly large proportion of their lives together. It is imitated in the relationship between older married sister and younger unmarried sister. Brother–sister relations and mother–son relations come some way behind and the husband–wife relationship (except in the case of young, modern, educated couples) is not necessarily emotionally close at all.

In most of their leisure-time activities, as in weddings and funerals, men and women are apart and engaged in different events. Men join open-air informal discussion groups which talk about politics, or compose poetry, or study Islamic texts. Some join football supporters' clubs or *tarabu* (arabesque) music orchestras. Women are keen participants in dance societies, girls' initiation groups, welfare societies or (especially in the past) spirit-possession groups, all of which take place in other women's houses most of the time. They also visit or are visited with great frequency. These close friendships, some based on kinship, are of great importance to both sexes and heavily relied on for emotional support and small favours. Almost all comment, gossip, and analysis of the events of the day – the exchanges which go to make up the full flowering of the individual's sense of self in the world – take place with members of the same sex. And of course it is here that rivalry and competition for prestige establish the details of social rank.

Homosexuals and lesbians in Mombasa

HOMOSEXUALS

The Swahili for a male homosexual is *shoga*, a word also used between women to mean 'friend'. Homosexual relations in Mombasa are almost without exception between a younger, poorer partner and an older, richer one, whether their connection is for a brief act of prostitution or a more lengthy relationship. In the former case there are fixed rates of payment, and in the latter, presents and perhaps full financial support for a while. But financial considerations are always involved and it is generally only the person who is paid who is called *shoga*. The older partner may have been a *shoga* himself in youth, but is very likely to be successfully married to a woman as well as maintaining an interest in boys. Only if he is not married and has an apparently exclusive interest in homosexual contacts will he perhaps still be referred to as a *shoga*. The paid partner usually takes the passive role during intercourse, but I think it is true to say that his inferiority derives from the fact that he is paid to provide what is asked for, rather than from the role he adopts. Slaves in the past were reputedly paid at times to take an active role with their masters, but this did not turn the masters into inferiors.[7] The paying partner is usually known as the *basha* – the Pasha, the local term for the king in packs of playing cards.

Boys of 12 or so begin to find that they are being approached by men in the new contexts they increasingly enter at this age: clubs, sports activities, secondary schools, or special occasions such as the all-night picnics held in the country just before Ramadan begins.[8] Many boys have homosexual experiences at this stage. People say that they can predict who will be a homosexual, even with boys as young as 5 or 6 years old at times. They seem to base their prediction upon prettiness and family circumstances; boys reared in all-female households by a divorced mother and several

sisters are likely to become homosexuals, they say, and the prediction is self-fulfilling since these are the boys whom men are
certain to approach. 'If he's not a homosexual yet, he will be', say
women of teenage boys from such households.

Most boys move on out of this homosexual stage into heterosexual adventures before marriage. There are prostitutes if they
can afford them, and well-born young men are at times approached
discreetly by married women through female intermediaries,
and embark upon highly clandestine affairs. Such relationships
are much more romantic than engagement and marriage, and
incidentally constitute one of the few really friendly meeting-
points between men and women. Some young men continue to
be *shoga*, however. What starts as 'earning a shilling to go to the
cinema', as one informant put it, moves gradually into more
clearly defined prostitution. This is not an all-or-nothing decision.
There are men who prostitute themselves from time to time
when they are insolvent and perhaps have other jobs too. Such
men have usually had some liaisons with women. Others live
more permanently from prostitution – often those with few
alternative sources of income and none that would offer them, at
least for a few years, such a high standard of living.

Some young men never move beyond affairs with men they
have met socially, and friends of these men. Others begin to
frequent bars along the road that runs down to the docks and seek
out partners of other nationalities among the sailors and tourists.
While this latter alternative is well-paid, homosexuals appear to
prefer a situation where they are well enough known to remain at
home and be visited regularly by known patrons on a longer-term
basis. It is exceedingly rare for a patron's main residence to be
with a homosexual lover.

While they are still young, homosexuals bask in their glory,
boasting of their lovers and sometimes making a good deal of
money. A homosexual interviewed by Wilson in the 1950s
proudly showed him his Post Office Savings Bank book with a
credit balance of over £600 in it, a huge sum at the time. Another
owned at least £150-worth of jewellery given him by admirers
(Wilson 1957: 3). The financially astute are able to buy a house
and as they get older they can begin to live from renting rooms
out. Homosexuals spend much of their free time in one another's
company. Men like to relax together in the open air every day in

the late afternoon, but they meet in status-equal groups on these occasions. Homosexuals are thus not to be seen in the same *barazas* (informal discussion groups) as their patrons. They have their own *barazas* in certain well-defined corners of the town as do most other men, beggars and cripples included. In the evenings homosexuals may be found with patrons, most usually at home. Homosexuals are also regularly found in the company of women at various times of day and on certain formal occasions, notably weddings. How should we interpret this?

It is a common error to suppose that segregation rules in Muslim society apply equally to men and women. This is not so: women are kept away from many of the activities of men, but select categories of men may freely enter the company of particular women. The Koran's ruling on this is quite clear:

'tell the believing women . . . not to reveal their adornment except to their own husbands or fathers or husband's fathers, or their sons or their husband's sons, or their brothers or their brothers' sons or sisters' sons, or their women, or their slaves, or male attendants who lack vigour, or children who know nothing of women's nakedness.'   (Surah XXIV: 31)

In Mombasa the letter of the law is fairly closely adhered to. Nowadays there are servants instead of slaves (male, non-Muslim Africans, as a rule) and there may be the occasional elderly poverty-stricken non-kinsman who comes to the house for food and is fed in the kitchen by women, but otherwise only close adult kinsmen and children are to be found with women. Some men spend very little time at home but those (homosexual or not) who are only semi-employed or unemployed may spend several hours a day in the house, rather than drift around the town, and only leave the company of women for the reception room if a male guest appears.

Homosexuals are also found in houses where there are no discernible kinship links, though they tend to be introduced as 'siblings' or 'children'. Men in such households treat them like teenage children or wives' younger brothers – as inferiors, at any rate, boy–men whose status is too low to constitute a sexual threat. The use women make of them supports this interpretation. They are not given women's tasks to do, but are rather used as junior male kin are – for errands such as shopping, or taking a child that has hurt itself to the public clinic.

Thus the problem is not to explain why men allow homosexuals to mingle with their kinswomen, but rather to understand why homosexuals enjoy being with women. The answer is, I think, that they are of more account among women and are better treated. Homosexuals are low-ranking among men not only because they earn money in a way which is not entirely respectable, but also because they are young and poor. Men like to have dependants from among more important men than these, when building a reputation as a generous and honourable man. Among women – older ones on the whole, who have also begun to construct a little circle of loyal dependants – men are valued additions even if they are homosexuals. A homosexual is worth more to a woman because it adds to her prestige to have dependants who are not all women and small children, and because a man can come and go, and give entertaining accounts of events in the men's world where so many more interesting things happen.

Some homosexuals enjoy being invited to women's ceremonies at weddings. They are seen in big, important weddings where they might be too low-ranking to be welcomed at the men's events but have a certain prestige at the women's. Women enjoy dressing up for weddings and casting their normally quiet behaviour aside; homosexuals too, if they come, often put on bits and pieces of female dress, and wear jasmine posies and cosmetics. Weddings are lighthearted occasions and homosexuals enjoy dancing and being the centre of attention. Similar behaviour would, however, be totally inappropriate in another formally segregated situation – mourning. When someone dies, male and female kin and friends gather in sex-segregated groups in different rooms of the bereaved household, and pray and read the Koran aloud for three days. Here, a homosexual would be expected to attend the men's gathering or not attend at all. It would be quite wrong to suggest that homosexuals ought always to be in the company of women in situations where there is formal segregation.

LESBIANS

Lesbian couples in Mombasa are far more likely to live together than male homosexual couples and I would like to stress from the outset that a *physical* relationship is meant. There are plenty of all-female households in Mombasa, but these are not necessarily lesbian. The word is used to mean lovemaking between women which usually, but not always, implies the abandonment of physical relationships with men, and often leads to the establishment of a household. The word in Swahili glossed as 'lesbian' is *msagaji* (pl. *wasagaji*) – 'a grinder'. The verb *kusaga* (to grind) is commonly used for the grinding of grain between millstones, but the close interplay between the two usages is illustrated, perhaps, by the fact that the upper and lower millstones are known as *mwana* and *mama* respectively: 'child' and 'mother', strictly speaking, or simply 'young woman' and 'older woman'.

Lesbians in Mombasa are mostly involved in two kinds of activity. Firstly, of course, there is the private relationship between pairs of women; secondly, groups of lesbians meet regularly in one another's houses as members of club-like groups focused upon individual women who become their leaders. At this more public level, comparison may pertinently be made with the other clubs, cults, and societies found among men and women on the Kenya coast. In all cases, the formal reason for meeting is only part of the picture, and the groups are also used as arenas of rivalry for power.

The main lesbian group in Mombasa is centred very much in the Old Town, though some of its members live in quarters outside it. Other groups are based in the suburbs. Each is composed of an inner circle of relatively wealthy older women who are friends, and then of their lovers, women poorer and usually younger than they are.

During the afternoons, when domestic responsibilities are over for a while, Swahili women sleep or do handicrafts, or go visiting kin and friends. Younger, lower-status women visit older, higher-status women as a rule: it is a mark of status to stay put and let others bestir themselves. Wealthy lesbian women hold court during the afternoons in this way, visited by friends and lovers. Like any other hostesses with guests they will be certain to offer them tea or cold fizzy drinks. In addition, at lesbian gatherings, *mira'a* (ghat) – a bitter narcotic leaf – is sometimes offered as well, together with sweetners such as peppermints. *Mira'a* is expensive, a bunch costing the daily wage of an unskilled labourer in 1974, and several bunches are required for an afternoon's entertainment. So few women can afford it, and gatherings where it is offered are attractive. What is perhaps more important for our understanding is that men do not pay for women's *mira'a*-eating (while they would within reason finance tea and cold drinks offered to guests by their female dependants) and so women cannot spend money on *mira'a* unless it is their own. *Mira'a* is really regarded as a male prerogative. Young men chew *mira'a* rather as they drink alcohol, in defiance of what they regard as Muslim norms, and usually leave it behind once they approach middle age. So women who use *mira'a* are defining themselves as independent spirits who, in so far as they are imitating men, are imitating young non-conformist men.

While it cannot possibly be said that non-lesbian women never use *mira'a*, if it becomes known that a particular woman has begun to eat it regularly with friends, whispers about her begin to circulate. What *is* true is that there is always a correlation between *mira'a* eating and the ability of a woman to spend money for which she is not accountable to a man.

Weddings are the most important occasions in ordinary life for all Mombasa's Swahili women, for here they meet a wider range of kin, friends, and acquaintances than anywhere else. Women's ceremonies for weddings are more numerous than men's, and are only partly concerned with the bride. In addition, there is much competitive jockeying for prestige. Individuals try to outdress one another; dance groups outperform one another; the whole wedding itself is compared with other weddings that season according to how many women from Mombasa's highest-ranking families came to it, how many events were staged, and the quality and quantity of food offered at it. At the same time certain formal changes of status, for particular categories of girls or women, are demonstrated. Girls who have been through the period of teaching and the initiation ceremony (*unyago*) which follows upon puberty, come to the unmarried girls' part of the wedding and perform *kiuno*, the sexually provocative dances their instructresses have taught them, for the approval of an audience of married women. They and even smaller girls also look forward to the chance to dance the *chakacha*, in which conga-lines of girls dance in unison to the calls for style variation from the band leader. Newly married young wives and older women enjoy their right to attend events for married women

256 The Cultural Construction of Sexuality

only, and cheer the bride with the prospect of soon being one of them.

Lesbian women come to weddings for a variety of reasons. Firstly, *all* lesbians are or have been married and so rank among the more important wedding guests. As such they compete with other women in luxuriousness of dress, perfume, and jewellery. Lesbians also dress their lovers finely for weddings and in this compete with one another. Non-lesbians will add that lesbians come to weddings partly to look at the newly initiated young girls dancing *kiuno* and *chakacha*, comparing their looks and style. Lesbians do not sit apart from other women, though as groups of friends some will tend to congregate together. They encourage other women to come and sit with them, but while older non-lesbian women are easy in their company, younger girls are half frightened of them. Older lesbians display their power over their lovers by ordering them about, having them fetch food and light cigarettes for them, and so on. Lesbians, unlike male homosexuals, quite often live together and have a long-term and full relationship with one another. Probably for this reason the two partners are referred to by a single term despite the wealth and status difference which exists between them, and which in the case of male homosexuals is indicated in the *basha/shoga* terminology.

What draws a woman into such a type of relationship? Such Swahili women as I have heard speculating on this question are clear in their minds about the attraction of being a lesbian for women who are poor or of lowly birth. Such women are most unlikely to be able to contract marriages with men having wealth or status sufficient to offer them financial security or social eminence, whereas a wealthy lesbian lover can offer both. So much of the acquisition of prestige among women is concerned with having jewellery, several pairs of shoes, and a stream of new dresses that a sexual partner who will offer these is likely to be welcomed with gratitude. A young woman may long for an escape from an unhappy marriage, but perhaps lacks a natal family able to take her in if she returns and is unable to support herself in any other way because of having several young children. Lesbian women will at times support such women as lovers, and offer a new sort of freedom to them. Very occasionally a wealthy lesbian woman will help a girl who has not married

but remains miserably caught within the constraints of unmarried womanhood while all her peers have moved forward.
Such a girl is usually of such high birth, or so well educated, that
men hesitate to make offers for her since the parents refuse all
suitors. Slight miscalculation may find her still unmarried in her
late twenties or early thirties, and the rigidity of the division
between the never-married and the married, among women, is
such that adult freedoms can *only* come through marriage. A
lesbian woman who wants to help such a girl will find a man prepared to make a marriage of convenience and give him the money
with which to go to the girl's parents and make an offer. The
couple are divorced shortly after the marriage and the girl goes to
live with her lesbian benefactor.

For the wealthy partner in a lesbian relationship it seems, to an
observer, that being a lesbian brings freedom from the extreme
constraint normally placed upon high-ranking women in Muslim
societies. A wealthy Swahili woman can only marry a wealthy,
high-ranking man, because of the Sharia's *kafa'a* injunction
which states that Muslim women must be given in marriage to
their equals or superiors; such a marriage brings a great degree of
seclusion for the woman and her wealth must be administered
for her by her husband. She cannot easily avoid this by looking
for a poor husband with little authority – power to prevent her
making such a marriage – again because of the *kafa'a* rule. Thus if
she wishes to use her wealth as she likes and has a taste for
power, entry into a lesbian relationship, or living alone as a
divorced or widowed woman, are virtually her only options.

Financial independence for a woman certainly offers the
opportunity of converting wealth to power. By paying for the
marriages of others, like a rising New Guinea Big Man (Sahlins
1963: 292) or offering economic support in return for loyalty, a
circle of dependants is created. Women who successfully support
numerous dependants are paradoxically admired as much by
men as by women. A few women, some of them lesbians, have
achieved positions of real influence in Mombasa. In 1974 one was
a city councillor and another campaigning to become one; several
were regularly approached at election times by would-be politicians aware of the size of their following and hoping to harness it,
in the way they would have gone to voluntary-association
officials and prominent male individuals; one lesbian woman

owns a kebab restaurant (an unheard-of activity for a woman) which she and a handful of other women of similar standing use as a *baraza* – a regular street meeting-place of a kind normally created only by men.

Since it is possible to wield influence as a wealthy woman *without* being a lesbian – as a divorced or widowed woman, for instance – we still have to go one step further in explaining the attractiveness of being a lesbian for some. The answer is complicated. It is not entirely respectable for a woman of under 45 or 50 to be without a spouse, for she is assumed to be sexually available. Some women retain a good deal of autonomy combined with respectability by contracting a nominal marriage with a man of suitable status who lives entirely with another wife. In this case the woman largely supports herself. Such an arrangement fulfils the criterion of decency, but it is a somewhat lonely alternative which offers little or no satisfaction for sexual needs. Living as a lesbian is less respectable than being a nominal second wife, but more respectable than not being married at all, as far as it is possible to measure. Such sexual fulfilment involves no loss of autonomy for a wealthy lesbian and indeed takes place in the highly positive context of the fond and supportive relationships women establish among themselves anyway.

The acceptability of male and female homosexuality

In some parts of the world, homosexuality has an institutional role in allowing a gender switch to individuals, who can be fuller members of society if they do so (Devereux 1937; Evans-Pritchard 1970; Whitehead 1981). Since it is argued here that the sexual choices of male homosexuals and lesbians enable them to participate more fully in Mombasa life – by some criteria, at any rate – it is important to establish whether they do this by effecting a gender change.

GENDER SWITCHING

Economic activities

Homosexual men are not required to make domestic work an aspect of the relationship with the men whom they sleep with.

They compete with women for the attention of wealthy men by charm, grace, engaging conversation, perfume, and ornament, but not by domestic competence. Indeed it is my strong impression that older men who like homosexual company do so precisely because homosexuals are *not* women. Homosexuals may poach on female preserves, but do not thereby become female.

Women who become lesbians – whether dominant or dependent – continue to cook, clean the house, rear children, sew. Although dominant lesbians may spend more of their time on other activities, and delegate some household tasks to others, they are careful not to fail at the domestic competence by which women judge one another.

Dress

Style of dress is somewhat problematic for any diagnosis of gender change because modern governments may ban the wearing of clothing that individuals would choose for preference. In Oman, for instance, the wearing of female dress by homosexuals is forbidden, and they wear pastel-tinted men's clothes (Wikan 1977: 305). Yet Rigby reported that in Zanzibar in the 1860s, 'numbers of sodomites have come from Muscat (Oman), and these degraded wretches openly walk about dressed in female attire with veils on their faces' (Russell 1935: 342). Similarly in Mombasa, homosexuals wear a slightly flamboyant version of male dress in the streets, but away from the police, in private, among women at weddings, they may put on far more female attire to amuse and flatter women.

Lesbians dress entirely as women. Their wealth enables them to dress in a rich and feminine way (or be so dressed) and, though dominant lesbians are more assertive in manner and conversation than most other women, they make no attempt to look like men. When they go out they wear the veil (*buibui*) like all other coastal women.

Segregation

Homosexuals enjoy relaxing in the company of women but on serious – that is, religious – occasions, men and women segregate according to their biological sex. Homosexuals pray at the mosques with men, not at home with women, and once they have performed the ablutions for prayer they lose their ritual purity through touching women (even if they have never slept with one), not through shaking hands with men.

Women who are dominant lesbians do not obey strict seclusion rules. As household heads they welcome male visitors to the house and sit with them in the reception room, and they frequently go out of the house. However, they are not to be found in the company of men in public in places such as mosques, male *barazas*, or men's ceremonies at weddings and funerals.

Behaviour

Homosexuals tend to employ the gait and voice which are the international signals of homosexuality. These seem to be imitated from other homosexuals, not from women, and the modesty and quietness of ideal Swahili womanhood are quite absent in homosexual behaviour. Homosexuals are not required to seclude themselves and the only direct imitation of female behaviour I have witnessed is to be seen when homosexual men dance like women in weddings.

Dependent lesbian women are expected to behave like ordinary women. Dominant lesbian women display energetic personalities very similar to those of active, intelligent *non*-lesbian women and are thus, again, not unique in this respect.

It should be clear from the foregoing that homosexuals and lesbians do *not* closely model themselves upon heterosexual women and men respectively, either in attributes or in the assumption of rights and duties. Homosexuals play at looking like women from time to time, but do not imitate anything else about them; dominant lesbians opt to support women and perhaps their children, but do not try to look like men or force an entry into their lives. Neither men nor women think of lesbians as virtual men or homosexuals as virtual women, but judge them as members of the sex they were born into. So the basis for the relative acceptability of homosexuals and lesbians cannot be that they blend into the background by gender switching. Rather, the explanation is to be found in a combination of three factors: the importance to the Swahili of Arab culture, economic pragmatism, and rank.

ARAB CULTURE

Arab culture is emulated and admired in Mombasa, and the fact that there is a long tradition of acceptable male homosexuality in many Arab countries is relevant. Homosexuality is forbidden in the Koran (Surah 4: 20) but Arabic literature contains both jocular stories about homosexuality such as those in the *Arabian Nights*, and fine love poetry to homosexuals (Arberry 1965; Gibb 1963).

Richard Burton heard in Shiraz of a pious Muslim father publicly executing his son for homosexuality (Brodie 1971: 82); at the other extreme in the Siwa oasis in the Western Desert of Egypt, Cline in 1936 found that every single male except one immigrant was or had been a homosexual (Cline 1936: 43); homosexuality is a part of daily life in Aden (Ashworth and Walker 1972: 153) and in Oman (Wikan 1977), and is the subject of popular love songs in Afghanistan (Dupree 1970: 361). Significantly for our understanding of the Swahili, homosexuality is common in the two original areas of most of the Arab immigrants to East Africa: South Arabia and Oman. Their incorporation into Swahili life was often as superiors – traders, rulers, wealthy settlers – and their attitudes to homosexuality must have been influential.

Homosexuality is very much an urban phenomenon in East Africa, following the routes by which Islam spread through trade. Non-Muslim town-dwellers are very rarely homosexual, and even village Swahili seem to be less likely to be homosexual than townsmen.

References to lesbians in the Middle East are rare, but al-Katib mentions their existence in tenth-century Baghdad and Medina (cited in Musallam 1983: 154, n. 8) where they explained their choices as being made in order 'to do without men', and 'to avoid scandalous pregnancies'. The same author refers to *male* homosexuality as also essentially a form of contraception, incidentally.

Interestingly, though, lesbians on the East African coast are unlikely to have acquired their sexual preferences in imitation of Arab women, for very few ever immigrated to East Africa. On the whole the men who came took local women as wives and concubines. It seems likely that they imitated the pattern of male homosexuality which they saw locally, as in the past they imitated men's competitive dance societies (Ranger 1975: 167–70). Alternatively we may argue that the great segregation of Arab life in East African coast towns, by contrast with that in adjacent rural areas, automatically produces the conditions for homosexuality to emerge. Whatever the reason, the local development of lesbianism is perhaps suggested by the fact that words for male homosexuals – *shoga, hanithi, basha* – are all of Arabic or Persian origin, while *msagaji* is a purely local Bantu word.

ECONOMIC NECESSITY

Many Swahili understand that homosexuals and lesbians have been able to improve upon their social and/or economic situation by the choices they have made, and find it reasonable that people try to make the best of their circumstances in life. A man who complained that he disapproved of his sister becoming a dependent lesbian when she was divorced by her husband, was roundly told off by his cousins. 'How can you blame her?' they said. '*You* haven't offered to take her and her children!' It would be universally accepted, I think, that passive homosexuals have gained some financial security only by also taking on low social status, which nobody would do if it could be avoided; yet low status is better than starving, begging, or stealing.

THE IMPORTANCE OF RANK

The third and to me most important explanation for the acceptability of male and female homosexuality is to be found in attitudes to rank in Mombasa. This point of course draws also on the previous one. Rank, compounded of wealth, the strength of the ability to claim Arab ancestry, and degree of Muslim piety and learning, is here both birth-ascribed and personally achieved. Men and women expect to rise in rank over a lifetime, not only because age brings importance but also because property will hopefully be acquired and a circle of dependants created. Rank rules dictate who can marry whom, who can command the loyalty of whom, who runs the errands, and who sits and waits. When we look at homosexual or lesbian relationships it is striking that, though they break the implicit rule that sexual intercourse should take place between a heterosexual pair, they do not break any *rank* rules. A marriage between a poor husband and a rich wife would be, I think, more shocking to the Swahili than a homosexual or lesbian liaison where the dominant partner is better born and richer than the dependent one. To put it another way, lesbians and homosexuals have been unable to establish the relationships they want within a heterosexual framework – relationships which grant power and freedom for a wealthy woman or a more secure living for a poor man – without doing violence to rank rules. To the Swahili, the physical details of the liaisons between lesbians or between homosexuals have no definitional interest; they appear to view them not as perverse imitations of heterosexual coupling, but as patron-client relations given a sexual dimension.

It is suggested that, since rank is so important in Mombasa, the divisions in society which it creates must logically push the gender division into second place. Men do not strive to be thought more *male*: they strive to be thought more *Arab*, better *Muslims*, more *important*, bigger *patrons*. And it can be noted that these aims are not sex-specific. Yet we know that gender organizes a great deal among the Swahili of crucial day-to-day importance. In what sense can we dismiss it as not particularly significant?

Conclusion: rank, gender, and homosexuality

The main characteristic of gender in Mombasa is its utter clarity. All social males are biological males and all social females are biological females. The presence of numbers of lesbians and homosexuals, that is to say, does nothing to cloud the boundary line. The implications of this are very interesting. If dominant lesbians and dependent homosexuals are not called upon to take on even partial local colour as social males and females respectively, as they are in some cultures, then their biological *sex* is much more important than their *behaviour* as a determinant of gender.

By contrast, the biological sexes in Britain and America must constantly bolster biology with 'male' or 'female' behaviour if they wish to avoid conventional censure. We have a host of words for accusing one another of failing to conform socially to biological 'givens'. Men may be dubbed 'effeminate', their tears 'womanish'; some male homosexuals are called 'queens'. Successful assertive women may be regarded as 'masculine', 'butch', 'the ones who wear the trousers'. Such language hedges us about with rules which threaten us with crossing a gender threshold without meaning to, and finding ourselves social outcasts.

In Mombasa, gender holds none of the punishing power it does for us, for rank rules are the powerful ones which order behaviour. Where social inequality is accepted as a basic premise, a weak, foolish, or indeed homosexual man need not be classified as one who has strayed into femaleness, but as a *low-ranking, unimportant* man. Whereas Britons and Americans use *gender* to elaborate metaphor about acceptable and unacceptable behaviour, and to describe power relations in figurative form, Mombasans allow metaphorical meaning to cluster around the notion of *rank*.

Gender, in a notionally egalitarian society, is the only incontrovertible difference officially recognized. Thus any attempt to rank men against men or women against women will draw on maleness versus femaleness to make the point. The insights of Strathern (1976: 50) and Moore (1977: 94) help to illuminate this process. So homosexuality, transvestism, and so on may all be attempts to grapple not only with gender, but also with the power relations which are expressed by analogy with gender. We can contrast the scorn some British and American women have felt for 'feminine' styles of dressing (because they symbolize the shackles which help to subordinate women to men) with attitudes in rank-ridden Mombasa. There, the most powerful lesbian women wear beautiful, expensive dresses, perfume, and make-up to help them compete for superiority with other women.

And of course, any society which makes gender an irreducible distinction – and where women are subordinated to men – is likely to be uneasy about homosexuality. Once gender has been allowed to accrete layers of metaphorical meaning on the subject of dominance and subordination it becomes a symbol of great power.[9] The Anglican marriage service, for instance, asserts that bride and bridegroom in their union symbolize the religio-political authority relationship between Christ and the Church – Heaven and Earth.

Gender's symbolic assimilation to so much else in our society means that the inversion of gender roles may be read as threatening the overthrow of a greater order. This is why societies like Britain and the USA have had such an exaggerated horror of homosexuality – the sexual invert is assumed to have subversive political attitudes as well, should be banned from high office, and until recently was considered not merely as a potential, but as an actual criminal. It is also why some feminists find it easier to fight as lesbians.

On the other hand, rank downplays the differentness of the two sexes for certain purposes and instead highlights common birth status. In Mombasa – where finally every family is ranked against others on the basis of previous prestigious or unsuitable alliances made – brothers and sisters are strongly united by their social position. The sex roles allotted to them domestically by Islam are secondary to the shared public face presented to outsiders. They have more in common with those of their own social rank, that is to say, than with those of the same sex in other ranks. Even though many events, especially weddings, are notable for their sexual segregation, the hierarchical jockeying that goes on inside each domain is more important socially than the sexual segregation itself.

THE INCIDENCE OF HOMOSEXUALITY

To return to the fundamental questions asked at the beginning of the paper: some societies have homosexuality and some do not; it is genuinely unknown in many precapitalist societies, for instance.[10] Empirically it would seem that where young men and women have easy sexual access to each other, homosexuality does not occur. (I realize this statement begs questions about Britain and America, and return to our own culture in a moment.) Even though societies such as the Maasai do not allow their young men to *marry* for many years, prepubertal girls and the elders' wives in fact provide ample sexual outlets. Conversely, in the rare cases where the elders could withhold young men's access to women completely, then homosexuality occurred, even in a remote precapitalist society such as that of the Azande when Evans-Pritchard studied them (1970).

The withholding of unmarried women becomes more common as societies become increasingly stratified by wealth and status. And as the marriages of sisters begin to have social implications for those their brothers might be able to make, virginity becomes more and more important. Prostitution is almost certain to be found as the concomitant of a virginity cult and so, it would seem, is a degree of homosexuality among young men. But the fact that homosexuality is found in stratified and sexually segregated societies provides only one level of explanation. *Within* the category 'stratified societies' attitudes to homosexuality vary widely, being strongly condemnatory in some, and accepting in others. And homosexuality is actually found in both. How are we to explain this?

FERTILITY AND SEXUALITY

At this point, I found Ortner's reanalysis (1981: 395ff) of Goody and Tambiah (1973) extremely useful. As she points out, there are two sorts of hierarchically organized societies, patrilineal-exogamous and cognatic-endogamous. The former is associated with dowry for women, the severance of a woman's ties with her natal group, and therefore rare divorce. The latter is associated with women's inheritance, continued rights in the woman's natal group, and easy, frequent divorce. For a woman in the former system (this is not Ortner's point, but it follows from her groupings) kinship rights and the identity they conferred are all but extinguished at marriage and can only be rebuilt with new kin – children. But a woman in the latter system enjoys her natal kinship rights permanently, and her sense of who she is has two dimensions, that of kinswoman as well as that of affine.

In societies where large numbers of children are desired to help with the family farm or herd, sexuality and procreation are ideas which need never be conceptually distinguished. But in towns, the two ideas begin to exist independently of one another as circumstances place a limit on the desired number of children. Procreation is curbed, by one means or another, but sexual desire continues much as before. The only difference is that sexuality begins to be a pastime, as some of its economic function – the provision of a workforce – is lost. But children are still desired – so long as they are the right children, by a suitable spouse of the correct social status – so the sexuality of the individual tends still to be the concern of a variety of people. When we come to look more closely at Ortner's typology, we can see that in the patrilineal-exogamous model, female sexuality and fertility are the property of the husband, handed over lock, stock, and barrel in a bargain struck at marriage. Because the girl's natal kin give her up, she has no way of resisting her husband. In cognatic-endogamous systems, on the contrary, her children – and therefore her sexuality, I would argue – are partly the woman's own property, as a representative of her natal kinship group. High divorce (and remarriage) rates suggest that the woman can choose to bestow or withhold her sexual and procreative faculties without constant reference to others with rights in them. In Mombasa, implicit difficulties in the discord between the importance, for other kin, of sisters' alliances, and the *actual* freedom which the system grants women, are resolved by the placing of great importance on the *first* marriage for a woman and a relative lack of interest in the post-virginity subsequent ones.

In the first type of hierarchical society, complementarily, the husband's total responsibility for his wife makes him vulnerable if she shames him sexually. His identity is deeply rooted in his ability to control her, and if she misbehaves he cannot easily shed her through divorce. Though he may visit prostitutes or have the odd adulterous affair, he cannot be said to be his own man in these circumstances. In cognatic-endogamous societies, the woman's greater freedom also frees the man from some of the burden of responsibility for her and the possibility of divorces and remarriages means that his sexuality and procreativity are not defined by any particular union.

CONCLUSION

On the basis of these important differences, I hope it is not stretching a point to try to bring homosexuality back into the picture. I would propose the hypothesis that the more fertility and sexuality are seen as personal property in any society, the less opprobium will be attached to homosexuality. If the individual chooses to 'spend' his or her sexuality and fertility in a non-reproductive context, there are two ways of accepting it. It can be said that it is the individual's own business, and it can further be noted that the individual is not irresponsibly producing children when they are not wanted. Conversely, the more the individual's sexuality and fertility are the property of others, the more those particular rights are slighted by homosexuality, and the more they are cheated of children who might have come from a conventional fertile union.

Such a hypothesis not only explains the Swahili data with which I began, but also makes it possible to think about British and American homosexuality from a slightly different standpoint. Divorce in these areas was a rare and major scandal forty years ago, and is now as common as it is among the Swahili. We can link this to greater economic independence for women and a decreased reliance upon marriage as the chief career of women. Concomitantly, in recent decades, homosexuality has become legal and a great deal more acceptable, and has in consequence become more common. At the same time the increased availability of contraception has 'privatized' almost all kinds of sexual activity between single people. It is only after marriage that there begin to be constraints upon the free use of one's own sexuality, and these come because joint property, including children, may be jeopardized. It is for reasons to do with the desire to escape the economic conventions of marriage, I suspect, that some individuals not only avoid heterosexual marriage but even heterosexual pre-marital relationships. They, too, like Mombasa's lesbians and homosexuals, have taken stock of their economic resources present and future – and have probably made the most rational decision in the circumstances.

Notes

1 This paper is based upon the results of casual observation rather than intensive research. It relies too little on personal statements to me by directly involved informants, and too much on the evidence of kin, affines, and acquaintances of homosexuals and lesbians, offered at times as gossip and anecdote. My own observations were sometimes uncomprehending at the time and had to be rethought in the light of what I was told afterwards. The paper attempts to allow for all this, but is still an imperfect record.

2 In an attempt to steer away from the clinical, I use the term *lesbian* for female homosexuals and *homosexual* for male homosexuals, when writing of Mombasa. The two categories are far from being mirror images of one another, as will become clear.

3 As does all blood. The blood of animals, or of boys when they are circumcised, is as polluting.

4 Women seem to enjoy wearing veils. The *buibui* is a flattering garment, which young girls look forward to being old enough to wear, and at times it provides valuable anonymity.

5 Sharifs, descendants of the Prophet, are an exception. Their membership of patrilineages with international ramifications is of importance

to them and they have a lively knowledge of large numbers of patri-lateral kin.

6 On the 1976 pilgrimage to Mecca only half a dozen pilgrims returned of a planeload which had flown from Mombasa to Jedda on package-tour terms. The rest had reputedly absconded illegally in Saudi Arabia to look for work.

7 M. Gilsenan (personal communication) reports servants taking a similar role in present-day Lebanon.

8 Lamu, a Swahili town north of Mombasa, used in the 1950s to have clubs where boys dressed as girls performed a sort of strip-tease to older men and then paired off with them (Wilson 1957: 1).

9 Such a line of argument sheds interesting light on Mediterranean macho. Where gender and power are tangled together, actions such as the seduction of women, which increase a man's maleness in his own eyes, may also increase his metaphorical maleness and endow him with power and influence. By the same token he can withhold increased stature at his expense from other men, by keeping a tight grip on the purity of his women.

10 I am not considering in this essay either ritual male homosexuality at puberty (as found, for example, in New Guinea) nor the transvestism once found among North American Indians. This latter case is very different from the sort of homosexuality discussed here, as White-head's excellent paper (1981) makes clear.

References

Arberry, A. J. (1965) *Arabic Poetry*. Cambridge: Cambridge University Press.

Ashworth, A. E. and Walker, W. M. (1972) Social Stratification and Homosexuality: a Theoretical Appraisal. *British Journal of Sociology* 23: 146–58.

Brodie, F. (1971) *The Devil Drives: a Life of Sir Richard Burton*. London: Penguin.

Bujra, J. (1968) An Anthropological Study of Political Action in a Bajuni Village in Kenya. Unpublished Ph.D. thesis, University of London.

Cline, W. (1936) *Notes on the People of Siwah and El Garah in the Libyan Desert*. General Series in Anthropology No. 4. Wisconsin: George Banta Publishing Company, Menasha.

Devereux, G. (1937) Institutionalised Homosexuality of the Mohave Indians. *Human Biology* 9: 498–527.

Dupree, L. (1970) Aq Kupruk: a Town in North Afghanistan. In Louise E. Sweet (ed.) *Peoples and Cultures of the Middle East, Vol. 2*. New York: Natural History Press for the American Museum of Natural History.

Evans-Pritchard, E. E. (1970) Sexual Inversion among the Azande. *American Anthropologist* 72: 1428–434.

Gibb, H. A. R. (1963) *Arabic Literature* (2nd revised edn). Oxford: Clarendon Press.

Goody, J. and Tambiah, S. J. (1973) *Bridewealth and Dowry*. Cambridge: Cambridge University Press.

Moore, J. (1977) The Exploitation of Women in Evolutionary Perspective. *Critique of Anthropology* 3 (9 & 10): 83–100.

Musallam, B. F. (1983) *Sex and Society in Islam*. Cambridge Studies in Islamic Civilization. Cambridge: Cambridge University Press.

Ortner, S. B. (1981) Gender and Sexuality in Hierarchical Societies: the Case of Polynesia and Some Comparative Implications. In S. B. Ortner and H. Whitehead (eds) *Sexual Meanings*. Cambridge: Cambridge University Press.

Ranger, T. O. (1975) *Dance and Society in Eastern Africa: the Beni Ngoma*. London: Heinemann.

Russell, Mrs C. E. (1935) *General Rigby, Zanzibar and the Slave Trade*. London: Allen & Unwin.

Sahlins, M. (1963) Poor Man, Rich Man, Big-Man, Chief: Political Types in Melanesia and Polynesia. *Comparative Studies in Society and History* 5: 285–303.

Shepherd, G. M. (1982) *The Comorians in Kenya: the Establishment and Loss of an Economic Niche*. Ph.D. dissertation, London School of Economics.

Strathern, M. (1976) An Anthropological Perspective. In B. Lloyd and J. Archer (eds) *Exploring Sex Differences*. London: Academic Press.

Strobel, M. (1975) *Moslem Women in Mombasa, Kenya, 1890–1973*. Unpublished Ph.D. dissertation. University of California, Los Angeles.

Tanner, R. E. S. (1962) The Relationship between the Sexes in a Coastal Islamic Society: Pangani District, Tanganyika. *African Studies* 21 (2): 70–82.

Topan, F. M. T. (1972) *Oral Literature in a Ritual Setting: the Role of Spirit Songs in a Spirit Mediumship Cult of Mombasa, Kenya*. Unpublished Ph.D. thesis. University of London.

Whitehead, H. (1981) The Bow and the Burden Strap: a New Look at Institutionalized Homosexuality in Native North America. In S. B. Ortner and H. Whitehead (eds) *Sexual Meanings*. Cambridge: Cambridge University Press.

Wikan, U. (1977) Man Becomes Woman: Transsexualism in Oman as a Key to Gender Roles. *Man* n.s. 12 (2): 304–19.

Wilson, G. M. (1957) Male Prostitution and Homosexuals. Appendix to *Mombasa Social Survey*. Nairobi: unpublished mimeograph, Government Printer.

10 Celibacy as a solution?
Mahatma Gandhi and *Brahmacharya*[1]

Pat Caplan

Since the second wave of feminism began in the 1960s, it has been common for some feminists to assert that heterosexual activity is dangerous for women. Given the weight of conditioning with which men enter into relationships with women, given the way in which western society operates, it is argued that an egalitarian sexual relationship between a woman and a man is just not possible. However, since this second wave of feminism is decidedly post-Freudian, its proponents have assumed that sex must find an outlet, and for many women, the only choices possible have been lesbianism or masturbation. Until very recently, celibacy has neither been advocated, nor viewed as a positive option.

Celibacy forms an important ideal in many world religions – Hinduism, Buddhism, Christianity, for instance – but it is an ideal for specific categories of people. It is not advocated for everyone, except perhaps at particular stages of the life cycle, much less for married couples for virtually all of the time.

This article focuses on the ideas of Gandhi, who did advocate virtual celibacy for all. His argument is little understood in the West, where he is known primarily for his advocacy of non-violence and his role in the Indian nationalist movement. Indeed, even the recent rediscovery of Gandhi's ideas in the West, first by the civil rights movement in America, and more recently, by the peace movement, pays little attention to this aspect of Gandhi's thought. If it is acknowledged at all, it is dismissed, in a somewhat embarrassed fashion, as one of his 'fads'. For Gandhi, however, the link between celibacy and non-violence was crucial.

Gandhi was seeking a transformation of Indian, and ultimately human, society. This he felt could only come about through a change at the level of the individual's body and soul, as well as in his or her relations with others. He realized that in this process, sexuality had to be redefined, and male–female relations transformed before other changes could take place. Why he chose to solve this problem through an advocacy of celibacy can be explained partly by his own personal circumstances, and partly through the influence of strands of thought emanating from both Hinduism and Victorian England.

Gandhi's life

Mohandas Karamchand Gandhi was born in Porbander, a town north of Bombay, situated in a petty principality of which both his father and grandfather had been prime ministers. Gandhi grew up in a joint family household, and at the age of 12, although he was still at school, he was married to Kasturbai, and began to live with her immediately. In his autobiography (Gandhi 1927), he tells us that he sought to control his wife's movements, and would not allow her to go anywhere without his permission. This provoked bitter quarrels between husband and wife:

> 'The restraint was virtually a sort of imprisonment. And Kasturbai was not the girl to brook any such thing. She made it a point to go out whenever and wherever she liked. More restraint on my part resulted in more liberties being taken by her, and in my getting more and more cross.'   (Gandhi 1927: 9)

None the less, he records that he was inordinately fond of her, and thought about her constantly, even when he was at school or helping to nurse his sick father: 'Every night whilst my hands were busy massaging my father's legs, my mind was hovering about the bedroom' (1927: 21). One night, when he was 16, Gandhi was relieved of the task of massaging his father by his uncle: 'I was glad, and went straight to the bedroom. My wife, poor thing, was fast asleep. But how could she sleep when I was there? I woke her up' (1927: 21). As Gandhi and his wife were having sexual intercourse, a servant knocked on the door to say that Gandhi's father was dead. Gandhi never forgave himself for what he perceived as a gross dereliction of duty to his father. His sin, as he saw it, was compounded by the fact that Kasturbai was at the time heavily pregnant, and therefore he should not have had relations with her at all. He also blamed himself for the fact that the child born soon afterwards lived only for three days. These two deaths, of his father and his child, appear to have haunted Gandhi for the rest of his life, and many commentators have suggested that they had a profound effect on his thinking, leading to his equation of sex with violence and death.

Even so, during his youth, Gandhi deliberately broke every rule of his orthodox household in secret and, with a friend of his, indulged in meat and alcohol: he also visited a prostitute, although he admits that neither on that occasion, nor later when he was taken to a brothel by a ship's captain, was he able to perform.

At the age of 19, Gandhi went to London to study law. This move was very much against the wishes of his relatives; his mother made him take a vow in the presence of a Jain monk not to touch meat or alcohol, and in London he appears to have honoured this promise. Indeed, in London he met with many 'Indophiles', such as Theosophists, who enabled him to see his own culture through new and perhaps more positive eyes. He also came into contact with the ideas of such thinkers as Ruskin, Thoreau, and Tolstoy.

Soon after his return to India, he left again for South Africa to serve as a lawyer to the Indian community. He also set up a community – Phoenix Farm – to put into practice some of the ideas he had gained from Ruskin and Tolstoy. In addition, Gandhi began to organize the Indians to protest against racial injustice. The method he evolved there, based upon a mixture of Hindu and Jain ethics, he termed *satyagraha* – truth force – and it was based upon non-violence – *ahimsa*.

Ahimsa is particularly important for Jains, but also significant for Hindus and Buddhists. *Satya* – truth – in Hindu ethics aims at self-sufficiency and freedom from external ties; it seeks individual autonomy rather than social service. However, Gandhi's idea of *satyagraha* projects the traditional ethical laws into the realm of social action (Bondurant 1958: 105). Later Gandhi was to use these techniques with varying degrees of success when he returned to India in 1915, and became one of the leaders in the nationalist struggle. He evolved such methods as the *hartal*, a strike during which people devoted themselves to prayer and fasting, and other forms of mass civil disobedience. One of the most famous was the Salt March, in which thousands joined him in a walk to the sea coast, where they proceeded – illegally – to make salt, which the British had put out of reach of the masses by imposing taxes on it.

Apart from campaigning for Indian independence, Gandhi also preached the abolition of untouchability to his fellow Indians, re-naming those outside the Hindu *varna* system 'Harijans' or children of God. He also sought to maintain Hindu-Muslim unity, and vigorously opposed the partition of India. Gandhi also had much to say on the subject of women, many thousands of whom, with his active encouragement, joined his campaigns. He opposed early marriage, and advocated remarriage for widows. There is no space in this article to consider all of Gandhi's ideas and campaigns, and I focus henceforth on his ideas concerning sexuality and gender.

SEXUAL ABSTINENCE AND OTHER FORMS OF BODILY CONTROL

In 1906, at the age of 36, Gandhi took the vow of *brahmacharya* or total sexual abstinence. In one of his numerous little pamphlets, he defines it thus:

> '*Brahmacharya* literally means that mode of life which leads to the realization of God. That realization is impossible without practising self-restraint. Self-restraint means restraint of all the senses. But ordinarily *brahmacharya* is understood to mean control over the sexual organs and prevention of seminal discharge through complete control over the sexual instinct.'
>
> (Gandhi 1948: 42)

Mere refraining from sexual intercourse is not, however, enough, for Gandhi goes on to say that:

> 'So long as the desire for intercourse is there, one cannot be said to have attained *brahmacharya*. Only he who has burned away the sexual desire in its entirety may be said to have attained control over his sexual organ. . . . His speech, his thought, and his actions all bespeak possession of vital force.'
>
> (Gandhi 1948: 44)

Sexual intercourse between a married couple for the purpose of procreation of a child did not, Gandhi felt, negate the state of *brahmacharya*, although he counselled that one child per couple was sufficient, even if that one child was a girl and not, as is preferred in India, a boy.

What then is the reason for taking this vow of *brahmacharya*? First of all, Gandhi believed that semen ('the vital fluid') should be used for enhancing spiritual, physical, and mental energy:

> 'Once the idea that the only and grand function of the sexual organ is generation possesses man and woman, union for any other purpose they will hold as criminal waste of the vital fluid, and consequent excitement caused to man and woman as an equally criminal waste of precious energy.' (1941: 70)

The idea of semen as a 'vital force' is a pan-Indian one. In his study of high castes in a Rajasthani village, Carstairs describes it thus: 'Everyone knew that semen was not easily formed; it takes forty days, and forty drops of blood to make one drop of semen' (1968: 83). However, a man who had a good stock of semen was thought to be a kind of superman whom one informant described as 'glowing with health'. Carstairs describes the preoccupation of many of his informants with a disease they called *jiryan* which he translates as 'spermatorrhea' and their frequent request to him as a medical doctor (as well as an anthropologist) to treat the weaknesses which they believed it caused.

However, ideas about the conservation of semen are not only concerned with bodily health but also relate to spiritual well-being. In many respects, they symbolize control over the body by the soul, and in this regard, they are part of a powerful Hindu tradition which extols asceticism and the performance of *tapas* (bodily mortification) as a means of gaining greater spiritual power. Thus for Gandhi, as for other Hindus, control over one's sexual behaviour and, even more importantly, sexual desires, symbolized in an important way control over all of one's behaviour and emotions.

FASTING

In many respects, Gandhi's ideas on food and fasting are analogous to his ideas on sexual abstinence. 'A genuine fast cleanses body, mind, and soul. It crucifies the flesh and to that extent sets the soul free. It is an intense longing of the soul for even greater purity' (Gandhi 1965: 8). Gandhi's ideas on fasting, are, like his ideas on sexual abstinence, complex, and contain many strands. It must be remembered that for Hindus, food is a vehicle of pollution and purity. It has to be of an acceptable kind, and cooked and served by an equal or superior, in order to avoid polluting the eater. Furthermore, the pollution conferred by food is greater than that potentially incurred by sex, at least for a man, because food pollution is internal, and cannot be easily cleansed, whereas that of sex is external, and can be removed by bathing. The foods on which Gandhi lived for most of the latter part of his life – fruit, vegetables, and nuts – are, perhaps not insignificantly, relatively less prone to carry pollution. Gandhi wrote many times that people should only eat sufficient food to keep their bodies healthy. 'Food should be taken as a matter of duty . . . to sustain the body, never for the satisfaction of the palate' (1948: 24). He advocated vegetarianism, and the avoidance of foods which in the Hindu schema fall into the category of 'hot' and which are thought to inflame the passions, such as spices. He also condemned the use of tea and coffee, and above all of intoxicants such as alcohol, marijuana, and tobacco, which precipitate loss of control. Another reason for fasting, Gandhi stated, was to 'mortify the flesh':

'Man tends to become a slave of his own body, and engages in many activities and commits many sins for the sake of physical enjoyment. . . . He should therefore mortify the flesh whenever there is an occasion of sin. A man given to physical enjoyment is subject to delusion. Even a slight renunciation of enjoyment in the shape of food will probably be helpful in breaking the power of that delusion. Fasting in order to produce this effect, must be taken in its widest sense as the exercise of control over all the organs of sense with a view to the purification of oneself or others.'   (1965: 17)

In this passage, Gandhi again reveals the influence of the Hindu ascetic tradition, in which bodily privation and the performance of *tapas* lead to greater control over oneself and others, and also the strong Hindu belief that all attachment, including that to the delights of the senses, is illusion. He couches these ideas, moreover, in language which would not seem strange if it came from a Christian, for example when he speaks of 'mortification of the flesh', just as he often spoke, as above, of 'crucifying'. Indeed, he was fond of telling Protestant Christians, whom he said appeared to dislike fasting, that it had good biblical authority.

Throughout his life, Gandhi was also preoccupied with bowel movements, making frequent use of enemas. Like his mother, he seems to have suffered from chronic constipation. Again, it is difficult to separate his use of enemas for physiological ends from their use for reasons of purity ('inner cleanliness'), but certainly, it was a part of his desire to control every aspect of his body.

Like all Hindus, then, Gandhi viewed the body as inextricably linked to the soul and spirit, and also as a microcosm of the social. It is thus not surprising to find that his political campaigns were often intimately linked with bodily functions. His campaign for the abolition of untouchability, for example, was also linked with a campaign to persuade Indians to use latrines, and for each person to be responsible for the disposal of his or her own excreta, thus obviating the necessity for the existence of an untouchable caste of sweepers to clean up faeces. On one occasion, Gandhi scandalized a group of Congress politicians with whom he was staying by sweeping the areas where they had defecated outside the house. He also forced his wife Kasturbai to participate in such activities by asking her to empty the chamber pots of guests, a request with which she finally complied only with the greatest reluctance. Similarly Gandhi did not only fast for health and for spiritual strength and communion with the divine, he also used fasting as a weapon in his political armoury.

Food, unlike sex, is a necessity for personal survival, and it is for this reason that Gandhi's fasts, unlike his sexual abstinence, could be turned into an immediate and public political weapon. An early instance of this was when Gandhi was living in South Africa. While on a visit to Johannesburg, he received news of the 'moral fall' of two inmates of his community Phoenix Farm. He relates what happened next: 'I felt that the only way the guilty parties could be made to realize my distress, and the depth of their own fall, would be for me to do some penance. So I imposed upon myself a fast for seven days and a vow to have only one meal a day for a period of four months and a half' (1965: 11).

Fasting in this way, he was convinced, had a beneficial effect upon the penitent (i.e. the faster), upon the wrongdoer, and upon the congregation which witnesses the act.

The Rudolphs have characterized Gandhi's ideas on bodily control as a theory of 'sexual and moral hydrostatics' (Rudolph and Rudolph 1967). It has obvious similarities to Freud's theory of sublimation (Cantlie 1977). Indeed, Margaret Sanger, in her debate with Gandhi, accused him and his followers of 'sublimating their sex energies into creative action, into the activities of his [Gandhi's] own National Congress' (Gandhi 1941: 59). In this respect, both pre- and post-Freudian thought seems to argue for a 'limited good' theory of human energy. There is, however, an important difference between the thought of Gandhi and that of Freud: whereas both saw the repression of the libido as connected with cultural creativity, Freud also saw it as leading to neurosis, a view which Gandhi rejected.

Towards the end of Gandhi's life, it became publicly known that he had for a number of years been sharing his bed with young women, particularly his 19-year-old greatniece Manu Gandhi. He explained this action not only in terms of bodily warmth at night, but in order to test his self-control (Bose 1974: 153).

His actions are consonant with a particular strand in Hindu thought, that of Tantrism, in which sexual energy is generated by ritual sexual practices between male and female, but in which orgasm must be inhibited and 'the energy which would have been expended in them should be turned back and totally sublimated into a radiant inner condition' (Rawson 1973: 24). However, although Tantrism views sexuality positively, it is chiefly as a means for men to increase their spiritual power. Women, as Allen (1982: 13) points out, are merely a means to an end (just as were Gandhi's greatnieces).

Male and female sexuality and relations between men and women

Although one reason for taking the vow of *brahmacharya* was to increase control over one's senses, another reason which Gandhi wrote about at some length was that it changed the nature of the relationship between the sexes. Man, he felt, is a brute, and only rises above the animal in so far as he observes restraint (1927: 234).

'Sexual intercourse for the purpose of carnal satisfaction is reversion to animality, and it should therefore be man's endeavour to rise above it' (1942: 99).

Sex, even between husband and wife, he equated with lust. (The Sanskrit word is *kama* and there is some debate about whether this is best translated as 'desire' or 'lust' (see Copley 1981: 25)). Gandhi engaged in a vigorous debate with the American birth-control propagandist Margaret Sanger when she visited India and asked for his support in her campaigns. Gandhi opposed all forms of artificial birth-control, preaching abstinence instead. Part of their debate was about the nature and meaning of the sex act. Sanger spoke for a new set of ideas about sex between women and men: 'Sex love is a relationship which makes for oneness, for completeness between husband and wife, and contributes to a finer understanding and greater spiritual harmony' (Gandhi 1941: 59). But Gandhi rejected such ideas firmly: 'Love becomes lust, the moment you make it a means for the satisfaction of animal needs. It is just the same with food. If food is taken only for pleasure, it is lust' (Gandhi 1941: 59).

The arguments of Gandhi and Sanger echoed debates current in the West at the time between advocates and opponents of birth-control. The former were not only concerned with population increase, poverty, and 'eugenics', but some also argued that sexual abstinence was harmful for health, reflecting the influence of Freud. Opponents of birth-control used the argument that, on the contrary, restraint was good for health, that availability of contraception would lead to immorality, and that the highest love was not expressed sexually at all.

Gandhi was not a lone voice in preaching this latter gospel in India. Muthulakshmi Reddy, for example, a doctor, feminist, and social campaigner, wrote in 1930 that:

'It is premature for this country to practise birth control. Instead of birth control, we ought to teach them self-control. Science and experience have proved that continence is conducive to health, and incontinence is productive of diseases. India, famed for its eminent philosophy, religion and spirituality, should give the message to the world.'   (1930: 191)

Gandhi, Muthulakshmi, and others thus rejected entirely the message of the post-Freudians – that sexual repression was harmful and that all human beings had sexual urges which must find expression. Indeed, Gandhi felt strongly that sexual expression was a learned, and not an innate, factor. Instead of being given the licence to sexual expression which early marriage (such as his own) encourages, Gandhi urged that young people should be taught that it is immoral to have more than three or four children, and that after they have had that number, they should sleep separately. 'If they are taught this, it would harden into custom' (1941: 61). Here Gandhi seems to be suggesting that sexual desire is constructed by the socialization process.

When Gandhi took his vow of *brahmacharya*, he did not consult his wife. He mentions several times that she did not appear to be particularly interested in sex: 'To be fair to my wife, she was never the temptress' (1927: 149); however, she rarely resisted him, although she often showed disinclination. Gandhi felt that his youthful insistence upon conjugal rights degraded his wife, whereas his vow of *brahmacharya* freed her from his authority, as well as freeing him from slavery to his own appetite. He thought that his wife was inferior to him when she was an 'instrument of lust', but ceased to be so when she slept with him 'naked as a sister'.

Again these ideas are consonant with much of Hindu thought. In the role of wife, women are inevitably subordinate. A wife becomes merged on marriage into the persona of her husband, and this merging lasts beyond death. A dutiful wife (*patrivrata*) worships her husband, regardless of his worth or character, as if he were a god.

Wadley explains that the concept of the female contains an important duality. On the one hand, she is conceived of as fertile, benevolent, the bestower, but on the other hand, she is also aggressive, malevolent, the destroyer. Within herself, woman contains *sakti*, the tension between cohesion and disintegration, often translated as 'energy': 'All creation and all power in the Hindu world is based on femaleness – there would be no being without energy/power' (Wadley 1977: 115). Women are also associated with nature, i.e. non-culture, and this combination of energy/power plus nature spells danger. Good females, therefore, are those who are controlled by males (i.e. by culture). Benevolent goddesses, for example, are those who are properly married, and have transferred control of their sexuality to their husbands (see Tapper 1979: 15; Babb 1970: 142, 146–47; Fuller 1980: 347). Women who control their own sexuality are seen as highly dangerous, representing both fertility and death, malevolence as well as benevolence.

Such a set of beliefs helps to explain the restrictions with which Hindu women are surrounded at various stages of their life cycle. As young virgins, women are considered to be extremely pure, and at certain festivals are worshipped by other members of their households, including their own parents. However, this purity is lost when a girl begins to menstruate and becomes capable of bearing children. For this reason, orthodox Hindus, until relatively recently, tried to ensure that girls were married, and therefore under the control of their husbands, before menstruation began.

As a wife, the dominant virtue which women must manifest is chastity. This means that they must be faithful to their husbands in thought as well as in deed. It is believed in many parts of India that a truly chaste woman can cause miracles to happen, if she prays for them (see Hart 1973, Jacobson 1978, Minault 1981).

In the Malayalam novel *Chemeen*, about fisherfolk on the Kerala coast, the heroine loves her childhood sweetheart, but struggles to remain faithful to her husband. When she finally gives way to her lover, her husband is drowned at sea, for it is believed that the safety of fishermen is only ensured by their wives' chastity (Thakazhi Pillai 1962). In this case, as in many others, there is a clear equation between sex and death in Hindu thought. Chastity is a source of great power to a woman, yet however chaste, the role of a wife is both ambiguous and ambivalent. On the one hand, sex is necessary for procreation. In Hinduism, a man who dies without a son to carry out his funeral rites is spiritually disadvantaged: in a more worldly sense, sons are necessary to inherit property and continue families. On the other hand, the women who bear these sons are, at least in most of north and central India, strangers to their husbands and their families. A vast literature depicts the lowly status of a newly married wife in such a situation. Women themselves will thus ardently desire children, because once they have borne a child, especially if it is a son, their status in the joint family changes dramatically, from that of subordinate wife to that of mother.

Women's own interests in bearing children, plus the role laid down for them to be obedient to their husbands, thus makes it unlikely that women will refuse sex. However, it is widely believed in India that in fact a woman's sexuality is greater than that of a man. Indeed, this is seen as an additional reason for having her sexuality tamed and controlled by a man.

Carstairs's study of a village in Rajasthan, for example, states that his informants 'were agreed that women, like men, varied among themselves as to the intensity of their sexual appetite; but in general, their need for sex was felt to be more imperative and they were described as taking the initiative in suggesting sexual intercourse' (1968: 73). Women who did not get their marital dues at least once a month were felt to be in danger of straying.

Other studies too seem to indicate that this belief is widespread. Tapper's work on Andhra Pradesh finds men 'highly concerned with women's sexuality, since it is one of the rationales they use to justify the necessity for their domination and authority over them. . . . Such notions derive directly from the idea of women's *asa* – their compulsive emotionalism and passion' (1979: 7).

Similarly Berreman reports that a woman is believed to have seven times the sexual energies that a man has (1972: 170). Such views resonate with the classic Hindu text *The Laws of Manu*, written early in the Christian era: '[Women] give themselves to the handsome and the ugly. Through their passion for men, through their mutable temper, through their natural heartlessness, they become disloyal to their husbands, however carefully they are guarded in this world' (Bühler 1969: 327–30).

But not all Indian women do in fact enjoy sex. Apart from Gandhi's own wife, we have a good example in Buribai, one of Jacobson's informants:

'I've never liked [sex]. From my youth until now in my old age, I've never liked that work. I never enjoyed it. I always thought "what kind of business is this?" I really have disliked this from the beginning, Bai . . . I never got pleasure out of it; I'm very definite about that. . . . I even tell him [her husband] that. . . . It's difficult for me to do it even once (a night) . . . I've never done it twice. I tell him plainly "Brother, I can't·do that. If you like it so much, bring another wife. I don't do that stuff."'

(1978: 116–17)

Is this difference in whether women enjoy sex with men a cultural one, or based merely upon personal differences? Certainly the situation in which many young Indian couples spend at least the early years of their married life – often with not even a room to themselves if they live in a joint family household and with the wife subject to the demands of her mother-in-law so that she may have to go to bed only after the work is completed, and rise early in the morning – is scarcely conducive to the development of an easy relationship between husband and wife. In addition, they are forbidden to show any signs of affection, or even pay attention to each other, in the presence of other family members. This may well militate against a wife being able to feel sexual passion for her husband, yet the bedroom (i.e. the sexual arena) is the only one in which husband and wife meet alone. Sex is the wife's greatest weapon in her attempts to gain her husband's affection (see Bennett 1983: 174), and it is also necessary if she is to bear him a son. None the less, it is a double-edged weapon, for every act of sexual intercourse, as already described, is thought to weaken her husband, and threatens to shorten his life. Given this belief, it is not surprising that women are seen as highly dangerous to men, even when they are faithful wives.

Information about specifically female sexuality is difficult to obtain from the literature on India, whether the classic texts or empirical studies. It is unclear, for example, whether by abstaining from sexual intercourse, women can build up a storehouse of power within themselves, as can men. Gandhi himself seems to suggest that it is possible (see quote on p. 275), as does some anthropological evidence.

Tapper, writing of Andhra Pradesh (1979), notes that while a male *sadhu*'s (ascetic's) austerities, which entail denials of normal bodily functions, ultimately give him control, so in a similar way, a perfect wife who denies her natural female *asa* (tendencies to be sexually uncontrolled and selfish) also gains control of extraordinary power. He goes on to suggest that 'perhaps the fact that females are attributed with greater *asa* than males means that if they can control it, they can harness a greater mystical power'.

However, Hershman, working in the Punjab, comes to a different conclusion. In the Punjab:

'While male sexuality is a socially positive force so that stored-up semen may be channelled to form spiritual power, female sexuality is something which is dark and polluting, and ultimately

man-devouring. Semen is regarded as the quintessential substance of male energy and a woman is considered capable of
having sexual intercourse far in excess of any man; so that while
excessive sexual practice debilitates a man, it is thought to have
no such weakening effect upon a woman.'   (1977: 271–72)

Hershman's male informants were, however, divided in their
opinion, some maintaining that women had far greater sexual
appetites than men, others that they 'suffered' sex simply in
order to have children.

Thompson (1983) suggests that men's ability to control seminal
fluids makes them superior to women, who cannot control their
bodily secretions, especially menstruation.

Gandhi himself was equivocal on this subject, although plainly
believing that women did not enjoy sex. He furthermore maintained that married life, with its domestic concerns and responsibilities, and the inevitability of sexual relations, is a hindrance to
social service. Gandhi did often tell students and young people
that they should think only of social service, and he even maintained (heretically for a Hindu) that marriage was not actually
necessary, unless and until children were desired. Obviously,
such an ethos of sexual puritanism made it much more acceptable
for young men, and particularly young women from 'respectable'
families, to leave home and join his ashrams and his campaigns.

Gandhi urged men to regard women as sisters or mothers, that
is as non-sexual beings. Sisters are regarded as nearly the equals
of their brothers in Hinduism, while mothers are in many
respects considered the superior of their sons. It is to a consideration of the role of mother that I now turn.

Women as mothers

While Hinduism accords women as wives a subordinate place,
women as mothers are highly honoured. The *Laws of Manu* state
that: 'The father is a hundred times more venerable than the
teacher, but the mother is a thousand times more [so] than the
father' (Bühler 1969: 56–7).

Allen notes that

'The positive evaluation of the mother in Hindu mythology,
folklore, contemporary cinema, political ideology and every

day family life is so well known that it needs little elaboration. Throughout India, the very idea of a mother is accorded massive respect, and it is generally believed to be a role of great spiritual power.'   (1982: 9)

He goes on to point out, however, that this does not necessarily result in female autonomy, for mothers are honoured above all for their self-effacing love and compassion.

Bennett shows how in Hindu Nepal, motherhood, associated with constancy, purity, breast-milk, and selfless asexual love, purifies the dangerous affinal women, the sexually subordinate stranger wives of one generation, and transforms them into the consanguineal women of the next (1983: 255).

In certain contexts, the word 'mother' can even be applied by one male to another. Tapper records that a village man begging a gate-keeper for admittance to a hospital in Andhra Pradesh addressed him as 'Amma', a manipulative use of the term, indicating both pleading and affection (1979: 18).

All of this positive evaluation of motherhood actually disguises a paradox, for beneath the oft-repeated view of the mother, and mother goddesses, as benign carers for their children, there is a fear of them as capable of unleashing destructive powers. Women as mothers in India do wield great power over their children, especially their sons, even in adult life, and their power both within the domestic arena and the wider society stems from their role as mothers. Such views are also projected on to deities. Shulman, in a study of Tamil temple myths, for example, discusses the goddess as mother:

'The mother is by nature ambiguous: benign and threatening, nourishing and destructive. In the context of the marriage myths, she is both erotically tied to her son, yet precluded from sexual contact with him; the goddess as mother remains virginal and powerful, her power being used in both creative and destructive ways.'   (1980: 266)

Copley suggests that it is because of the 'excessive' emotional demands of the mother upon the son, as well as the fear of the loss of seminal fluid posed by women as wives, that males in India tend to feel highly threatened by women (1981: 26).

None the less, it is perhaps because aspects of Hindu thought do allow women an active role, one that is powerful and dangerous, that we can find explanations for acceptance of women in positions of political power, for 'It is the mother who gives, who must be obeyed, who loves, and who sometimes rejects' (Wadley 1977: 124). However, as Hershman points out, it is only anthropologists who are likely to posit this contradiction between the negative views of women as wives, and the largely positive ones of women as mothers (1977: 290). Within the culture, the paradox is contained.

Gandhi, however, never referred to women in conjunction with *sakti*, and indeed, he often termed women 'passive by nature'. When he wrote about women as mothers, it was to extol their self-sacrifice as the epitome of desirable human behaviour; he ignored the fact that mothers withhold as well as give.

How do we explain the fact that Gandhi ignored this important aspect of Hindu thought concerning women, and viewed them as essentially passive? Jayaraman (1981) has suggested that it is perhaps because Gandhi came from the Gujarati area, which is strongly influenced by Jainism, whereas some areas of India such as Bengal or Tamilnadu have strongly developed cults of powerful mother goddesses. However, another important strand in Gandhi's thought, which I have not yet explored, is that of Victorian England. Bondurant's study of Gandhi characterizes his ideas as 'essentially syncretic' (1958), and Mies, in her assessment of his views on women, terms them a mixture of the *patrivrata* and the Victorian 'clinging vine' (1975). Perhaps, in fact, Victorian ideas and those of Hinduism have more in common when it comes to their views of women than might be supposed, as Stein has perceptively suggested (1978). The next section considers nineteenth- and early twentieth-century ideas concerning sexuality and women.

Sexuality in Victorian Britain

One of the most striking parallels between Hindu India and Victorian England was the belief that production of semen is highly weakening to males. Masturbation was thought in the nineteenth century to be extremely dangerous, leading not only to sickness but also to madness. Even as late as the 1920s, conservation of semen was thought to result in health and strength (see Lindlahr 1975: 231).

Chastity for both men and women was a key ideal in the Victorian value system. As Basch points out: 'The Protestant middle classic ethic required the man to repress his instincts and manifestations of pleasure and eroticism; he was thereby wasting precious energy required for work and production' (1974: 271).

As with India, we have far less information about female sexuality, one reason being that women were thought to be much less interested in sex than were men. It is apparent, indeed, that during the eighteenth century, a radical change in the attitude to woman had taken place – she was no longer considered inherently weaker and more immoral because of her stronger sexual appetite. Rather, the cult of the lady, which reached its apotheosis in the nineteenth century, completely split sex from marriage and domestic life. Women were either 'ladies', in which case they were supposed neither to have nor manifest any sexual feeling, otherwise they were considered to be 'fallen women'. Houghton claims that 'The sexual act was associated by many wives only with a duty, and by most husbands with a necessary if pleasurable yielding to one's baser nature' (1957: 353). Similarly, Moore's study of Victorian wives shows that women designated as ladies were not supposed to have any knowledge of sex: 'It was the exception for any "nice" girl to know anything of the facts of life before marriage and very often the ensuing shock put an end once and for all to any hopes of a satisfactory physical relationship between husband and wife' (1974: xv).

The Victorian era did, however, recognize that men had their 'baser instincts', and to cater for these there grew up in the cities of nineteenth-century England a veritable army of prostitutes, who, as 'fallen women', were permitted some sexual feeling, as indeed were women of the working class, from whose ranks many of the prostitutes were drawn.

Women of the upper and middle classes were thus progressively desexualized during the nineteenth century: 'Love of home, children and domestic duties are the only passions they feel', wote Acton in his famous study *The Functions and Disorders of the Reproductive Organs* (1857). Although his book, incredibly, did not discuss the reproductive organs of women at all, it does give an interesting insight into contemporary attitudes on sexuality.

For the wife, the ideal consisted of submitting to her husband, impelled by the spirit of sacrifice and the desire for motherhood.

Women were assigned the task of being the 'angel in the house'. Homes of the middle and upper classes had been considerably transformed by the rise in their standard of living during this period; this, coupled with an enormous increase in the number of domestic servants, freed such women from domestic labour, and enabled them to play a new role, primarily confined to the home. The home became a place apart, a 'walled garden', uncontaminated by the competitive spirit of industrial capitalism, a 'temple of purity, a haven of peace in a hostile and impure world' (Basch 1974: 7).

However, this vision of womanhood which gave women 'nobler natures', and laid upon them the task of purifying their husbands through their love (untainted by lust), was in the latter part of the century used by women as an argument for them to be allowed to take part in public life, the better to purify and ennoble it. It was on this basis that women came to engage in large numbers in philanthropic work, although later similar arguments were used by women campaigning for the vote and for other public and political rights for women.

Houghton's study of the Victorians discusses what came in the 1860s to be called 'woman worship'. He cites as a typical example a picture entitled *The Triumph of Woman*, in which a 'new and divine ideal of her sex' carries a cross in her right hand as an emblem of self-sacrifice (1957: 350).

Houghton also points out that boys were taught to view women as objects of respect, even awe: 'An image wonderfully calculated not only to dissociate love from sex, but to turn love into worship, and worship of purity' (1957: 355). Of all the women in the world, he continues, the most pure (and therefore most useful in promoting adolescent chastity) was Mother:

'Every young Victorian heard his father's voice sounding in his conscience: "Remember your dear, good mother, and never do anything, think anything, imagine anything she would be ashamed of." In that way, filial love, already increased in the Victorian family by the repression of sexual emotions, was exaggerated in the cause of moral censorship and control.'

(Houghton 1957: 355)

Recent historians have viewed Victorian sexual ideology in a more complex way. Cott suggests that it was characterized predominantly by what she terms 'passionlessness' – the concept that 'women lacked sexual aggressiveness, that their sexual appetites contributed a very minor part . . . to their motivations, that lustfulness was simply uncharacteristic' (1978: 220). Other historians have suggested that it was an ideology invented by males for their own convenience – to help gentlemen cope with the problems of their own sexuality, as Cominos (1972) puts it. Although such a view may appear to be attacking Victorian morality, as well as demonstrating its relationship to the growth of industrial capitalism, it does nothing to attack the notion that women are essentially passive pawns, victims of male ideas as well as behaviour. Cott points out that women may well have colluded in the view of themselves as desexualized, and in promoting passionlessness through the temperance and social purity movements, asserted some semblance of control in the sexual arena, even if that control consisted of denial. On a practical level, it enabled married women to say 'no' to their husbands or to promote 'voluntary motherhood' (see Gordon and Dubois 1983), and thus limit their childbearing, as well as their exposure to the venereal disease which some husbands brought home from the brothel. Perhaps most importantly, passionlessness served women's larger interests by downplaying altogether their sexual characterization, which was the cause of their exclusion from significant 'human' (i.e. male) pursuits (Cott 1978: 233). Thus for many women, the notion of passionlessness (or what Havelock Ellis called 'female anaesthesia') was an assertion of moral integrity, the 'retrieval of their identity from a trough of sexual vulnerability and dependence' (Cott 1978: 236).

Gandhi's views on women

Many of the ideas concerning women, sexuality, and proper relations between the sexes, discussed in the previous section, were available to Gandhi. We know, for instance, that he read Ruskin who stated, in his influential lecture '*Of Queens' Gardens*' (1871), that for woman, 'Her true function is to guide and uplift her more worldly mate'. Gandhi too wrote frequently of woman's 'nobler nature'. It was for this reason that he wanted women to join the nationalist struggle, because he was convinced that they would be better able than men to use the weapons of *satyagraha*: 'Since resistance in *satyagraha* is offered through self-suffering, it is a weapon open pre-eminently to women. She can become the leader in *satyagraha* which does not require the learning that books give, but does require the stout heart that comes from suffering and faith' (1942: 187).

These qualities in women, Gandhi was convinced, stemmed from the fact that women gave birth – all were actually or potentially mothers, and thus differed from men: 'The duty of motherhood, which the vast majority of women will always undertake, requires the qualities which men need not possess' (Tendulkar 1960: 227). However, this very fact, as Gandhi saw it, meant that women's participation in public life would be limited: 'I do not envisage the wife, as a rule, following an avocation independent of her husband. The care of the children and the upkeep of the household are quite enough to fully engage her energy' (1942: 21).

It is for statements like these that some have castigated Gandhi for deradicalizing a growing women's movement (e.g. Mies 1975) and constructing the image of an ideal woman and wife. But as other commentators have pointed out, he did actually break away from nineteenth-century reformist traditions in India by preaching equality between women and men:

> 'Woman is the companion of man gifted with equal mental capacities. She has the right to participate in the minutest details of the activities of man, and has the same right to freedom and liberty as he. . . . By sheer force of a vicious custom, even the most ignorant and worthless men have been enjoying a superiority over women which they do not deserve and ought not to have.'   (*Young India* 26 March, 1918)

In passages like this, Gandhi is closer to thinkers like Mill than Ruskin (Millett 1973).

None the less, Gandhi was equivocal in his view of the growing women's movement. In reply to a speech given by Muthulakshmi Reddy when he visited Madras, in which she asked for his support in campaigns concerning women's rights, Gandhi castigated both her and the audience: 'You have pointed out that woman is of paramount importance in India. Poor people do not know anything of that. . . . Understanding the difficulties of the poor means the beginning of the freedom of our country' (Muthulakshmi Reddy 1964: 55).

On another occasion, he wrote in *Young India*, in reply to a letter from Muthulakshmi Reddy, that women should realize that in the villages, there did not exist the problems on which the women's associations were concentrating, and that these were largely confined to upper-caste and class urban women:

> 'Before, therefore, reform on a large scale takes place, the mentality of the educated class has to undergo transformation. And may I suggest to Dr. Muthulakshmi that the few educated women that we have in India will have to descend from their Western heights and come down to India's plains?'
>
> (Muthulakshmi Reddy 1964: 114)

In many respects this dialogue is intrinsic to many political struggles: which is paramount, women's emancipation or the freedom struggle? gender or class? Those who believe the latter can relegate the women's struggle to the background by labelling their problems 'élitist' or 'western', as did Gandhi.

Gandhi was also equivocal in exactly how he wanted women to participate in the freedom struggle. For example, initially he did not want women to come on the Salt March, saying that they would 'complicate things' (Muthulakshmi Reddy 1956: 73). He also justified their exclusion on the grounds that the British would not attack women, and thus their participation was no test of the effectiveness of *satyagraha*. Gandhi thought it would be better for women to stick to the picketing of liquor and foreign cloth shops as 'They could make a more effective appeal to the heart' (Muthulakshmi Reddy 1956: 73). Nevertheless, many women did join the march, and some were arrested. As more and more men found themselves in gaol, women became increasingly prominent in the nationalist movement.

Many commentators, then, see Gandhi's action in enrolling women in the nationalist struggle as absolutely crucial to their future equality in an independent India (Mazumdar 1979: vii). As Mazumdar has said, 'Gandhi was the only one who went beyond customs and individuals, and sought a new social and moral role for women outside sex relationships. But even he could not free himself altogether from the familial images and the language of reformers' (1976: 66). Forbes has also pointed out that only a few people such as Gandhi were actually able to understand that the 'separate worlds' concept so prevalent in Hindu society is related to deep-seated notions about female sexuality (1981: 63).

But Gandhi's solution to this problem of sexuality, as we have seen, was to sublimate it. For him, sex meant heterosexual intercourse, leading to orgasm for the man, and hence a loss of the 'vital fluid'. For the woman, whom he saw as having no sexual desires, sex was distasteful and acquiesced in because of the duty of pleasing her husband, and the need to procreate. Given such a set of premises, then, there were doubly good reasons for taking the vow of *brahmacharya* – to conserve semen, and thus increase physical and mental health and well-being, as well as to achieve greater control over the senses, and also to free women from their subordinate role as wives to men.

He, like those for whom his message was intended, assumed that sexual desire and aggression are part and parcel of the human, and particularly male, condition. One way for society to control this situation is by means of institutions such as *purdah* (see Papanek 1982). Another is to repress it, as was done in Victorian England. But Gandhi suggested a third route. Working on the same set of premises, he taught that *purdah* and seclusion of women (what Papanek terms 'symbolic shelter') were detrimental to the status of women. If women were to be protected from male lust and aggression, if they were to be full human beings, capable of taking part in public life, they had to cease to be sex objects and become 'sisters', i.e. sexually forbidden. The only way for this to happen was for sex to be tabooed as an activity, or at least, any sex which was not meant for procreative purposes. By preaching *brahmacharya*, Gandhi believed that he was freeing women from the yoke of sexual servitude and, at the same time, enabling men to control the 'animal' part of their nature. Given the mode of thought and the social structure in which he operated, this is not an unreasonable conclusion.

Note

1 This article owes its inspiration to a number of sources. The first and most important of these is a brief article by Brian Morris 'Gandhi, Sex and Power' (1985). I am also grateful to Brian Morris, Gill Shepherd,

and Lionel Caplan for reading drafts of this article and making useful suggestions.

After I had finished this article, Gerry Forbes drew my attention to a recent article by Madhu Kishwar, 'Gandhi on Women' (1985); although our articles overlap in many respects, hers is more broadly based than my own. She makes a number of important points, including the fact that there is a gap between his stated views on women's role, and the practice of his own life: 'even while insisting that a woman's real sphere of activity was the home, he was instrumental in creating conditions which could help women break the shackles of domesticity' (1985: 1691). One of the ways in which he did this was to break down the barrier between the private and public spheres; for example, the use of salt and the wearing of *khadi* (homespun cloth) became important political symbols. Kishwar also points out that Gandhi drew his political inspiration for non-violence and passive resistance from women, especially his mother and his wife.

References

Acton, W. (1857) *The Functions and Disorders of the Reproductive Organs in Youth, in Adult Age, and in Advanced Life*. London.

Allen, M. (1982) The Hindu View of Women. In M. Allen and S. N. Mukherjee (eds) *Women in India and Nepal*. Canberra: A.N.U. Printing.

Babb, L. A. (1970) Marriage and Malevolence: the Uses of Sexual Opposition in a Hindu Pantheon. *Ethnology* 9: 137–48.

Basch, F. (1974) *Relative Creatures: Victorian Women in Society and the Novel, 1837–67*. London: Allen Lane.

Bennett, L. (1983) *Dangerous Wives and Sacred Sisters: Social and Symbolic Roles of High-caste Women in Nepal*. New York: Columbia University Press.

Berreman, G. (1972) *Hindus of the Himalayas: Ethnography and Change*. Berkeley, Los Angeles, and London: University of California Press.

Bondurant, J. (1958) *The Conquest of Violence: the Gandhian Philosophy*. Princeton, NJ: Princeton University Press.

Bose, N. K. (1974) *My Days with Gandhi*. Bombay: Orient Longman.

Bühler, G. (1969) *The Laws of Manu (Manu dharma-sastra) (Sacred books of the East, vol. XXX)*. New York: Dover.

Cantlie, A. (1977) Aspects of Hindu Asceticism. In I. M. Lewis (ed.) *Symbols and Sentiments*. London: Academic Press.

Carstairs, G. M. (1968) *The Twice-born*. London: The Hogarth Press.

Cominos, P. T. (1972) Innocent Femina Sensualis in Unconscious Conflict. In M. Vicinus (ed.) *Suffer and Be Still*. Bloomington, Ind.: Indiana University Press.

Copley, A. (1981) Reflections in Attitudes towards Women in Indian Traditional Society. *South Asia Research* 1 (2).

Cott, N. F. (1978) Passionlessness: an Interpretation of Victorian Sexual Ideology, 1790–1850. *Signs* 4 (2).

Forbes, G. (1981) The Indian Women's Movement: a Struggle for Women's Rights or National Liberation? In G. Minault (ed.) *The Extended Family*. Delhi: Chanakya Publications.

Fuller, C. (1980) The Divine Couple's Relationship in a South Indian Temple: Minakshi and Sundareswara at Madurai. *History of Religions* 19 (4).

Gandhi, M. K. (1927) *An Autobiography or the Story of My Experiments with Truth*. Ahmedabad: Navajivan Publishing House.

—— (1941) *To the Women*. Karachi: Anand Hingorani.

—— (1942) *Women and Social Injustice*. Ahmedabad: Navajivan Publishing House.

—— (1948) *Key to Health*. Ahmedabad: Navajivan Publishing House.

—— (1965) *Fasting in Satyagraha: Its Use and Abuse*. Ahmedabad: Navajivan Publishing House.

Gordon, L. and Dubois, E. (1983) Seeking Ecstasy on the Battlefield: Danger and Pleasure in Nineteenth Century Feminist Thought. *Feminist Review* 13, spring.

Hart, G. (1973) Women and the Sacred in Ancient Tamilnadu. *Journal of Asian Studies* XXXII (2).

Hershman, P. (1977) Virgin and Mother. In I. M. Lewis (ed.) *Symbols and Sentiments*. London and New York: Academic Press.

Houghton, W. E. (1957) *The Victorian Frame of Mind, 1830–70*. Connecticut: Yale University Press.

Jacobson, D. (1978) The Chaste Wife: Cultural Norm and Individual Experience. In S. Vatuk (ed.) *American Studies in the Anthropology of India*. New Delhi: Manohar and American Institute of Indian Studies.

Jayaraman, R. (1981) *Caste, Class and Sex: the Dynamic of Inequality in Indian Society*. New Delhi: Hindustan Publishing Company.

Kishwar, M. (1985) Gandhi on Women. *Economic and Political Weekly* XX (40, 41).

Lindlahr, H. (1975) *Philosophy of Natural Therapeutics*. Ed. and revised by J. Parry. Kent: Maidstone Osteopathic Centre.

Mazumdar, V. (1976) The Social Reform Movement in India: from Ranade to Nehru. In B. R. Nanda (ed.) *Indian Women from Purdah to Modernity*. New Delhi: Vikas Publishing.

—— (1979) *Symbols of Power: Studies on the Political Status of Women in India*. Bombay: Allied Publishers.

Mies, M. (1975) Indian Women and Leadership. *Bulletin of Concerned Asian Scholars* 7: 56–66.

Millett, K. (1973) The Debate over Women: Ruskin versus Mill. In M. Vicinus (ed.) *Suffer and Be Still*. Bloomington, Ind.: Indiana University Press.

Minault, G. (1981) Sisterhood or Separation? The All-Indian Muslim Ladies Conference and the Nationalist Movement. In G. Minault (ed.) *The Extended Family*. Delhi: Chanakya Publications.

Moore, K. (1974) *Victorian Wives*. London: Allison & Busby.

Morris, B. (1985) Gandhi, Sex and Power. *Freedom* 46.

Muthulakshmi Reddy, S. (1930) *My Experience as a Legislator*. Madras: The Current Thought Press.
—— (1956) *Mrs. Margaret Cousins and Her Work in India*. Adyar, Madras: Women's India Association.
—— (1964) *Autobiography*. Madras. (Unpublished.)
Papanek, H. (1982) Purdah: Separate Worlds and Symbolic Shelter. In H. Papanek (ed.) *Separate Worlds: Studies of Purdah in South Asia*. Delhi: Chanakya Publications.
Rawson, P. (1973) *Tantra: the Indian Cult of Ectasy*. London: Thames & Hudson.
Rudolph, L. and Rudolph, S. (1967) The Traditional Roots of Charisma: Gandhi. In L. Rudolph and S. Rudolph *The Modernity of Tradition*. Chicago: University of Chicago Press.
Rudolph, S. (1966) Self-control and Political Potency: Gandhi's Asceticism. *The American Scholar* 35 (1).
Ruskin, J. (1871) Of Queens' Gardens. In J. Ruskin *Sesame and Lilies*. London: Allen & Unwin. (First published 1865.)
Shulman, D. (1980) *Tamil Temple Myths: Sacrifice and Divine Marriage in the South Indian Saiva Tradition*. Princeton, NJ: Princeton University Press.
Stein, D. (1978) Women to Burn: Suttee as Normative Institution. *Signs* 4 (2) winter.
Tapper, B. E. (1979) Widows and Goddesses: Female Roles in Deity Symbolism in a South Indian Village. *Contributions to Indian Sociology* 13 (1).
Tendulkar, D. G. (1960) *Mahatma* (vol. 2, 2nd edn). Delhi: Ministry of Information, Publications Division.
Thakazhi, Sivasankara Pillai (1962) *Chemeen*. London: Gollancz.
Thompson, C. (1983) Women's Fertility and the Worship of Gods in a Hindu Village. In P. Holden (ed.) *Women's Religious Experience*. London: Croom Helm.
Wadley, S. (1977) Women and the Hindu Tradition. In Wellesley Committee (ed.) *Women and National Development: the Complexities of Change*. Chicago: University of Chicago Press.

Name index

Abramson, A. vii, 13, 18, 20, 24, 193–215
Acton, W. 2, 287
Adam, B. 37, 42–3
Allen, M. 278, 284–85
Allen, S. M. 150–53
Altman, D. 41
Arberry, A. J. 261
Ardener, E. W. 15–16
Ardener, S. G. vii, 15–16, 113–37
Arnold, K. 228–30
Ashworth, A. E. 240, 261
Atkinson, T. G. 9
Augustine, St 89

Babb, L. A. 281
Barrett, M. 10
Basch, F. 3, 287–88
Bateson, G. 14
Baubo 120–21
Beauvoir, S. de 124
Bennett, L. 15, 283, 285
Berreman, G. 282
Bloch, I. 34
Blum, L. 86
Boadella, D. 91
Bondurant, J. 273, 286
Bontecon, L. 125
Bose, N. K. 278
Boserup, E. 185

Brake, M. 2
Brandes, P. 188–89
Bray, A. 40
Brecher, E. M. 53, 62
Brodber, E. 152
Brodie, F. 261
Brody, E. 146, 150–55, 158
Brown, B. 10
Brown, E. 153
Browne, S. 52, 64
Brownmiller, S. 9
Buhler, G. 282, 284
Bujra, J. 224, 247
Burton, R. 261

Califia, P. 46
Campbell, B. 67
Cantlie, A. 278
Caplan, P. vii, 1–25, 222, 271–92
Caro Baroja, P. 170
Carstairs, G. M. 275, 282
Cassidy, F. G. 162
Cavell, S. 85
Chesser, E. 72
Chicago, J. 126–28, 131–33
Chodorow, N. 97–9
Christian, B. 156, 159
Clarke, E. 147, 150, 155
Clarke, S. C. 149, 151–52
Cline, W. 261

Cohen, A. 221, 234
Cole, E. 61
Comfort, A. 73
Cominos, P. T. 289
Copley, A. 279, 285
Cott, N. F. 3–4, 289
Coveney, L. 40
Coward, R. 10, 14, 38, 53
Cutrufelli, M. R. 169–71

Dank, B. 43
Darwin, C. 33
Davenport, W. 153
Davis, J. 167–68
DeCecco, J. P. 47
Demeter 118–19
D'Emilio, J. 37, 41–2
Descartes, H. 84–5, 94
Devereux, G. 137, 258
Douglas, M. 14, 113, 154, 180–81, 189
Dove, L. 124
Draper, A. vii, 18–20, 23, 143–63
Dubois, E. 4, 289
Dupree, L. 261
Durkheim, E. 137
Dworkin, A. 9, 134
Dyehouse, C. 71

Ehrenreich, B. 4, 59
Eichinger Ferro-Luzzi, G. 135
Ellenberger, H. F. 33
Ellis, H. H. 4, 34–5, 53–63, 66, 75, 289
El Saadawi, N. 15
Elwin, V. 13
English, D. 4, 59
Evans-Pritchard, E. E. 21–2, 258, 265
Eyles, L. 61

Faderman, L. 5, 40, 44
Falk, C. 104

Fee, E. 11
Féré, C. 34
Ferguson, A. 10, 46
Figes, E. 235
Firestone, S. 125
Flandrin, J.-L. 18
Forbes, G. 292
Foucault, M. 4–8, 25, 37–40, 49, 82–6, 89–95, 100–08, 193
Freeman, D. 13, 193–95, 204, 207
Freud, S. 6, 11–12, 34, 38–9, 85, 95–101, 105–07, 120, 278
Fromm, E. 91
Fruzzetti, L. M. 15
Fuller, C. 281

Gagnon, J. H. 39
Gallichan, W. 69, 71
Gallop, J. 31
Gandhi, K. 272–73, 277, 280
Gandhi, M. K. 22–3, 271–92; on abstinence 274–75; on fasting 275–78; life of 272–78; on relations between men and women 278–84; on women 286, 289–92
Gibb, H. A. R. 261
Gilligan, C. 86, 104
Gleason, P. 37
Goddard, V. viii, 20, 24, 166–91
Goffman, E. 37, 114, 137
Goldman, E. 104
Gonzales, V. D. 145–48, 155
Gooden, S. S. 151
Goody, J. 18, 168, 266
Gordon, L. 4, 289
Gough, K. 14
Graf, F. 120
Gramsci, A. 49
Greer, G. 119–20, 123–24
Greg, W. R. 3
Griffin, S. 9, 94–6, 99–102, 106, 134

Haire, N. 60, 63
Hall, R. 65–6
Hart, G. 281
Hegel, G. W. F. 184
Heider, K. G. 22
Helman, C. 155
Henriques, F. 233
Herdt, G. H. 11
Hershman, P. 283–84, 286
Hertz, R. 14
Hewitt, L. 153–54, 157
Hirschfeldt, M. 34
Hirschman, A. 87
Hobsbawm, E. J. 6
Hocquenghem, G. 44
Hodge, M. 147–48
Hosken, F. P. 15
Houghton, W. E. 287–88

Iambe 118–19, 121
Ignatieff, M. 84

Jackson, M. viii, 8, 22, 52–79
Jacobson, D. 281–82
Jayaraman, R. 286
Jeffreys, S. 54
Johnson, V. 52–3, 72–5
Jones, E. 95
Jordanova, L. 158
Jung, C. 99

Kaan, H. 33
Kaplan, C. 46
Kant, I. 86–7, 91
Kantarowicz, E. 214
Katz, J. N. 41
Kelly-Gadol, J. 17
Kennedy, J. G. 15
Kenyatta, J. 13, 220
Kerr, M. 155
Kinsey, A. C. 43, 53, 72
Koedt, A. 52, 74
Kore 118–19

Krafft-Ebing, R. von 33–6
Krieger, S. 44
Kuhn, A. 10
Kupfermann, J. 136

Leach, E. 14
Leakey, L. 222–23
Leenhardt, M. 199
L'Espérance, J. 36
Leslie, C. 154
Lewis, J. 71
Lindlahr, H. 287
Littlewood, M. 71

MacCormack, C. P. viii, 18–20,
    23, 143–63
MacFarlane, A. 18
McIntosh, M. 5
MacIntyre, A. 83
McNeely, J. 129
Malinowski, B. 11–13, 208
Manderson, L. 154
Marcuse, H. 6, 95, 101
Martin, C. E. 43
Martinez-Alier, V. 172–73, 179
Massiah, J. 145
Masters, W. 52–3, 72–5
Mathieu, N.-C. 16
Mayer, I. 114
Mazumdar, V. 291
Mbiti, J. 221
Mead, G. H. 39
Mead, M. 12–13, 39, 193–95, 207
Midgley, M. 85
Mies, M. 286, 290
Millett, K. 8, 290
Minault, G. 281
Minson, J. 48
Mitchell, J. 39, 134
Mitchell, M. F. 154–55
Moll, A. 34
Montagu, M. F. A. 12

Moore, J. 264
Moore, K. 287
More, H. 4
Morgan, K. B. 153
Mukerjee, D. 150
Mulvey, L. 129
Murphy, V. J. 151
Murray, M. 139
Musallam, B. F. 261
Muthulakshmi Reddy, S. 279, 290–91

Nadel, S. F. 234
Nelson, N. viii, 5, 23–4, 217–39
Nkwain, F. 116
Nochlin, L. 135–36

Oakley, A. 59
Okely, J. 15
Okin, S. M. 88–9
Ortner, S. B. 16–17, 266

Padgug, R. A. 19
Papanek, H. 292
Parker, R. 128–29, 133–34
Parkin, D. 233
Parrinder, G. 235
Patterson, O. 144–45
Peristiany, J. G. 167, 171–72
Persephone 118–19
Peterson, K. 125
Phillips, A. S. 149
Pitt-Rivers, J. 167–68, 188
Plummer, K. 37–8, 42–3
Polhemus, T. 113
Pollock, G. 128, 133–34
Pomeroy, W. B. 43
Powell, D. 151, 153–54, 157

Ranger, T. O. 261
Rapp, R. 18–19, 25
Rawson, P. 278
Re-Bartlett, L. 54–5

Reich, W. 6, 91, 105, 107
Rich, A. 6, 45–6, 76
Richards, A. 14, 222
Richardson, N. J. 118
Rickles, N. K. 120
Ritzenthaler, R. 116
Roberts, G. W. 149–50, 153, 155
Robinson, P. 53
Rorty, R. 85
Rose, B. 130–31, 135
Rose, J. 39
Ross, E. 18–19, 25
Rousseau, J.-J. 87–9
Rowbotham, S. 52, 104
Rubin, G. 10, 16
Rudolph, L. and S. 278
Ruehl, S. 67
Ruskin, J. 289
Russell, C. E. 259

Safa-Isfahani, K. 15
Sahlins, M. D. 213, 257
Saint-Phalle, N. de 129
Sanger, M. 61, 278–79
Santoro, S. 128–29
Schapera, I. 13
Schneider, J. and P. 169–70, 179
Schrader, H. 121
Scott, C. S. 159
Seidler, V. J. viii, 8, 22, 82–110
Semmel, J. 129
Sennett, R. 89–93, 107–08
Severson, A. 124–25
Sharaf, M. 105
Shepherd, G. ix, 2–3, 20–1, 23–4, 240–69
Sheridan, A. 83–4
Shively, M. G. 47
Shulman, D. 285
Sieberling, D. 129
Simon, W. 39
Sinclair, S. A. 149–50, 153, 155
Smith-Rosenberg, C. 5, 17

Snitow, A. 3, 45
Snowden, R. 156, 159
Socarides, C. W. 39
Sophocles 184
Spencer, H. 11
Stack, C. B. 19, 154
Stansell, C. 3, 45
Stein, D. 286
Stekel, W. 69, 71
Stone, H. and A. 72
Stone, L. 18
Stopes, M. 64–7
Strathern, M. 156, 264
Strobel, M. 243, 247–48
Sullerot, E. 233
Sutherland, A. 15
Swantz, M.-L. 234

Tambiah, S. J. 168, 266
Tanker, N. 19
Tanner, R. E. S. 242–43
Tapper, B. E. 281–83, 285
Tendulkar, D. G. 290
Thakazhi Pillai, S. 281
Thompson, C. 284
Thompson, S. 3, 45
Thompson, T. 150
Tickner, L. 134
Tillion, F. 169, 179
Topan, F. M. T. 241, 248
Turner, V. 14, 161

Ulrichs, K. H. 33

Vance, C. S. 2, 10–11
Van de Velde, T. H. 59, 62–4, 68

Wachtel, E. 225
Wadley, S. 280, 286
Walker, W. M. 240, 261
Walkowitz, J. 5
Weiner, A. 17
Weeks, J. ix, 5, 20, 31–49,
    52
Westphal, C. 33
White, E. 42
Whitehead, A. 18
Whitehead, H. 16–17, 258
Whyte, L. 224–25
Wiegand, T. von 121
Wikan, U. 21, 259, 261
Wilkes, H. 126
Wilson, E. 31
Wilson, G. M. 251
Wilson, J. J. 125
Wooming, P. 153–54, 157
Wright, H. 67–8
Wright, P. 147

Yalman, N. 15, 173, 180–81

Zeitlin, F. 118–24

Subject index

abstinence 221; *brahmacharya*
  (q.v.) 22–3, 271–92
adulthood 149–54
anthropology 10–20
Arab culture 261–63; *see also*
  Islam
art 125–34, 136–37

Bakweri 115–18
Balong 116
birth 143, 148–49
body 14–15, 113–14; imagery
  125–36, 146–49, 154–61;
  margins and orifices of 113–14,
  154, 161, 189–90; and
  repression 93–8; symbolic
  123–24; *vs.* spirit 235–37,
  276–78
Brahmacharya 22–3, 271–92;
  Gandhi's life 272–78; his views
  on women 286, 289–92 breasts
  135–36

caste system 180–81, 189–90; *see
  also* Hinduism
celibacy 221; *brahmacharya (q.v.)*
  22–3, 271–92
children, as status symbol 143,
  146
Christianity: in Fiji 210–11;

Kikuyu 232–33, 235–37; view
  of sexuality 89–91
circumcision 219–20; female 4,
  221, 238n
clitoridectomy 4, 221, 238n
clitoris 67
contraception 65, 151–52,
  157–58, 279
control: desire and 98–102; of
  women's sexuality 166–91
courtship 56–8; in Naples 173–79
Cuba 172
cults, female 118–23; *see also*
  virginity

Darwinism 33
death 199–200
desire, sexual: control and
  98–102; female 3–4; male 4,
  98–102, 104–05
doctors 3–4, 36, 59, 62; and sex
  manuals 58–71, 73–4

fasting 275–78
feminism 54–5, 84; and
  heterosexuality 74–8, 271;
  lesbian 44–6; radical *vs.*
  libertarian 9–10; and sexology
  52–3

fertility 23–4, 124; and death 199–200; and sexuality 266–67
Fiji 193–215; contradiction (politics of sexuality) 208–13; female virginity 198–204; transgression 204–08, 213–14
films 124–25
food: Gandhi and 275–78; Hindu 189–90; in Naples 186–87
frigidity 68–71
functionalism 195–96

gender 1–3, 196–98; iconography see vagina; roles 242–50, 258–65; and sexuality 16; social vs. biological basis of 12–13

heterosexuality 2; and feminism 74–8, 271; marriage manuals 58–71; model of 59–74; and sexology 52–79
Hinduism: body and spirit 276–78; pollution 180–81, 189–90, 243, 276; sexuality 280–84; women as mothers 284–86
history 18–20
homosexuality 2–6, 20–2; in Mombasa (q.v.) 240–69; politics and 41–3; see also lesbianism
'honour' 15, 167–73

iconography, gender see vagina
identity 20–4, 31–49; as choice 43–7; as destiny 32–7; development of 95–8; group 180–90; and relationships 47–9; psychoanalysis and 95–100; as resistance 37–42; sexual 31–2, 104–05
imagery, body 125–36, 146–49, 154–61
India: caste system 180–81,

189–90; Gandhi 271–92; see also Hinduism
infidelity 177–78, 219–20
initiation rituals 14, 162–63
instinct, sexual 33–5
Islam 242–43, 252, 261–62

Jamaica 143–63; adulthood 149–54; body imagery 154–61; class and gender 145–46; menstruation 155–59; navel string 161–63; slavery 144–45; status 146–49

Kenya see Kikuyu; Mombasa
Kikuyu 217–39; female sexuality 220–21; free vs. married women 225–26, 230–32; male sexuality 219–20; 'sex for sale' 224–27; sexual behaviour 221–24; views of sexuality 227–37
Kom 116–17

language 98–105
lesbianism 2, 5–6; and heterosexuality 76; in Mombasa (q.v.) 240–69; political 44–6
libertarian feminism 9–10

madness 82–93
malaya 230–33
mana 201–02
manuals, sex 58–71, 73–4
marriage 11–12; manuals 58–71, 73–4; in Mombasa 255–57; in Naples 173–79
masculinity: and madness 82–5; and reason 85–9
masturbation 4, 286
Mathare Valley see Kikuyu

medicalization of sex 3–4, 36, 59, 62; *see also* manuals
menstruation: meanings of 155–59; onset of 149–50
Mombasa 240–69; friendship 249–50; gender roles 242–50; gender switching 258–63; history of 240–42; homosexuals 250–53; lesbians 253–58; rank 262–65
motherhood 284–86

Naples 166–91; courtship and marriage 174–79; food 186–87; honour and shame 167–73; women as carriers of group identity 180–90; work 173–74, 185, 187
naturalism 74–8, 195
navel string 161–63

oppression 6–8; eroticization of 56–8; and heterosexual model 59–74
orifices, body 113–14, 154, 161, 189–90

paintings *see* art
pathology, sexual 33–4
patriarchy 6–8, 53–4
penis 73–4, 135
permissiveness 6
Peru 228–30
politics of sex 8–10; homosexuality 41–6
pollution 180–81, 189–90, 243, 276
polygyny 219, 233
pornography 9, 100–02, 134
power: mechanisms of 7, 102–04, 108; slavery and 144–45
pregnancy 152
prostitution 5; *see also* Kikuyu

psychoanalysis 7–8; and anthropology 11–12; and identity 38–9, 95–100; and repression 95–6
puberty 12–13; Fiji *(q.v.)* 193–215; Kikuyu 236–37

radical feminism 9–10
rank, and gender 258, 262–65
rape 9, 57, 213
reason 82–93; masculinity and 85–9
relationships, and identity 47–9
religion 3; Christian view of sexuality 89–91; in Fiji 210–11; Islam 242–43, 252, 261–62; Kikuyu 232–33, 235–37; *see also* Hinduism
repression 93–8
ritual: female 118–23; initiation 14, 162–63

Samoa 12–13, 193–94
scientific model of heterosexuality 59–74
self 91–3; *see also* identity
Serea 198–214
sex 1–3; manuals 58–71, 73–4; politics 8–10, 41–6
sexology 8; early 33–6, 40–1, 53–8, 289; and feminism 52–3, 74–8; and heterosexuality 52–79; marriage manuals 58–71
sexuality 2–3; and fertility 266–67; Hindu 280–84; history, western 3–8, 53–8, 289; male 82–110; and power 102–04; scientific model of 59–74; in Victorian Britian 286–89; *see also* heterosexuality; homosexuality
'shame' 15, 167–73

Sicily 169–71
slavery 144–45, 162
spirit *vs.* body 235–37,
    276–78
statuettes 121–22
status 146–49; *see also*
    rank
Swahilis *see* Mombasa
symbolism, body 123–24

Thesmophoria 118–19, 124
titi ikoli 115, 117–18, 124
transsexuality 21
transvestism 211–13, 259

uterus: images of 146–49, 160;
    symbolism 123

vagina 15–16, 113–37; in art
    125–34; body symbolism
    123–24; 'educating the' 67–8;
    insults to 115–18; and ritual
    115–23
virginity: in Fiji 193–94, 198–208;
    Kikuyu 236; in Naples 175–77
vulva 123–24

womb *see* uterus
work: in Naples 173–74, 185,
    187; *see also* Kikuyu